THE
AUTHORITARIAN
CENTURY

China's Rise and the Demise of
the Liberal International Order

Chris Ogden

BRISTOL
UNIVERSITY
PRESS

First published in Great Britain in 2022 by

Bristol University Press
University of Bristol
1-9 Old Park Hill
Bristol
BS2 8BB
UK
t: +44 (0)117 374 6645
e: bup-info@bristol.ac.uk

Details of international sales and distribution partners are available at
bristoluniversitypress.co.uk

British Library Cataloguing in Publication Data
A catalogue record for this book is available from the British Library

ISBN 978-1-5292-0511-4 paperback
ISBN 978-1-5292-0513-8 ePub
ISBN 978-1-5292-0512-1 ePdf

Cover design: blu inc
Front cover image: Stocksy/Smokey Spartacus © Christian B

Bristol University Press uses environmentally responsible
print partners.

Printed and bound in Great Britain by TJ Books, Padstow

for Nestor

Every road has two directions

Russian proverb

China is a sea that salts all
the waters that flow into it

Chinese saying

Contents

About the Author

Chris Ogden is Senior Lecturer in Asian Affairs at the University of St Andrews, where he teaches on the international relations of China and India. His research interests concern the interplay between foreign and domestic policy influences in East Asia (primarily China) and South Asia (primarily India), as well as contemporary great power politics, national identity, Hindu nationalism and global authoritarianism.

Chris's other books include *A Dictionary of Politics and International Relations in China* (Oxford University Press, 2019), *A Dictionary of Politics and International Relations in India* (Oxford University Press, 2019), *China and India: Asia's Emergent Great Powers* (Polity, 2017), *Indian National Security* (Oxford University Press, 2017), *Hindu Nationalism and the Evolution of Contemporary Indian Security: Portents of Power* (Oxford University Press, 2014), *Indian Foreign Policy: Ambition and Transition* (Polity, 2014) and the *Handbook of China's Governance and Domestic Politics* (Routledge, 2013).

For more information, see http://chris-ogden.org.

Acknowledgements

Many thanks to Stephen Wenham at Bristol University Press for inviting me to write this book back in 2017. Your insights – as well as those of the initial reviewers – have been invaluable. I am also indebted to my research assistants at the University of St Andrews who worked on this project. In no particular order, many thanks to Alison Strongwater, Asya Wu, Caleb Reynolds-Snell, Elisabeth Speyerl, Jake Steiner, Katie Scheibner, Leonard Seyfried, Märit Eriksson, Rahul Srivastava and Rupert Schulenburg.

Preface

China's current rise to prominence as an economic, military and political powerhouse will significantly determine the nature of modern geopolitics in the coming decades. As China's stature increases, it will allow the country to determine the functioning of the international system, and thus the parameters of international order itself. Such a new order would underscore China's supremacy in political, economic and diplomatic terms, and echo the country's specific domestic values, including its authoritarian political basis, which are deeply engrained in the mindsets of its leaders, thinkers and people. As these values directly structure and inform both the interests and the actions guiding China's global interactions, appreciating this worldview has never been so critical. This is especially apparent as these attitudes frequently diverge from those in the liberal international order regarding democracy, free market economics, universal human rights and hegemony. This book thus asks: is this the start of an autocratic era in international politics that will profoundly affect all of our lives? And hence, the beginning of the end of democracy as we know it?

Researching this book came about at a pertinent time in international affairs. In particular, the coronavirus pandemic pulled back the curtain on how countries would act in times of extreme national emergencies and the powers that they would be willing to use. It also brought into sharp relief the extent of our freedoms in such circumstances, and the willingness or not of leaders to either protect or curtail these rights. That China was at the epicentre of the pandemic, was the first to react to it and the first to be scrutinized for its reaction, also focused the world on its authoritarian basis. As the virus spread in China, we saw doctors silenced, apartment blocks sealed, quarantines enforced, entire cities and regions shut down, and internal and external communications blocked. Recognizing these tensions and trying to imagine what would happen when coronavirus reached the UK, in February 2020 I had a letter published in *The Guardian*[1] suggesting that such – until then – apparently unthinkable actions would also become necessary in my home country. Hitting a nerve, this was followed up by an interview with BBC Radio 4's flagship PM[2] news programme, among others, where I was met with some scepticism that such measures would ever be required or could ever be adequately enacted in a democracy.

However, it rapidly became clear that the methods of authoritarianism – although not necessarily deployed to the same degree as in China – were going to be a looming inevitability within global responses to combat COVID-19. Moreover, as deaths and infections subsided in China, the raw efficacy of the Chinese Communist Party's (CCP's) autocratic rule was clearly evident. Almost learning from this success, or at least seeking its advantages, within weeks the UK was in a full lockdown. The inconceivable had now become reality as individual freedoms to move and associate were radically reduced, access to services were diminished as schooling and nurseries were closed, the health service reprioritized to deal with the infected and dying, and workplaces and homes merged. As the West faltered in its response and as the risks of the pandemic were denied by US President Donald Trump, China reopened its economy and speedily created a vaccine, further evidencing not only their differing policies but also the raw efficacy of them. It also seemed as though not a day went by without some reference to the West being in decline, that authoritarianism was on the rise or that Big Tech and surveillance were a threat to democracies worldwide. By the end of 2020, authoritarian thinking and behaviour – including the ones that China had rapidly brought in – became the norm and were enacted by our governments through existing emergency laws. Social, political and economic freedoms were reduced globally, as the spectre of authoritarian control became something that suddenly affected us all.

Despite these seismic impacts, the greatest of all the curtains to be pulled back was that which showed the deep-seated power underpinning China's authoritarianism, and the willingness of Beijing to enact such measures that simply extended their existing practices. To many observers this came as a shock, yet, as long-term China watchers have known for many years, this underlying reality was nothing new. It was clear that China was authoritarian, if not at times in its history totalitarian, and that its rulers in Beijing were willing to do whatever they could to severely control a large and restive population, so as to achieve their political, economic and global ambitions. What was also evident was that Western governments and their corporations had discreetly closed this curtain in order to benefit from China's economic boom over the last 40 years. This book seeks to cast aside this curtain to show how – despite clear evidence of China's authoritarian basis – the West purposely cultivated and facilitated its rise, and vainly tried to usher it into Western-led institutions and understandings in the hope of socializing and assimilating China into the current international order. This embrace was underpinned by the belief after the Cold War in the universality of a US-created and US-led *liberal international order*, wherein globalized free trade would spur on unavoidable democracy and associated liberal human rights in China.

The story that this book reveals is that rather than submit entirely to this order, China's economic and military strength skyrocketed and quickly outstripped many of the countries in the West. This rise was buoyed by the weight of being a 2,000-year-old civilization, and of having a differing global outlook influenced by Confucianism and driven by the ambitions of the CCP. Such countervailing forces are now succeeding in presenting a different vision of the world, an alternative outlook to the West that challenges its exclusivity and shows that liberal economic growth can go hand in hand with continued autocratic rule and control. In these ways, Beijing is currently presenting *and realizing* an alternative way of ordering the world, an order informed by very clear Chinese characteristics embodied in a resolutely authoritarian outlook. This challenge is also coming in the context of an ever weaker and declining West, whose legitimacy in the 21st century has been successively undercut by its flawed military escapades after 9/11, the 2008 global credit crisis and the storming of the US Capitol in early 2021. This vulnerability merged with the strategic naivety that wrongly thought that China could be successfully assimilated into the US-led liberal international order. Together these forces are turbocharging and legitimizing this new international order, one which is highly China-inspired, profoundly authoritarian, and potentially indicates the dawning of a long authoritarian century.

Chris Ogden
Edinburgh
April 2022

Introduction:
Whose International Order?

> [W]e have achieved the first centenary goal,
> comprehensively build[ing] a moderately prosperous
> society, ... [and are] now striding forward high-spiritedly
> toward the second centenary goal of comprehensively
> building a great, modern, socialist country.[1]

The rise of authoritarian tendencies represents an increasing and
accelerating illiberal trend in international politics over the last
decade.[2] A rapidly rising and modernizing China is at the vanguard
of this phenomenon. The ruling Chinese Communist Party (CCP)
under the leadership of President Xi (as quoted above) typifies the
core characteristics of repressive authoritarian rule. It does so by
rejecting universal democratic principles; denying the legitimacy
of political opponents; utilizing security forces and surveillance
capabilities against its people; and curtailing the civil liberties of
opponents, including human rights activists, religious activists and
the media. As China amasses more economic, institutional and
military power, the world is witnessing an accompanying power
shift that is depleting the relative influence and stature of Western
countries. This shift is undercutting the West's associated structural
power as built on the articulation and promotion of its own specific
values and worldviews, which is simultaneously delegitimizing
liberal democracy globally and legitimizing authoritarian
practices. As Beijing increasingly determines the functioning of
the international system, China will be able to more effectively
define the parameters of the international order, which will reflect
its autocratic principles.

1

For China, such an alternative vision of the international order is based on different economic, institutional and normative settings that are becoming increasingly recognized across global politics. At their most profound, these values and consequent behaviours frequently diverge from – and thus challenge – those central to the West's liberal order broadly built on democracy, free market economics, universal human rights and US hegemony. This contestation comes at a time when Western democracies are facing their own significant political upheavals and domestic crises from populism to coronavirus to Brexit – events which are diluting their core political values. Growing authoritarian and populist traits across the world – often supported by domestic populations negatively affected by globalization, increased migration and growing economic disparities – accelerate the viability of this trend. Such an authoritarian wave is not limited to smaller states but increasingly typifies the underlying political nature of the international system's other foremost powers – in the guise of Russia, the United States (US) and India – all of which are facilitating and normalizing authoritarianism as a dominant global political phenomenon. If these trends come to dominate global politics, at best the remaining liberal democratic rights enjoyed in the West will be fundamentally threatened, and at worst they will be entirely subsumed and replaced by repressive authoritarian governments.

Underpinning this development is a growing realization that authoritarianism and democracy are not opposing political systems but are deeply interrelated traits on one continuum. All too often, the characteristics of these systems appreciably intertwine, overlap and influence each other. In this way, democracies are not immune to authoritarian tendencies (and vice versa) and are susceptible to such tendencies creeping into everyday politics and being active even in well-established liberal countries. As we will see throughout this book, not only have authoritarian traits been present in the world's major democracies for many decades, as displayed by many of their dominant political parties and some of their most prominent leaders, but these traits have also rapidly accelerated in the 21st century and increasingly mirror those in authoritarian countries such as China and Russia.

Amid a 'democratic recession', a 2021 survey pertinently showed that only 8.4 per cent of the world's population live in a fully functioning democracy.[3] Signifying a global decline apparent since the 1970s, such 'democratic backsliding' is intensifying a broader sense within many populations of an impending authoritarian future. For many people across the world, a phenomenon that 'could never happen here' is now visibly taking place. Recent events in the world's major democracies appear to underscore such a threat. These include – amid a highly polarized, intolerant and volatile political environment – the violent storming on live television of the US Capitol in January 2021 by supporters of President Donald Trump looking to reverse the result of the 2020 US election. Elsewhere, in the UK, the populist government of Prime Minister Boris Johnson unlawfully suspended Parliament (in 2019) and passed laws inhibiting the right to protest, restricting the right to vote, and limiting the ability of the media and judiciary to provide independent oversight of the government.[4] Such visible manifestations serve to accelerate democratic backsliding globally, which over the last decade has occurred in democracies ranging from – but by no means limited to – Hungary, Poland, Slovenia, Israel, Peru, Myanmar, India, Mali, Afghanistan, Serbia, Morocco, the Philippines and Turkey.[5] The ever-increasing usage of social media across the world, which is increasingly driven by fear, anger and abundant misinformation, is frequently fuelling this phenomenon.

In such a context, the essence of the liberal international order appears on the verge of an assimilation and capitulation to China's preferred political basis, and the realization of the 21st century as an *authoritarian century*. Realizing such a China-inspired international order would underscore its supremacy in political, economic and normative terms, and directly echo the country's specific domestic values. These include its deeply engrained authoritarian political basis. Such an outlook also directly structures and influences the interests and aims guiding China's global interactions, whereby its authoritarian basis permeates the country's foreign policy interests and actions. Together these factors interlink to produce a *China-centric authoritarian international order*.

Identity and authoritarianism

My core approach to analyze this contestation between different political systems, and the transition to a new – authoritarian-centred

– international order, rests on exploring the dynamics underpinning the formation and realization of identity in global politics. In this book, 'identity' refers to 'varying constructions of nation- and statehood ... [through which] the process of construction is typically explicitly political and pits conflicting actors against each other'.[6] Such identities are specific to countries, and reflective of the worldviews, interests and aims of their leaders and peoples. At their heart, these identities are built on certain sets of values, principles and practices. Such values – often referred to as norms – have themselves been solidified via particular historical experiences and events, as well as the ongoing selection and repetition of core guiding narratives, whereby language and discourse act to legitimize and normalize dominant worldviews This repetition allows these narratives to become dominant in society, which are then used by ruling elites to set their domestic and international agendas, and ultimately to pursue and obtain power.

By taking such a standpoint, this analysis of international relations is not 'culture-free' or 'preconception-free',[7] and does not seek to claim that all countries respond to or conceptualize the world in the same way. Instead, it argues that the world is not 'as it is' (as rationalist and ahistorical approaches would claim) but is 'a project under construction, as becoming rather than being'.[8] As such, the world – and its prevailing nature (its 'order') and its actors (the various identities of its constituent countries) – is regarded as being an evolving, ever-changing and essentially organic entity. This approach allows me to first consider the specific norms and worldviews underpinning China's identity, along with the particular historical precedents and experiences that have built this identity. Such a basis can then be compared with the identities and worldviews of other countries so as to compare and contrast competing international orders. From such a comparison, we can ascertain what kind of new international order is emerging.

Authoritarianism fits into such accounts of constructed identities as it is a political system based on a certain set of values, practices and understandings of the world. However, despite its frequent usage, there is a 'terminological Babylon'[9] of inconsistent definitions that plagues the study of authoritarianism. Part of this problem is related to the desire by political scientists to produce an absolute – and thus generalizable – definition that classifies and encompasses all types of political regimes. Casting such a wide net places together political systems based on rule by a monarch, by the military or by civilians, and across a range of geographical and historical contexts.[10] To overcome this issue, the most seminal work identified three core features of authoritarian regimes: rule by a small number of leaders through systems that limit political and social pluralism (thus narrowing political opinion); limited political participation and mobilization (both during and outwith elections); and seeking legitimacy via collective mentalities, psychological predispositions and values (rather than ideologies).[11]

Other scholars also recognized the deeper *continuum* and interconnection between different political systems over time through the presence of *hybrid regimes*. These regimes displayed both authoritarian and democratic traits, resulting in a 'blurring' and shifting quality rather than being absolute in nature. Such scholars refer to 'pseudo-democracies'[12] and 'democratically disguised dictatorships'[13] that mimic but do not adhere to democratic practices. Others identify 'electoral authoritarianism',[14] whereby elections are held but are rigged by those in power, and 'competitive authoritarianism' whose 'formal democratic institutions exist ... [but the] incumbents' abuse of the state places them at a significant advantage vis-à-vis their opponents'[15] via the widespread abuse of state resources, restricting media access, harassment, bribery and violence. In turn, additional thinkers refer to 'illiberal democracies'[16] or 'semi-authoritarianism' wherein civil liberties lag behind political liberties and do not meet a full range of 'democratic conditions'.

Several popular measures attempt to capture this assortment of factors. The Polity data series (Polity IV) notes that democratic regimes must possess (1) 'institutions and procedures' that permit citizen political commentary and (2) 'institutionalized constraints on the power of the executive'.[17] In turn, the Economist Intelligence Unit's *Democracy Index* focuses on 'electoral process and pluralism; civil liberties; the functioning of government; political participation; and political culture',[18] while Freedom House's *Freedom in the World Report* measures civil liberties and political freedom across 25 different factors. Collectively, such measures are useful for indicating democracies and authoritarian regimes, and also show how we can explain fluctuating political systems both in countries and in the international system as a whole. Categorizing countries on sliding scales *across time*, such as from 'hereditary monarchy' to 'consolidated democracy' (Polity IV) or from 'full democracies' to 'authoritarian regimes' (*Democracy Index*) or from 'most free' to 'least free' (*Freedom in the World Report*), further helps to endorse the interconnection – and *continuum* – between different political systems.

Building on these ideas, I define authoritarianism as 'a type of government based on strong central authority and limited political freedoms'. This core definition encompasses influences from Levitsky and Ziblatt's *four indicators of authoritarian behaviour*, namely: '1) rejection of democratic rules of the game; 2) denial of the legitimacy of political opponents; 3) toleration of encouragement of violence; and 4) readiness to curtail civil liberties of opponents, including media'.[19] As such, authoritarian regimes display notable and longstanding deficiencies concerning:

- *a lack of political pluralism* – whereby political discourse is typified by limited political participation and activism, a restricted set of political viewpoints, and the frequent domination of politics by a singular leader or single party;
- *a legal system based on rule by law* – that a government applies to its population but not to itself. This contrasts with systems based on *rule of law* that have an independent judiciary, fair and open rules that uniformly apply to all citizens, a transparent and participatory law-making process, and a predictable legal process that provides reliable oversight of ruling elites;
- *a moribund civil society* – the part of a country's social fabric that lobbies for national causes, and which in a democracy would be separate and independent from government and business;
- *a lack of nationwide democratic elections and universal suffrage* – that in a functioning democracy facilitates the peaceful transition and alternation of power between different political actors; and
- *a high degree of control via accompanying personnel and technologies* – that limits the political, economic and social lives and possibilities of the population at large, including highly equipped security forces and widespread state-led surveillance.

These terms encompass Schedler's 'chain of democratic choice',[20] whereby a government or regime is considered to be authoritarian if it violates *even one of these elements*, a criterion that I also deploy here. It demands that democracies ought to be assessed to the highest standards possible and *avoid any back-sliding at all costs*.

These standards will be used to assess the presence of authoritarianism in China, and how such understandings affect its domestic affairs, its particular vision of international order, and the various dimensions of its international relations. From this basis, the criteria will then be used to reveal deeper potential political, cultural and institutional commonalities *throughout the international system*. This analysis will incorporate the application of the criteria to those countries in some of China's key global relationships, but also, more tellingly, other great powers – here the US, Russia and India – in order to reveal if and how authoritarian tendencies are also present and expanding within these countries. Such shared understandings are crucial in determining commonalities between their political systems and worldviews, and if present will underpin and validate the emergence of an authoritarian-oriented international order. Moreover, given the vital role that these great powers perform as the shapers and creators of accepted behaviours and practices in the international sphere, I argue that as they become more authoritarian in nature so too will the dominant international order.

What is 'international order'?

International order as a concept in international relations has come to designate the overall allocation of authority and influence among its leading countries: that is, its 'system-determining' great powers. Also often referred to as 'world order', apart from being hierarchical and relative between countries, this power distribution – in terms of military and economic but also institutions, values and perceptions – has encapsulated the nature of world politics at any given time. As Ikenberry relates, it is quintessentially a search for 'a stable peace', as leading countries attempt 'to establish a wider array of political and economic rules and principles of order, ... [in order] to create a congenial environment in which to pursue their interests'.[21] The construction of such an international architecture provides the global scope of a resultant *international order*. By being based on interactions between countries, international orders are also social in nature. From this basis, international orders are not solely based on material power but also the political and domestic values and outlooks of countries. As such, it is the parallel core values, perceptions and understandings radiating from the more influential countries that regulate the alignment, substance and physiognomy of the international system that they co-constitute. This confluence produces unique international or world order architectures that are specific to particular time periods and are reflective of the dominant countries in the international system in that particular era.

We can highlight the creation of various orders at different points in history. These include the Concert of Europe, dating broadly from the 1814–15 Congress of Vienna until 1914, which balanced power between Austria, France, Prussia, Russia and the United Kingdom (UK). In turn, the Cold War bipolar balance of power between the US and Soviet Union can also be regarded as a particular form of international order, as can US unipolarity between the end of the Cold War and the international terrorist attacks of 11 September 2001 on the US (referred to as 9/11), wherein the US constructed international politics around its liberal democratic outlook. As power fluctuates within the international system, in the midst of its constituent countries' competing ambitions and worldviews, such orders periodically come under pressure, as evidenced by the rise of Nazi Germany and Imperial Japan in the 1930s, and the contemporary rise of China and Asia. Periods of domination – hegemony – by certain powers have been designated as *Pax Romana* (the Roman Empire, 27 BC–180 AD), *Pax Sinicas* (the Han Dynasty, 202 BC–220 AD; the Tang Dynasty, 618–907; the Ming Dynasty, 1368–1644; and the Qing Dynasty 1644–1912), *Pax Mongolica* (the Mongols, 1271–1368), *Pax Britannia* (the British Empire, 1815–1924) and *Pax Americana* (the US, 1945 until the present). Notably, only the last two of these examples were truly global in terms of their power and capabilities.

After the end of the Cold War, US leaders proclaimed a New World Order – a term that has been frequently deployed to signify a desired – or actual – dramatic change in world affairs. To be built on multilateral institutions and international cooperation, then US President George H.W. Bush stated in 1990 that this new international order would be one 'in which the nations of the world, East and West, North and South, can prosper and live in harmony'.[22] The term 'new world order' has further permeated thinking in other fields of study, from anthropology and architecture to biotechnology and business, so as to signify a new ground-breaking paradigm of thinking. These new understandings have frequently been *in reaction* to broader changes that have taken place within international politics, and the seismic consequences that such shifts have resulted in. The term has also been frequently invoked by thinkers *pre-emptively*, in order to analyze how an upcoming shift or an emergent phenomenon will be particularly transformational.

This study concerning China's rise to international pre-eminence – frequently envisaged as a new *Pax Sinica* – and its accompanying worldview based on authoritarianism coming to dominate the nature of world politics (a potential '*Pax Autocratica*') straddles these two domains and is a spectacle that is concurrently occurring and emanant. Notably, the phrase 'new world order' has also featured prominently in various conspiracy theories arguing that there is a secretive global elite (including members of the Freemasons and the Order of the Illuminati, among others) who are orchestrating global crises to create an authoritarian world government. These embedded tropes in Western culture obliquely inform fears over China's rise concerning its authoritarian basis, political opaqueness, potential accumulation of power on a hitherto unseen scale, and alleged aims of global domination.

'Western' international order

The current international order is one that has emanated from the Western world. Emblematic of its principal creation, maintenance and dominance by the US (with some European influences), it is underpinned by specific social, political and economic values stemming from the US's national identity and historical experience. Originating in the aftermath of the First World War, US President Woodrow Wilson's agenda for post-war peace sought to 'reflect distinctive American ideas and ideals'.[23] These ideals imagined an order based on collective security and shared sovereignty, and liberal principles of democracy and universal human rights, accompanied by free trade and international law. As US hegemony increased during the 20th century, these aims were evermore reinforced, giving it the ability to provide security to other countries in order to create open global markets, as well as to sponsor core practices and accompanying institutions. Moreover, a sense of national exceptionalism underpinned this vision, as based on 'a pervasive faith in the uniqueness, immutability, and superiority of the country's founding liberal principles, and ... [the belief] that the US has a special destiny among nations'.[24]

The resultant hierarchical international order gained many monikers from 'liberal hegemonic order', 'American-led liberal world order' or 'American-led liberal hegemony', to 'the free world', 'the West', 'the Atlantic world', '*Pax Democratica*' or '*Pax Americana*'.[25] After many iterations, this liberal international order came to be centred mainly on the consent of countries to the US's broad 'provision of security, wealth creation, and social advancement'.[26] Through its emphasis on international law, US-dominated institutions were the bedrock of this order. In the economic sphere (as will be explained at length in Chapter 3), these included the creation by Washington of the World Bank in 1944, the International Monetary Fund (IMF) in 1945 and the General Agreement on Tariffs and Trade (GATT) in 1947 (the predecessor to the World Trade Organization (WTO)). In the security sphere (as will be investigated in detail in Chapter 4) – and reflecting a creed of collective and cooperative security, so as to ensure a stable international environment – the United Nations (UN) was founded in 1945 and the North Atlantic Treaty Organization (NATO) in 1949. Notably, these bodies emerged in the aftermath of the Second World War, which had confirmed the US's global pre-eminence, and reflected its national beliefs in the social and political, economic and military realms. Though formulated within the West, US leaders believed that these values would extend outwards to non-Western and developing countries.

Three realms

In the social and political realm, and as espoused through the UN's 1948 Universal Declaration of Human Rights, the liberal international order sought to guarantee rights on an individual level. These promoted freedom of thought and expression, of religion, of movement and association and of sexual orientation, whereby 'any particular freedom is to be respected only insofar as it does not violate the equal freedom of others'.[27] In turn, liberal democracy – that made ruling officials accountable to a country's voting citizens – was also central. Within a liberal international order, such 'rule by the people' encompassed freedom of political participation, representation, expression and association. It also included having regular free, inclusive and equal elections, the presence of accountable and transparent political institutions to guarantee the individual liberties and rights of citizens, and access to competing information. At its core, the US endorsed electoral democracy as the central and unquestionable pillar of its preferred international order. Such social and political rights are seen as being generalizable to the internal basis of all countries, and hence the whole international system. They also produced a sense of solidarity among Western countries concerning the preservation of a common social and political basis.

For the economic realm, and as the world's dominant power after 1945, the US arranged the world economy in line with its broader security and political interests. After the Second World War, economic growth and trade liberalization went hand in hand with the creation of modern social democracy, whereby economic prosperity would enhance individual social and political – especially democratic – rights. Economic liberalism thus upholds 'the rights of individuals to make any choices they please in the exercise of their labour and the use of their wealth and income, so long as they respect the liberty, property and contractual rights of others'.[28] Key to this vision were open global markets and free trade practices enshrined by anti-protectionist institutions through the rule of law. Such a basis married with a focus on cooperation, shared gains and interdependence, backed up by domestic welfare states. Underpinning this system was the US dollar as the premier international currency, with access to the US market and technology provided to countries that would be reliable partners and allies. Through the Washington Consensus, first posited in 1989 (and investigated further in Chapter 3), these ideals metamorphosized into the mantra of neoliberalism, which promoted free-market capitalism via policies that included privatization, deregulation and globalization, as well as lower government spending and austerity.

The final realm of the US-dominated liberal order rests on the use of force as a means to stabilize and strengthen its desired international order, with military intervention being regarded as necessary to protect and enforce liberal democracy and human rights. In this way, the 1950–53 Korean War sought 'to establish the rule of law in the world',[29] while the 1955–75 Vietnam War aimed to 'defend the frontiers of freedom'.[30] Defence planners also saw military power as vital to securing global markets and resources via the threat or use of military force, as well as a worldwide alliance system between the US and its regional partners, built on institutions and formal agreements. The US's 800 military bases across 80 countries (versus 70 held by all other countries)[31] underscores the centrality of military force to its international order, and its use to promote its goals, values and interests, whereby, as a former US president noted, if you 'speak softly and carry a big stick, you will go far'.[32] Compounding this importance, many of these bases were also established following demands by US allies for protection and deterrence against aggression. Military power has thus been used to strengthen the other realms of the US-led liberal international order, making 'access to resources and markets, socioeconomic stability, political pluralism, and American security interests – all … inextricably linked'.[33]

Dominance, hubris and China's challenge

The collapse of the Soviet Union and the end of the Cold War signalled the zenith of the US-led international order, which was unchallenged at the close of the 20th century. American thinkers proclaimed the irresistible triumph of the West's liberal international order as marking 'the end of history' – that is, 'the end point of mankind's ideological evolution and the universalisation of Western liberal democracy as the final form of human government'.[34] Moreover, with its main strategic competitor sidelined, and a dearth of viable alternatives, the liberal hegemony narrative presumed that rising powers such as China could be co-opted into the US-led international order. Such dominance led to an unashamed dawning of *Pax Americana*, with observers arguing 'Why deny it? Why be embarrassed by it?'[35] Notably, these claims entailed elements of myth and presumption, as not all the world – including China,

India, the former Soviet bloc, much of the Islamic world and many developing countries – had been subsumed into such a concept. This divergence indicated that the Western order was pre-eminent but not omnipotent and was thus a dominant *international order* but not necessarily a sweeping *world order*. It also overlooked the US's periodic support of various authoritarian regimes (such as in Pakistan, Indonesia and Iran), and its overthrow of democratic regimes (across South America, for example), factors which will be elucidated at length in Chapters 1 and 5.

As the 21st century began, the liberal international order experienced three major crises that called into question its global legitimacy and reputation. The first of these came after 9/11 and the subsequent invasions of Afghanistan and Iraq, and the resultant long period of occupation, instability and widespread deaths, which effectively undercut the acceptability of deploying overwhelming force in geopolitics. The use of torture, clandestine jails (known as 'black sites') and rendition, as well as the pursuit of nebulous political reforms, further questioned the validity of the military, social and political pillars of the US-led liberal international order. Washington's departure from Afghanistan in the summer of 2021, which led to the rapid political return of the Taliban – whose removal had been cited as the major aim of the US's 2001 invasion, and who re-took the country in weeks – further undercuts this legitimacy and in many ways signalled the death of 'liberal military interventionism'. In turn, the 2008 credit crisis served to challenge the core rationales of the Western-based international financial system, and hence the liberal economic pillar of the current international order. Going further still, the current coronavirus pandemic which began in 2020 has also revealed the seeming inability of the US (and other Western states) to comprehensively protect the wellbeing and security of their citizens. It also asked if the privileging of individual rights is the best basis for a society versus protecting the collective health of a population as a whole (as has been the norm for many other countries, especially in China and across East Asia).

As the credibility of the Western liberal international order has been called into question, the rise of China has presented a clear challenge to it – and an alternative vision of international order.[36] Socially and politically, China bears the hallmarks of an authoritarian system as it inhibits political pluralism, sanctions political participation, imprisons opponents, and uses state apparatuses to monitor, control and command the population. In turn, the country's slow embrace of liberal economics – but merged with state control and a blurring between public and private ownership – has resulted in an economic system defined as being *authoritarian-capitalist* (as investigated in Chapter 3). China's creation of different multilateral regimes, such as the Asian Infrastructure Investment Bank (AIIB) and the Shanghai Cooperation Organization (SCO), which are analyzed in depth in Chapter 4, also act as mechanisms to further project China's values into the global system. Together, these elements have produced a social, political and economic basis that contrasts to the core dynamics of the current liberal international order. They also act as an inspirational and non-ideological developmental model for other countries to follow, and by extension are engendering a new – China-inspired – *illiberal world order.*

Such challenges and creeping authoritarianism are not confined to the non-Western world. 'Anti-elitist', assertive and nationalist-minded leaders lead (or have led) the world's great – that is, the most influential economic, political, military and diplomatic – powers. These countries will also help to delineate the foundations of world politics – and thus of international order – in the decades to come. When in office, the populist US President Trump openly questioned civil liberties, attacked the media, and sidelined and undermined major bureaucratic and legal bodies. In Russia, an autocratic President Putin routinely silences liberal opposition groups, restricts free speech and controls media outlets. And in India, Prime Minister Modi's Hindu nationalist rule is typified by state censorship, the frequent banning of non-governmental organizations, and increased violence towards minority groups. Together with China's President Xi, the leaders of these countries all display highly personalistic leadership styles, along with a desire for centralized political control, an appeal to mass public audiences and a sustained intolerance of dissent. In 2016, according to the *Democracy Index*,[37] the US and India were considered to be 'flawed democracies', while Russia and China were classified as 'authoritarian'. These factors, and what are becoming clear commonalities, are analyzed in Chapter 6, especially concerning their adoption of ever-more powerful surveillance capabilities.

Approach and structure

To elucidate its underpinning arguments concerning the centrality of identity and values concerning the shift from a liberal to an authoritarian international order, this book utilizes five key themes.

Continuum

Authoritarianism and democracy are argued as not being opposing and exclusive political systems but are instead fundamentally interrelated on one single political spectrum. From this perspective, there is no fixed, binary – either/or – divide between democracies and authoritarian (and even totalitarian) regimes but rather they are essentially fluid, interconnected and impermanent entities. From this basis, democratic regimes can simultaneously display particular authoritarian inclinations, and vice versa.

Facilitation

As the world's great powers become increasingly authoritarian, I contend that so too will the resultant international order, because it is the domestic political identities – and associated values and mindsets – of these great powers that are able to inform, shape and dictate dominant *global* values and behaviour. In this dynamic, China acts as the critical agent that proactively stimulates this shift, but so too are foremost countries (such as the US and India) whose gradual use of authoritarian politics is also enabling this change.

Assimilation

Just as the predominant political basis of any country can develop, shift and evolve, so too does the basis of the prevailing international order. In these ways, the constituent parts of a China-centric international order – and arguably international and world orders more generally – are formed through processes of gestation and absorption. Such processes are apparent as China has acclimatized itself to Western-originating economic and institutional practices, but also as the Western countries increasingly integrate elements of China's political style into their domestic practices.

Normalization

As authoritarianism becomes a widely shared phenomenon among the world's leading – both established and rising – great powers, so too will it become the central feature of global politics as a whole. Such an adoption will span the political, cultural and institutional domains of global politics. It will mean that authoritarianism becomes an increasingly normalized reference point that many other countries will be progressively socialized into by China and other countries, or which they will actively seek to emulate.

Longevity

International orders are evidenced by the very extended periods of time that they are active. From this basis, time is not only central concerning normalizing the existence of a particular international order. It also indicates when the domination of a country's – or potentially a set of countries' – particular worldview, and its associated political, social, cultural and other values, eventually solidifies into an actual *order*. It also underpins my assertion that the 21st century will become an indisputable *Authoritarian Century*, inspired by and reflective of China at its epicentre.

From this basis, this book is structured as follows. Chapter 1 focuses on the particular principles, narratives and ideas that motivate how China's leaders seek to control modern China's domestic social and political fabric. Central to this basis is the continued practice of authoritarian governance resting on a singular and oligarchic figure or group, as based on enduring principles of *tian xia* ('all under heaven'). Chapter 2 then elucidates the various political principles, both ancient and modern, on which notions of a China-specific international order will be built. It outlines the core elements of its specific world vision and how the various influences on this process have evolved over China's existence. From this basis, Chapter 3 goes on to exemplify how China's gradual embrace of liberal economics – often merged with specific Chinese values and characteristics based on state control – has given it a system-determining capacity in international affairs. This capacity has allowed it to cast its own vision of authority and order within a contemporary geopolitical structure that has become highly dependent on China's ongoing economic success.

Chapter 4 shows how China's creation of new multilateral regimes is giving it a managerial role to govern and regulate international affairs. Underscoring this system-ordering potential, and also a necessary differentiation from existing groupings, China's particular beliefs concerning multipolarity, global governance, human rights, peaceful development and non-intervention are engendering a new form of international order. Chapter 5 next investigates China's regional standing, which acts as the fulcrum of its desired international order. Stemming from the country's physical dominance of East Asia, it shows how China is enacting core principles concerning *tian xia*, hierarchy, harmony and respect in its relations with the region. In turn, Chapter 6 expands our analytical scope from Asia to the global stage. Drawing on how hegemons not only create international order but also provide leadership, as well as territorial, financial and existential security, it discusses and evaluates how *increasing authoritarianism among great powers* is changing the conduct and nature of global affairs. In the Conclusion, each chapter's findings are synthesized to evaluate China's prospective impact on the international system, including looking at how a China-inspired authoritarian international order will function, the various kinds of futures that it may engender, and how it will affect people living in democracies.

1

Controlled Politics

Here I investigate the major values, narratives and motivations underpinning how the Chinese Communist Party (CCP) rules modern-day China. Through a political system that lacks political pluralism, nationwide democratic elections and an active civil society, as well as a legal system based on rule by law and a pervasive surveillance apparatus, daily life in contemporary China displays all the hallmarks of authoritarianism for its people. At the heart of these narratives is the CCP's desire for the continued control of China's domestic political and social fabric, which is perpetuated by the system of centralized authoritarian governance. Such a system appears to deeply contrast with the social and political realm of the current US-led liberal international order, which is based on an adherence to liberal democracy, universal human rights; accountable political institutions and the rule of law, and core freedoms of political participation, representation, expression and association.

Despite the CCP's ascent to power through a successful communist-based revolution in the 1940s, the Confucian values of the previous 2,000 years of China's history continue to permeate its rule. As we shall see in more detail in Chapter 2, such values sought to harmonize the country's social relations through the ordering system of *tian xia* ('all under heaven'), centred on paternalistic and hierarchical principles based on collective loyalty, reciprocity and interdependence. For the CCP, this system seeks to preserve stability and order, underpinned by the quest for 'great national unity' (*da yi tong*). More widely, Confucianism's contemporary presence includes Chinese citizenship being based more on obligations than rights,[1] welfare and health policies encompassing concepts of benevolence and morality,[2] and education being regarded as a form of personal development.[3] This persistence also allows these values to contest dominant Western liberal philosophies, while Confucianism's 'modernization' (*xiandaihua*) in contemporary China serves as a tool that effectively strengthens the ideological control of the CCP.

The constant realities of having a vast territory (the world's fourth largest), a huge population (the world's largest at nearly 1.4 billion people) and the joint highest number of neighbouring countries (14) further underscore the scale of the challenges faced by China's rulers. Such threats are augmented by the historical memory and experience of huge internal mass rebellions and bloodshed, resulting in a CCP that deeply fears unrest. All of these factors are reminders for the CCP of the necessity of maintaining autocratic control, as it is the central means by which the developmental, regional, global and status goals of its ongoing revolution can be achieved.

Characteristic of these concerns, protest is a daily occurrence in modern China as the country continues its rapid economic and social transformation. Such protests are personified by so-called mass incidents, defined as 'scale protests and acts of civil disobedience that result in rioting and the destruction of commercial, CCP or state property'.[4] Occurring in response to specific economic, corruption, environmental degradation, inequality or civil rights issues, they have risen in frequency from 8,700 in 1993 to 180,000 in 2010 (shortly after which official bodies in China ceased to publish annual numbers). The CCP also faces what are known as the 'three evil forces' (*san gu shili*) of terrorism, ethnic separatism and religious extremism that threaten national security, and which primarily emanate from Xinjiang and Tibet. As a result of these pressures, since 2010 China's spending on public security has *surpassed* spending on the military, and reached $212.49 billion[5] in 2019, a threefold increase over the prior decade.[6] Such increases, in the pursuit of 'stability maintenance', show the growing costs needed to maintain internal control within a political system that is highly sensitive to any sources of conflict. As we shall see, in the modern era such spending helps realize the CCP's increasingly proactive oppression of any sources of political opposition (including in the media, business and academia) and cultural difference (most clearly in Xinjiang and Tibet), as well as the building of the social credit system that is designed to create a peaceful society of 'socially harmonized and politically compliant subjects'.[7]

The CCP also needs to encourage sources of domestic legitimacy in order to maintain its 'mandate of heaven' (*tian ming*). According to Xunzi, a Confucian philosopher, although people can be subjugated by raw power and wealth, the only way to make them willingly submit is via a moral power that convinces them to voluntarily comply.[8] Thus, for the CCP, legitimacy does not solely come from the delivery of transformative economic wealth or the use of state violence to quell dissent but must include a display of moral leadership. CCP rule is therefore a balancing act emblematic of the Chinese saying that 'the leader who nurtures benevolence through morality is a king but the leader who rules only by might is a tyrant'.[9]

Culture of domination

The CCP that emerged in the first half of the 20th century, and which founded the People's Republic of China (PRC) in 1949, is a political grouping whose power rests on domination. In the early 20th century, this perspective characterized its rise against – and eventual defeat of – domestic opponents. These ranged from the remnants of the imperial system that had ruled China for the previous 2,000 years, to the nationalist Kuomintang, which was defeated by the CCP during the Chinese civil war that intermittently occurred between 1927 and 1949. It also applied to external foes, principally Japan, which had fully invaded China in 1937, as well as Western powers, which since the mid-1800s had reduced China's political and trade dominance in East Asia, resulting in the so-called Century of Humiliation (as detailed in Chapter 2). As a key influence on the formation of its identity – and by extension, that of China's political basis – these experiences all strengthened the CCP's resolve to monopolize China's one-party state. In such a political system, a single party forms the country's government, with all other political bodies either being prohibited from political activities or having severely restricted political participation.

The CCP is founded on principles of Marxist-Leninism, the ideology underpinning communism, resulting in 'socialism with

Chinese characteristics'. Most clearly pursued by Mao Zedong, it aims for the revolutionary attainment of a socialist state through the 'dictatorship of the proletariat', often using the entire population in mass campaigns. At its core is the principle of democratic centralism, a Leninist organizational principle which asserts that once decisions are made by a small group of leaders, they must be implemented throughout the party system. This concept underpins the structure of the CCP, from the main seven-member Politburo Standing Committee led by Xi Jinping to the Politburo (20–25 members), the Central Committee (300–400 members) and the National Party Congress (2,200 members), all of which serve to cascade policy instructions down through the various province, county, city, town and village levels of the Party structure. Such a process is reinforced through the CCP's 91 million members (in 2017), plus the 89 million members (in 2013) of the Communist Youth League of China. Within the CCP, the Central Commission for Discipline Inspection punishes any violation of CCP rules and regulations, defends party ideology and orthodoxy, and prevents corruption. In turn, the Central Propaganda Department deals with information management through the control and censorship of the country's media, and the granting of licences to media providers. Notably, liberal economic reforms introduced in the late 1970s downplayed the role of Marxist-Leninist 'class struggle' in favour of economic development and modernization, and saw their replacement by new mantras relating to China's 'socialist market economy'.

As the Party controls all major institutional appointments, there is a virtual inseparability of the CCP from the country's government institutions, as the CCP determines and guides China's political, social, economic and diplomatic policies. The CCP's infused presence is therefore a highly normalized aspect of everyday life in modern China. Apart from stemming from China's deep-seated cultural heritage of centralized political subordination (as engrained through at least 70 different dynasties since that of Yu the Great, circa 2070 BC), such authoritarian control is regarded by the CCP as the natural way to ensure stability and prosperity. Such a proclivity also allows for the pursuit of its domestic, regional and global ambitions 'without the distractions and abrupt course changes brought about by that inherently unstable system known as democracy, with its fixation on rival parties and alternation'.[10] Such a basis further allows for the CCP to protect China from unwanted external influence – a central legacy of the Century of Humiliation – and thus helps to block attempts by Western powers to influence China.

Significantly, and emblematic of a key theme of this volume, China's political basis has evolved and oscillated across the *continuum*, interlinking different political regimes. In the earliest decades of the PRC, this continuum extended beyond authoritarianism to totalitarianism, whereby the Chinese government controlled and managed *all* aspects of public and private life in China. Primarily characterized by the presence of one supreme individual leader, an official ideology, and the use of terror and propaganda as methods of control, totalitarian regimes desire the total domination and atomization of each individual in all spheres of life. Such a form of political rule typified China under Mao Zedong, who had absolute control over China from the 1940s to the 1970s. That system was exemplified by a Soviet-style command economy centred on collectivized agriculture and industry, as the CCP determined what needed to be produced and when. It was accompanied by the 'iron rice bowl' and its 'five guarantees' concerning access to housing, medical care, pensions, nurseries and schools, and cheap food and goods, meaning that the population was entirely dependent on the state. Finally, the nationwide use of communes served to regulate the social existence of the population, including when they could marry and have children, and virtually curtailed their right to free movement, resulting in very low social and geographical mobility. Each citizen also had a *dang'an* (or file) noting their social position, job and marital status. Within such a system, the CCP had total social, educative and economic control of its people.

This totalitarian rule ushered in periods of severe political, social and economic turmoil in China. These included the Great Leap Forward of 1958–62, an economic and social campaign intended to transform the Chinese economy through the rapid development of the country's agrarian and industrial capabilities. The campaign aimed to leap across the capitalist stage of development and achieve a socialist society. It ended in complete failure due to bad weather, poor communication and ill-placed ideological zeal, which arrested economic growth, intensified a widespread famine (that killed between 20 and 45 million people), and resulted in extreme shortages of food, goods and products. In turn, the 1966–76 Cultural Revolution sought to purify and preserve the ideology of the CCP in the form of a hyper-Maoism, while purging any elements associated with imperial China. Later, radical commitment to the ideological purity of the CCP was further accelerated by the Gang of Four (which included Mao's wife, Jiang Qing), resulting in widespread violence and instability across China. It also led to millions of people being persecuted, imprisoned and executed, as well as at least one million unnatural deaths[11] and a badly malfunctioning economy.

The totalitarian period only ended with Mao's death in 1976, and China's political system evolved to become more authoritarian, as shown by the gradual embrace of free market economic reforms in the late 1970s. Mao's successor, Deng Xiaoping, sought to reshape CCP rule away from mass campaigns, purges and divisive dogmatism to one based on consensus, ideological flexibility and the ability to adapt. Key phrases such as 'practice is the sole criterion for testing truth' and 'correct mistakes whenever they are discovered' also signalled to the population that criticism – even if still constrained – was now acceptable. It also showed the CCP that its popular legitimacy (and survival) could come from raising living standards and economic gains, as well as giving some power to the grassroots over the country's bureaucracy. These concessions were balanced, however, with continued authoritarianism and centralized control, as expedited by the CCP.

There was also some separation of the Party and the government, which limited the role of the CCP in day-to-day government and China's economic activities, and allowed for increased consultation with think tanks and impartial policy advisers. Deng further rejected Mao's mantra of 'red versus expert' (whereby ideological purity and professional skills were mutually exclusive) and replaced it with 'red and expert', which led to civil service reforms based on competitive recruitment and merit-based promotion. The importance of *guanxi* – the system of interpersonal social networks and influential associations used to expedite business, political and other dealings between individuals or groups in China and across East Asia – also persisted. It originated from Confucian thought in that it encapsulates concepts of hierarchy, trust, reciprocity and mutual responsibility as the means to ensure the stability of the wider economic and social order. As the CCP is the overriding arbiter of China's social and political basis, it acts as *guanxi's* main fulcrum.

The ascendancy of Xi Jinping to lead China has only reinforced rather than diluted the country's authoritarianism. If anything, it has even marked a regression towards the totalitarianism of the past. By removing the presidential term limit in 2018, Xi – who was born in 1953 – could possibly be China's president for the next 20 years, as an effective 'President of Everything' who is the 'Chairman of the Board' or the CEO of the CCP and the PRC.[12] Further echoing the earlier omnipotence of Mao, his rise to pre-eminence included the use of anti-corruption drives to purge his political rivals (including hundreds of ministers and millions of party cadres, as well as Zhou Yongkang, the former national security minister); a nationwide crackdown on civil rights lawyers, activists and minorities; increased internet and press censorship; writing himself into China's Constitution; and producing the eponymous Xi Jinping Thought, which includes the China Dream. Such actions have been accompanied by a carefully crafted cult of personality that further resonates with memories of Mao. Reinforcing the continuance of the CCP's authoritarian rule, at the 19th National Congress in October 2017 Xi reasserted China to be a feasible counter-model to Western liberal democracy, stating that 'no one political system should be regarded as the only choice and we should not just mechanically copy the political systems of other countries'.[13]

Sanctioned political participation

Through an ongoing process of co-option, limitation and coercion, political participation in the PRC is highly sanctioned, resulting in a system that is – despite some restricted forms of engagement – anti-pluralistic in nature. While China's economic liberalization demanded some social relaxation and mechanisms to incorporate non-CCP views into the political process, any consultations have been controlled. Expanding political participation continues to be seen by the CCP as being destabilizing, as evidenced during the Cultural Revolution and through events such as the

Hundred Flowers Bloom campaign of 1956–57 that encouraged the population to voice their opinions about the CCP, so as to promote socialism and invoke cultural change. Although initially conservative, this campaign escalated as Mao urged all opinions to be aired, leading to widespread criticism of the CCP, which led to the campaign being suspended. Similarly, the Democracy Wall protests of 1978–79 were initially allowed by the CCP in Beijing to vent public criticism of the Gang of Four, but were curtailed after they spread across China and led to calls for democratic and human rights reform. Most vividly, the Tiananmen Square protests of 1989 encapsulated various critiques against the CCP's political, social and economic policies and spread to 400 cities across China, involving over one million people. Despite occasional conciliation, the protests were ultimately seen as a threat to CCP legitimacy and were crushed by the People's Liberation Army on 4 June, leading to between 300 and 10,000 deaths according to either official or external sources.

Although other political groupings exist, such as the eight political groups and the All-China Federation of Industry and Commerce making up the United Front parties, they are assimilated into the centralized, hierarchical and subservient nature of the CCP. All of these parties were formed between 1925 and 1948 and were brought together to help the CCP form the PRC. While they are represented in bodies such as the Chinese People's Political Consultative Conference, they remain very small, with only thousands of members, and cannot in any sense be regarded as a formal political 'opposition'. The CCP's own deep-seated experience of revolution and civil war, and as a group that seized power from a small base, reinforces such domination. When alternative political parties have emerged, such as the China Democracy Party in 1998 (founded by individuals associated with the 1989 Tiananmen Square protests), they have been immediately banned and forced into exile. Similarly, when 303 activists and intellectuals signed the Charter 08 manifesto in 2008 demanding widespread political liberalization, they were imprisoned. Finally, and despite being initially permitted by the CCP, in 1999 the modern spiritual movement Falun Gong – with nearly 70 million members – was also proscribed, as it was seen to threaten China's national security and the survival of the one-party state.

Rather counterintuitively, elections were introduced for China's one million villages in 1988. Intended to help fill the organizational vacuum after the collapse of the commune system, they allow for self-governance in villages including the management of local budgets. They also form the lowest level of China's hierarchical electoral system, through which local people's congresses are directly elected via village elections. In a distinctly Chinese form of democracy, the elected members of these people's congresses then indirectly elect the higher levels above them, up to and including the National People's Congress (China's national legislature made up of members of the CCP and the United Front parties), which rubberstamps leadership decisions of the CCP. Heads of counties, districts, townships and towns, as well as provincial governors and mayors, are in turn elected by their respective local people's congresses. The fairness of village elections is often questioned, with many candidates being chosen by the CCP or there only being the same number of candidates as electable positions. The CCP's absolute control of political discourse and mobilization also dissuades any meaningful organized political opposition. It is estimated that 80 per cent (according to the CCP) to 10 per cent (unofficially) of all villages conduct regular elections.[14] In 2000, officials in Beijing also allowed direct elections in the 5,000 resident committees involved with urban governance. While there is periodic speculation that China's direct elections will be introduced beyond the village level, there is no real intention for the CCP or the state to be truly accountable to China's citizens.

Furthermore, all trade unions (referred to as 'mass organizations') are sanctioned by the CCP so as to incorporate them into the one-party state and to constrain their activities. Any such organizations have to register with a sponsoring state agency that oversees their activities, and any similar organizations are prohibited in order to limit their national presence. Although they pursue members' rights, and collectively represent in excess of 200 million members, these groupings are not independent as their very existence is dependent on the CCP's conditional support. There are also around 675,000 registered and an estimated three million unregistered non-governmental organizations (known as 'social organizations') in China[15] that are involved in private schools, hospitals, vocational training and other forms of activism. As they threaten CCP autonomy due to providing welfare functions where state provision is lacking, they too are forced to be affiliated with the CCP, which also dictates that no two organizations can campaign for the same thing, thus atomizing their activities to specific localities. From this basis, and if defined as an independent realm of autonomous political space essential for building a democracy and the rule of law, China's wider civil society is fragmented and dysfunctional. That stated, the use of an active complaints system within workplaces is deployed by the government to garner public opinion and to even shift policy, resulting in a form of decentralized authoritarianism that echoes similar Confucian practices conducted in ancient China.

Domestically, the CCP also asserts control over the state broadcaster China Central Television (CCTV), the official news agency Xinhua, and the *People's Daily* newspaper. In 2016, Xi toured the country's news outlets, telling journalists that 'they must love the party, protect the party, and closely align themselves with the party leadership in thought, politics and action'.[16] Such efforts stressed the CCP's active restriction of freedoms of speech and of the press and resulted in further constraints against a range of academics, novelists, feminists, actors and artists, as well as booksellers in Hong Kong.[17] As a result of such repression, in 2020 the *World Press Freedom Index* ranked China 177th out of 180 countries, noting that Beijing's systematic constraint and control of press freedoms are 'not just a danger for the people of China – they have more journalists in jail than anyone else – but it's trickling throughout our international information systems, ... they're trying to influence how we get and perceive information everywhere'.[18] Through content-sharing agreements, Beijing is also able to insinuate its worldview into international media sources, whereby 'hundreds of millions of news consumers around the world routinely view, read, or listen to information created or influenced by the CCP, often without knowing its origins',[19] which tacitly encourages its use of censorship abroad.

The China Global Television Network (known as CCTV International until 2016) has further internationalized the CCP's viewpoint, with international channels in English, Spanish, French, Arabic and Russian, and covering Africa, the Americas and Europe, and which aims 'to influence public opinion overseas in order to nudge foreign governments into making policies favourable towards [China]'.[20] Relatedly, in 2013 President Xi unveiled a project to develop 50–100 new state-affiliated and international prestigious think tanks with 'Chinese characteristics'. Intended to give China enhanced 'international discourse power',[21] such think tanks ought to be viewed as agents that work for rather than oversee the government, and which are intended to 'tell Chinese stories and spread Chinese voices'.[22]

Such practices have resulted in China increasingly pressurizing a host of countries and organizations to respect China's worldview. These include Cambridge University Press, which in August 2017 admitted to blocking access to 315 journal articles in *The China Quarterly* in China concerning the Cultural Revolution, Tibet, Xinjiang and the Tiananmen Square protests, at the request of Chinese censors. Cambridge University Press justified this decision as necessary to maintain further market access on other subjects in China, but it led to threats of a Western boycott and the decision was reversed three days later. Evident, too, is China pressurizing Western universities to change their curricula to reflect the CCP's historical perspectives,[23] including the use of overseas branches of the CCP to monitor staff and students[24] and physically attacking critics on overseas campuses.[25]

In 2020, the CCP also demanded that an exhibition by a museum in Nantes on ancient Mongolia remove all references to 'Genghis Khan', 'Mongols' and 'Empire',[26] which was rebuffed. In addition, the CCP attacked the awarding of the Nobel Peace Prize in 2010 to Charter 08 activist Liu Xiaobo, has banned foreign correspondents, civil society and human rights activists from entering (and leaving) China,[27] and in 2021 barred BBC World News from broadcasting in China. Anyone who is critical of CCP policy in Xinjiang has also faced censure, such as the manager of the Houston Rockets (which led to National Basketball Association games being taken off air in China[28]), UK MPs, lawyers and academics (leading to sanctions against them[29]), and Western fashion brands such as Burberry and H&M (resulting in the ending of contracts with many Chinese public figures[30]).

Rule by law and collective human rights

Reinforcing forms of sanctioned political participation, China's legal system is premised on notions of 'rule by law' rather than 'rule of law', whereby it has from the time of Confucius been 'an instrument of government for setting national direction and controlling the population, as well as achieving collective national aims'.[31] In this sense, a rule by law legal system – as instituted in China by former General Secretary of the CCP Jiang Zemin's 'socialist legality' – is one which is used 'for the resolution of people's disputes, to maintain harmony, but not to implement any social change or to check arbitrary governmental powers',[32] or to protect the fundamental human rights of the population. Instead, China's 'socialism with Chinese characteristics' requires a legal system that allows economic freedom (as per the 1970s liberalization reforms) but permits the CCP to sustain tight political control, and to mitigate against social and political reform. Rule by law is seen by observers as a way for the CCP to maintain its moral oversight of China, or what Confucius deemed to be 'rule by virtue'. As a result, in 2020, China ranked 88 out of 120 countries on the World Justice Project's *Rule of Law Index*.[33]

China's legal system is thus used against political opponents to achieve the CCP's interests and ambitions, and 'typically only applie[s] to ordinary people, ... by contrast, high-ranking government officials ha[ve] little or no legal accountability'.[34] Notably, the conviction rate in China is 98 per cent.[35] Fundamentally, the CCP's rule by law starkly contrasts with Western concepts of rule of law, all of which are a check on the power of the state: an independent judiciary; fair and open rules that apply uniformly to all; transparency and participation in the law-making process; and overall predictability and consistency in the legal process. Furthermore, as China's geopolitical and geo-economic interests expand, so too will its legal system act as a device by which the CCP's domestic authoritarian system is exported abroad, 'becom[ing] an intellectual competitor to Western rule of law, ... [and] may well write the blueprint for the legal systems of other countries'.[36] Typifying this view, Xi announced in 2017 that 'the rule by law is our historical mission'.[37]

These sentiments inform China's attitude towards human rights, which from the time of Confucius has emphasized collective duties over individual rights. Regarded as inalienable, human rights are a set of moral principles relating to particular criteria of human behaviour that encompass freedom of speech, voting rights, freedoms of thought, conscience and religion, and equality before the law, as well as the right to life, freedom from torture and slavery, and freedom of movement. While China recognizes that such rights are universal, and has signed the two core United Nations covenants relating to human rights in 1997 and 1998, the CCP insists that China is entitled (along with other countries) 'to interpret the international law of human rights in accordance with the traditional values of their societies rather than in accordance with the wishes of the West'.[38] Also done to protect itself from what it perceives as the damaging individualism of Western liberalism (and unwanted legal interference from the West in its internal affairs), China's attitude reflects a cultural adherence to collectivism that stresses the importance of the group over the self. This mindset is prevalent across East Asia, and informs Chinese society, China's one-party state and Mao's emphasis on the 'masses'; all 'see the community as an ideal organic harmony and the individual solely in terms of fulfilling a function or role in the whole that determines his or her rights and duties'.[39] Although placing it in opposition with many Western countries, China's attitude on human rights often aids its diplomatic ties with other authoritarian regimes, and further enables the export of an authoritarian international order.

Human rights in China must thus be seen through the lens of its one-party state that sanctions political participation and opposition groups, advocates a legal system premised on rule by law, and severely limits the role played by civil society, religious beliefs, the media and minority groups. As a result, most – if not all – of the freedoms listed in any universal definition of human rights (as above) are not present within the Chinese context. In addition, the 1982 Constitution removed the right to strike, as well as the four freedoms (known as the 'four Bigs' associated with the Democracy Wall movement) to speak out freely, air views fully, hold great debates and to write big character posters. The one-child policy carried out from 1979 (and phased out from 2015) to restrict population growth is also seen to violate universal human rights standards. So too is the widespread use of the death penalty, torture and re-education camps as forms of social and legal control, with international observers stating in 2019 that the number of annual executions in China are vastly under-reported and are probably in the thousands – the world's highest.[40] In 2018, China's prison population was estimated to be 2.36 million (not including those in detention camps in Xinjiang) or 167 out of every 100,000 Chinese citizens (versus 639 in the US, 331 in Russia and 35 in India).[41]

Censorship and surveillance

Coalescing this system of social and political control is the deep use of censorship in order to police, proscribe and punish what is written, discussed and shared in China. Underpinning such control is a desire to produce narratives conducive to the continued rule of the CCP, whereby 'to write history is the way to form and change memories and shape and alter worldviews and preferences, ... therefore, "history" functions as the *de facto* national and state religion in the Chinese world'.[42] Such practices date from the Qin Dynasty (221–206 BC), which had the censorate (*yushi tai*), later called *ducha yuan* in the Ming (1368–1644) and Qing (1644–1912) Dynasties, which exerted disciplinary power over all civil officials and discourse. From the time of the Ming Dynasty, communication with foreign countries was also forbidden and public opinion controlled through Confucian mantras such as 'loyalty to your emperor and nation'. These systems have been systematically deepened by the CCP.

Nowhere better is this combination of factors shown than in the regulation of the internet in China, which seeks to create a Foucauldian panopticon that encourages self-censorship and self-regulation. By doing so, the CCP aims to counteract Western arguments that assume a connection between 'technological advances and democratization',[43] which according to cyber-libertarians will facilitate regime change through the global free flow of information. In this regard, China sees 'internet freedom and US doctrines of [the] "free flow of information" a[s] tools hegemonic America penetrates'.[44] Instead, the CCP's goal has been to use the internet as a tool to enhance nationwide surveillance, constrain unsanctioned debate (including by pro-democracy activists and separatists), boost the legitimacy of the CCP and limit any negative side-effects through the overarching 'guidance of public opinion'.[45] In 2020, this aim applied to 988 million internet users in China, representing nearly a quarter of all global users,[46] as well as across Chinese social media platforms such as WeChat, Weibo, TikTok and Tencent. The overall intensity of censorship is initiated by the central government, then carried out by the Central Propaganda Department, the Ministry of Information Industry, the Ministry of State Security, the Ministry of Public Security and the People's Liberation Army, before being supported by internet service providers that commit to self-censorship (primarily in order to maximize profits), and then last of all circumvented, ignored or further policed by individual netizens.

Accompanying legislation, such as the 2017 Cybersecurity Law of the People's Republic of China, obliges domestic and foreign companies to localize their data collection in China, cooperate with law enforcement officials, and enforce online content restrictions. These actors work together with complex internet filtering software systems to produce the Great Firewall (also known as the Golden Shield), the term used to describe China's massive online censorship and surveillance system. Through such 'algorithmic governance', this system includes the active monitoring of internet traffic by at least 30,000 censors working for the Chinese government and the blocking of content and access to non-compliant websites and servers (inside and outside China). The '50-centers' are also hired to influence opinion online in favour of the CCP, ostensibly for 50 cents per post, and explicitly support the Party through the creation of positive comments or articles, the disruption of anti-Party discussions and the discrediting of political opponents. Reflecting the severity of the CCP's capacity to control debate, a 2017 study found that of the '43,757 posts [analyzed], only 281 were made by individuals or groups we could not identify, ... the remaining 99.3% were contributed by one of over 200 government agencies throughout the Chinese regime's matrix organizational structure'.[47] These powerful mechanisms are so widespread that they effectively block off China's internet from the rest of the world, thus delivering 'a blueprint for ... authoritarians elsewhere'.[48]

In turn, China's real name registration policy requires internet users to link their email and social media accounts with their

National ID, passport or mobile phone number, and to do the same if they wish to purchase or use a VPN (virtual private network). Observers have also reported how internet users 'will be charged with defamation if online rumours they create are visited by 5,000 internet users or reposted more than 500 times',[49] which aims to prevent the sharing of opinion, and to reduce association and collective expression. The internet is also providing fertile ground for nationalism relating to any foreign interference of Chinese sovereignty or apparent external criticism of China, especially concerning Japan, the US, Taiwan and the South China Sea. Moreover, China's surveillance mechanisms can be used to proactively respond to criticism, to direct public debate, and to target and discredit perceived opponents of CCP policy inside and outside China. Such agenda setting is a process through which the mass media acts as 'a central gatekeeper [to] construct the social reality in the public's mind'.[50] Revealing a range of perceived national security threats, and some personal sensitivities, in recent years China's censorship regime has banned Winnie the Pooh (due to resembling Xi Jinping), Peppa Pig (for encouraging 'unruly slackers'), children's books such as *James and the Giant Peach* (to stem an 'inflow of ideology' from the West), the meme app Neihan Duanzi (for its vulgar humour), George Orwell's *Animal Farm* and *1984*, and even – albeit briefly – the letter 'n'.[51]

Everyday authoritarianism

The CCP's compulsion for all-out authoritarian control, resting on a matrix of existential – including political, social, cultural and territorial – threats is best realized in Xinjiang. The vast region of 1.6 million square kilometres is China's largest autonomous region, making up 17.3 per cent of its total landmass. In line with the desire for an absolute political and social monopoly, and with a largely Muslim and culturally and linguistically distinct minority population of over 25 million, Xinjiang personifies the CCP's battle against the 'three evils' of terrorism, ethnic separatism and religious extremism. CCP policy also seeks to 'other' Xinjiang's Uyghur population from the majority Han Chinese, in order to present them as a fundamental threat to the stability of the entire PRC. Conversely, groups such as the Turkestan Islamic Party and the East Turkestan Liberation Organization actively wish to secede from China, and these and other groups have carried out several terrorist incidents in the PRC in the last decade, involving indiscriminate gun, knife and (suicide) bomb attacks. These attacks include the October 2013 car attack in Tiananmen Square that led to five deaths and 38 injuries, the March 2014 knife attack at Kunming train station that left 35 dead and 141 injured, and the May 2014 Ürümqi bomb attack that killed 43 and wounded 90. Such incidents have on occasion precipitated mass inter-ethnic violence such as the July 2009 ethnic riots in the capital Ürümqi that led to hundreds of deaths.

The CCP has tried to use economic development to stabilize the region, as shown through Jiang Zemin's Great Western Development (*xibu da kaifa*) project of June 1999, which sought to considerably increase the autonomous region's infrastructure investment concerning new roads, railways, telecommunications, power plants and oil and gas pipelines. It was, however, accompanied by high levels of migration from Han-dominant areas into the region, which heightened inter-ethnic tensions and the threat of cultural assimilation. In response to an upsurge in domestic tensions and unrest, the CCP promoted a policy of racial 'fusion' (*jiaorong*) as part of China's 'great revival', in order to unify the 'Chinese race' (*Zhonghua minzu*). As shown by documents leaked in 2019, purportedly central to such a policy is a vast chain of internment camps housing around 10 per cent of the autonomous region's population, which carry out a one- to two-year process of 'education transformation' and 'labour skills training', and earn points for 'ideological transformation', 'compliance with discipline' and 'study and training'.[52] According to observers, 'the purpose [of the camps is] … to try to indoctrinate and change an entire population'.[53] In 2018, a leading CCP official called the camps 'education centres',[54] and in 2019 another official noted that the aim of 'our center is to prevent terrorism thoughts from happening'.[55]

As part of Xi's Strike Hard campaign that seeks to build a 'great wall of iron' to safeguard Xinjiang, other policies attempt to further harmonize the Uyghur population. Adding to the five-year plan passed in January 2019 to 'guide Islam to be compatible with socialism', these include forbidding the Uyghur language in some schools,[56] demolishing Islamic religious sites,[57] splitting up families,[58] banning religious names for babies[59] and prohibiting 'abnormal' beards, the wearing of veils in public and behaviour that 'reject[s] or refuse[s] radio, television and other public facilities and services'.[60] In 2017, Human Rights Watch noted that authorities have collected 'DNA samples, fingerprints, iris scans and blood types of all residents in the region between the age of 12 and 65'.[61]

Such efforts inform the use of big data and artificial intelligence (AI) to fuel predictive policing programmes and are emboldened by the use of CCTV cameras with facial recognition and infra-red technologies placed at the region's countless security checkpoints. These are combined with 'Wi-Fi sniffers' to collect computer and phone data, and integrated with data systems that cross-reference health, banking, legal and vehicle records, so as to produce an overall 'trustworthiness' score that informs the possible detention of citizens.[62] Uyghurs must also use an app that automatically reports their browsing history and location history.[63] In Xinjiang, the ubiquity of these technologies have resulted in what one observer has called a 'high tech version of the Cultural Revolution',[64] and led one resident to remark that 'Uighurs are alive, but their entire lives are behind walls, ... they are ghosts living in another world'.[65]

Apart from informing other crackdowns on dissent, be it religious (for example, in Tibet) or political (most clearly in Hong Kong during and after the Umbrella Movement of 2014), the CCP's combined use of its technological, censorship and surveillance prowess in Xinjiang has acted as the testbed for its now nationwide social credit system. Referred to in 2016 as a 'centralized repository for citizen information, ... [intended to] creat[e] a robust socio-psychological service system',[66] it is a form of omnipresent surveillance authoritarianism supported by billions of dollars of state investment in China's techno-security industry.[67] Launched in 2020, and as in Xinjiang coalescing the CCP's political authority with the connivance of private corporations, the system combines recognition technology with lifestyle monitoring and the use of paid informants who report any unusual activity among fellow citizens to the police.[68] Underpinning its prowess, in 2020, there were 600 million surveillance cameras in so-called 'smart cities',[69] while in 2018 the national police's Skynet system was 'capable of identifying any one of China's 1.4 billion citizens within a second'.[70] From this basis, the social credit system seeks to 'record every action and transaction by each Chinese citizen in real time and to respond to the sum of an individual's economic, social and moral behaviour with rewards and penalties'.[71] In these ways, the system has drastically expanded each citizen's *dang'an* (file) and, as per Confucian values, is intended to 'forge a public opinion environment that trust-keeping is glorious [*sic*]'.[72]

Negative behaviours can involve all types of crime as well as lesser misdemeanours such as playing loud music, smoking in public or not walking a dog with a leash, while positive behaviours involve acts such as giving to charity, donating blood or praising the Party online. Achieved through processes of 'automatic verification, automatic monitoring and automatic punishment',[73] penalties for those with low scores include not being allowed to buy plane or train tickets (as affected 23 million people in 2018[74]), being barred from getting loans or high-speed internet, or banned from certain schools and universities. Based on a principle of 'once discredited, limited everywhere',[75] transgressions are listed (for at least three to five years) in publicly accessible and searchable blacklists and accompanied by public denouncements via large video screens in public squares, cinemas and on public transport. There are also similarly available red-lists of the most virtuous citizens, who enjoy benefits such as better job opportunities, hotel discounts and reduced hospital waiting times. Underlying such rewards and penalties is the belief that social harmony can be achieved through self-regulation, whereby 'as long as everyone plays their part, "peace will reign on earth" [*tianxia taiping*]'.[76] As part of the social credit system, in 2019 the CCP launched the Study (Xi) Strong Country app, which all its members are required to download and use every day. As a modern version of Mao's 'little red book' (on Mao's political thinking), app users must study Xi Jinping Thought, and earn points based on their reading of state media and taking online courses.[77]

Overall, such a system has made the CCP's authoritarian rule more resilient to unwanted political change, increased social and economic stability and fused these factors into a form of what some observers call – as we will see further in Chapter 3 – 'neoliberal autocracy'.[78] Moreover, and informing notions of a China-centric international order and the global projection of China's political and social values, the technologies and principles underpinning

China's algorithmic authoritarianism are being exported abroad. In 2018, these included the selling of intelligent monitoring systems and facial recognition technology developed by Chinese companies to 18 countries,[79] the training of local media elites and government officials from 36 countries[80] in China concerning new media or information management, and 38 countries buying telecom infrastructure, internet and mobile networking equipment installed by Chinese companies.[81,.82]

Harmonization, differentiation and exportation

This chapter has established the deep-seated presence of authoritarianism in China. Continuing Confucian traditions from the preceding millennia of dynastic rule (not excepting Confucianism being banned by Mao during the Cultural Revolution), the CCP actively seeks to maintain absolute control of China's political, legal and social fabric. This dominance has been achieved through the now very well-developed architectures of sanctioned political participation, indigenous rule by law and collective human rights, and a vast surveillance and censorship regime that has culminated in the omnipresent social credit system – all of which intend to harmonize China's population to CCP rule. In these ways, several of my key themes (as outlined in the Introduction) have also been present, including clear processes of *assimilation*, *normalization* and *longevity*, as well as concerning an interlinked political *continuum*, as shown by China's political system at times shifting towards totalitarian rule (most clearly under Mao until the 1970s and now arguably under Xi). Notably, these facets have also been informed by a history, fear and contemporary realization of instability in China, which have acutely embedded such practices into the country's ruling principles and narratives.

It also appears that the most extreme elements of China's political system are seemingly juxtaposed with the bedrock of the social and political realm of the current liberal international order. This contrast is most conspicuous in terms of Western human rights pertaining to political and social participation, representation, expression and association, and the rule of law. Within such debates however, the – highly limited – forms of authorized political activity in China are 'a reminder that all [countries] ... are constituted by combinations of practices that include both "democratic" practices of participation, accountability and justice and "authoritarian" practices of coercion, co-optation and arbitrariness, ... and whose dynamics are constantly interacting and evolving'.[83] That China has a longstanding political system based on differing – including Confucian – principles (as overseen by the world's longest ruling and second largest political party) also serves to significantly undercut Western claims regarding the universality of democratic systems. China's current export of its legal principles and surveillance capacity reinforces this challenge.

This success counteracts Fukuyama's popular 'end of history' narrative after the Cold War that authoritarian governments cannot compete with liberal democracies.[84] It is also notable, and despite assertions that democracy is an important pillar for a more non-violent system, that the US intervened at least 81 times (both overtly and covertly) in foreign elections from 1946 to 2000,[85] and engaged in 64 covert and six overt attempts at regime change against both authoritarian and democratic governments during the Cold War.[86] In the 21st century, this modus operandi was shown most vividly by the US's catastrophic attempts to democratize Iraq after invading the country in 2003. Such actions undercut the veracity of the US's democratic proclivities when it comes to the maintenance of its preferred international order.

Domestically, the US has also witnessed the systematic decaying of liberal political freedoms, institutions and declining representation, civil society and labour rights.[87] These include the 2001 Patriot Act that vastly increased the domestic and international surveillance of US citizens. As in China, this increased surveillance produced a 'conforming effect', forcing citizens to 'deny their own perceptions'.[88] These factors have all arguably contributed to a 'creeping authoritarianism' under successive US presidents. Under President Trump such political decay, mixed with suspicion and misinformation (or, as his former chief strategist Steve Bannon decreed, purposefully 'flood[ing] the zone with shit'),[89] led to the widespread denial among his supporters of the legitimacy of the 2020 US election result, which in many ways precipitated their storming of the US Capitol in early 2021. Observers regarded this event as 'the 9/11 of the 2020s: an assault on the citadel of US democracy'[90] that undermined the legitimacy of liberal democracy as a central pillar of the current Western liberal international order.

It is within this context that 'the decline of liberalism as a mainstream global political value creates an opportunity for other ideologies to compete for influence'.[91] This contention is the background to China's successful suppression of political rights in Hong Kong by undercutting the Basic Law that was intended to enshrine autonomy and continue democratic practices after the territory was returned to China by Britain in 1997. These democratic practices were regarded as an overt threat to Chinese authoritarianism. Their suppression included in 2021 'halv[ing] the proportion of directly elected representatives in the city's legislature, ... requir[ing] all candidates to be vetted for political loyalty'[92] and the draconian 2020 National Security Law used to crack down on pro-democracy activists following widespread protest and rioting. It has also included attacks on freedom of speech and of the press, such as shutting down newspapers, and seeking to harmonize Hong Kong's judicial basis with that of mainland China. Notably, the 2020 National Security Law applies to any critics of China *anywhere in the world*, leaving them open to prosecution in China, and could thus affect this book and the author of it, as well as those who voice its findings.

2

China's Worldview

This chapter elucidates the various values on which both ancient and modern China has been built, as well as how they have evolved over its existence. These principles have formed China's national identity and character, and by extension underpin and inform its specific worldview and hence desired international order, and – as we will see in later chapters of this book – its foreign policy proclivities. Their analysis underlines how ideas become dominant in societies and are then used to inform and justify the narratives deployed by ruling elites. Central to this basis in China is the continued practice of governance resting on a singular, oligarchic and – therefore – *authoritarian* figure or group, whose power has been derived from their domination of the state's bureaucracy.

Notably, and in a similar fashion to China's current one-party state, during the 2,000 years of Confucian-based rule that typified ancient China, the country's emperor was the dominant political figure. This period, which lasted until the demise of the imperial system in 1911, encompassed four *Pax Sinicas* totalling over 1,250 years. As part of these orders, China was the Middle or Central Kingdom (*zhongguo*) based on a self-perception of cultural and civilizational superiority, which was acknowledged and accepted by neighbouring countries and also those outside East Asia. China's neighbours were largely assimilated to the worldview and principles of such orders, and their mostly open recognition of China's superiority facilitated and normalized them over time.

China's professed dominance persisted until the Opium Wars of 1839–42 and 1856–60 that were lost to Great Britain. These losses and subsequent economic and territorial forfeitures marked the beginning of the Century of Humiliation (*bainian guochi*), which reduced China's international and regional stature. A later war (1894–95) with and then invasion (1937) by Japan, which was China's leading regional competitor, accompanied by internal instability and civil war (1945–49), only further enhanced this debasement. These experiences signified how 'historical suffering, memory, lack of ruling legitimacy, and domestic vulnerability, combined together [to form] China's feeling of insecurity'.[1] Despite the transition of the country's political basis to one centred on the Chinese Communist Party (CCP), core Confucian beliefs would continue to influence China's contemporary identity. These relate to how China is ruled domestically and also its vision of international order, in particular concerning core Middle Kingdom values regarding harmony, peace, hierarchy, respect and benevolence (centred on East Asia). Given that this identity and worldview is particular to China and built on China's specific historical experiences and geopolitical interactions, we can expect it to differ from the current international order broadly built on democracy, free market economics, universal human rights and an acceptance of US hegemony.

Confucian roots

Confucius (551–476 BC) was a Chinese philosopher, politician and teacher, whose name is a Latinization of his title 'Great Teacher', otherwise known as *Kongzi* or *Kong Fuzi*. His teachings are predominantly found in *The Analects* and centre on a belief in paternalistic and hierarchical structures based on collective loyalty (*zhong*), sacrifice and achievement. To these core sentiments can be added notions of justice, duty and public-spiritedness. Such was their influence on Chinese thinking beyond Confucius's death that Confucianism became the official culture of China between 202 BC and 220 AD and was formally adopted by the Han Emperor (140–87 BC). During the first millennium AD it also became a common heritage that was disseminated throughout much of East Asia, often facilitated by the geographical movement of the diasporic Chinese community. Acting as a set of rituals aimed at harmonizing inter-human relations, it came to be seen as a guide for social relations – a living tradition and conceptual worldview integral to all spheres of life. As it permeated Chinese culture, Confucianism also became a guidepost for China's leaders. In various forms, it further pervaded the social and political fabric of what would become modern Japan, Korea and much of South East Asia, including Indonesia and Singapore.

Confucianism is a regulatory concept which demarcates social relations in accordance with 'a patriarchal ethical order',[2] whereby paternalistic benevolent rule is combined with subjects willing and complicit to such an arrangement. The system rests on clearly delineated hierarchical relationships within the family from the father downwards, and between the family and higher levels of the government, culminating in the emperor. Such a system extends further, with the emperor himself being *tian zi*, 'son of heaven', with a moral responsibility to maintain harmony in Chinese society. Central to such a structure are ideas of intergenerational continuity and transference, ancestral reverence and filial piety (*xiao*), and collective responsibility (and collective dishonour), which are intended to engender social cohesion and social order. Reflective of these concepts, leaders of modern China are often referred to with a family moniker, resulting in, say, Grandpa Xi (for current President Xi Jinping) or Uncle Wen (for former Premier Wen Jiabao). Apart from providing a direct link between the ruler and the ruled, relations between an emperor and the people did not rest on absolute control and complete submission but on a softer and tacit acceptance of a 'natural' order. Thus, despite the tremendously authoritarian core of such a hierarchical system, principles of reciprocity (*shu*), respect and reliance via interdependence, as well as national dignity and pride, were also all vital hallmarks of Confucian rule.

Within such a deeply interconnected and relational modus vivendi, the conduct of China's emperors was of paramount importance. The correct form of this conduct rested on the adherence to several core principles. Among them is *ren*, that includes traits of benevolence and humaneness, and the belief that teachings should be passed on to the next generation. To this can be added *yi* – righteousness and having a moral outlook to do good in one's actions; *zhi* – the ability to determine right from wrong, especially in the behaviour of others; and *xian* – the capacity to act with integrity. In turn, *li* concerns acting properly in everyday life – from 'political protocol to court ceremony, religious rites to village festival, daily etiquette to disciples of personal conduct when alone'[3] – so as to enable harmony with the law of heaven. These principles were encapsulated in *dao* (the way), whereby 'the correct performance of ritual produced the highest type of power'[4] in the pursuit of self-perfection for oneself and one's people. This need for achievement placed an extra importance on education and meritocracy, whereby individuals worked for the gain of the collective through their ongoing self-improvement.

All of these principles connected human morality and proper conduct to the wider harmony of state and society. For Confucius, a ruler who achieved these principles could be called the 'true king' and would keep the loyalty of their subjects by maintaining peaceful harmony. As Confucius noted, 'the virtue of a gentleman is like the wind, and the virtue of a petty person is like the grass – when the wind moves over the grass, the grass is sure to bend'.[5] Such power is not unconditional but based on a legitimacy gained via performance, trust and responsibility, and is conferred from a collective society to the individual leader. From this basis, Confucian culture idealized harmony, making it a liberating attribute for wider society rather than a constricting threat to those whom it pulled together.

Tian xia

One of the most prominent themes of the current (and past) discourses of Chinese visions of international order is *tian xia*, commonly translated as 'all under heaven'. The term first served as an underlying principle of governance for the Zhou Dynasty (c.1046–256 BC), which sought to create an ordering system to govern a vast landmass and population made up of over 1,000 different tribes. It aimed to preserve stability and order and would play a key role in the building and maintenance of various dynastic empires in Chinese history. Over time, it came to signify an order that 'maximize[d] the interest and power for the autocratic and aristocratic rulers',[6] and was dominated by emperors whose 'mandate of heaven' (*tian ming*) permitted them to rule China. Concerning relations with surrounding countries, such supremacy reflected China's domestic system, which – while hierarchical –

rested on Confucian principles of benevolence maintained via tribute, whereby China's smaller neighbours needed to consent to China's authority in exchange for reciprocal trade and other incentives. This social and political hierarchy extended from the domestic sphere to the region and world, producing an organized and ordered system that leads to stability and seeks to maintain Chinese centrality through deference not dominance.

At the heart of *tian xia* is a concept of the world being composed of three elements: the earth, the 'hearts of all people' and a world institution, underpinned by a principle of 'worldness' that transcends the principle of 'internationality'.[7] The first factor describes the geographical area to which *tian xia* applies and was not constrained by the rigid frontiers of a country's borders but encompassed all of the territory that was under the influence of Confucian rulers. Such a dynamic, inclusive and perpetually contested outlook contrasts with the Western Westphalian system, whereby the sovereignty of countries gives them an inviolability within their own borders. The second element refers to a psychological aspect of governance over a specific territory and the moral acceptability of a ruling emperor or head of state, which is a non-material dimension within the Chinese concept of international order. Thus, rather than ruling through coercion, a ruler has to win the hearts and minds of the people, so that the latter willingly subscribe to Confucian rules: it is this adherence that then bestows legitimacy on the emperor. As such, *tian xia* can be seen as a soft – yet at times repressive – authoritarianism. The focus of all under heaven on gaining collective legitimacy based on performance – whereby the mandate of heaven is both conferred, and can be removed, by a population, as well as on collective benevolence and righteousness – also appears to somewhat supersede more legalistic Western principles of individuality, equality and democracy.

The third component of *tian xia* points to its ambition to be a universal global system. While the Westphalian model locates the nation-state at the centre, all under heaven instead includes all people and all countries, identifying world society as its ultimate referent object. It is therefore a civilizational order that is appreciably different from Western-derived international orders based on sovereignty and accompanying division and competition.

As Fairbank pertinently notes, the notion of a Chinese international order was thus built on 'a sense of superiority and hierarchy without the concepts of sovereignty, territorially-bounded nation states, or a balance of power. Rather, it was given order and unity by the universal presence of the Son of Heaven.'[8] At its pinnacle, *tian xia* hence 'advocates a singular sociopolitical system and thought-system, ... [acting as] the precondition for a new, better, more harmonious, and rational world order'.[9]

Within such a vision, which rests on the inclusion of all countries and peoples within the oneness of world society, *tian xia* is deeply informed by the Chinese concept of harmony. In this way, harmony is 'usually defined as reciprocal dependence, reciprocal improvement or the perfect setting for different things, as opposed to the *sameness (tong)* of things'.[10] The natural foundation of such harmony is based on the family and replicates its centrality to Confucianism on the domestic level as the lynchpin of a *social order*. In this regard, in *The Record of Rites* Confucius spoke of a *da tong* (great harmony) that describes family-like relations between all members of a society, whereby 'men practiced good faith and lived in harmony, ... therefore they did not regard as parents only their own parents, or as sons only their own sons'.[11] Such an understanding facilitates inclusive peaceful coexistence in the world by hyper-extending the basis of China's domestic system into the global sphere. Notably, such sameness has been interpreted in different ways, which arguably prioritizes actual family over strangers or favours those who are more closely connected to you socially. As such, the influence of Chinese civilization is the force that sustains China's supremacy over others, with China's hierarchical superiority over its inferior neighbours being the sole means to ensure a harmonious order.

China's historical orders

The realization of China-centric and *tian xia*-informed international orders peppers the last 2,000 years of the East Asian region. From the first period of *Pax Sinica* under the Han Dynasty (202 BC–20 AD) to subsequent ones under the Tang Dynasty (618–907), the Yuan Dynasty (1271–1368), the Ming Dynasty (1368–1644) and the Qing Dynasty (1644–1912), core principles of engrained hierarchy, dominance, tribute and stability have been evident in China's relationship with its region. Being geographically isolated courtesy of the Pacific Ocean to the east, the vast Gobi and Taklimakan Deserts and the Tibetan Plateau to the west, the inhospitable Siberia to the north, as well as malaria-infested tropical jungles to the south, aided these periods of dominance. China's territorial extent would fluctuate across time but slowly increased with each *Pax Sinica*, rising from 6.5 million square kilometres during the Han Dynasty to 11 million square kilometres during the Yuan Dynasty (established by Kublai Khan), before peaking at 14.7 million square kilometres by the time of the middle of the Qing Dynasty around 1750.

Stability through consolidation and domination was the lynchpin of the various *Pax Sinicas*, and since its unification in 221 BC all Chinese dynasties were persistently confronted by invasions and vast bloody domestic uprisings. Internally, these included – but were not limited to – wars during the Three Kingdoms period from 220 to 280 (which led to 38 million deaths), the An Lushan rebellion of 755–63 (up to 36 million deaths), the Ming-Qing transition of 1618–83 (25 million deaths), and the Taiping Rebellion of 1850–64 (between 20 and 50 million deaths). Such instability, along with recurrent natural disasters such as earthquakes, famines and floods, or abuses of power such as corruption, frequently contributed to emperors losing their mandate of heaven. Despite these upheavals, China persisted as a civilization and often absorbed those who threatened it, underscoring the singularity of the Chinese world, whereby repeated 'external invasions and influences, numerous conquering and rulings by the ungoverned 'peripheral' nations … and the mergers of many distinctive tribes and ethnicities, … made China a lasting, boiling at times, melting pot of many peoples and cultures'.[12] The fear of external invasion also motivated the building of the Great Wall from around 700 BC to 1643.

Vast military and naval power was amassed to counter the fear of instability but also to underscore China's ongoing regional supremacy, which was largely unsuccessfully challenged by China's neighbours with the exception of the 1215 invasion by Genghis Khan (as a precursor to the Yuan Dynasty) and the 1618 Manchu invasion (leading to the transition from the Ming Dynasty to the

Qing Dynasty). Such Chinese military capabilities were at times deployed as a way to punish or coerce neighbours towards China's power and its preferred regional order, whereby neighbouring countries were occupied (such as Vietnam for nearly 1,000 years until 907) or invaded (such as Japan in 1274 and 1281). Further highlighting the prowess of such capabilities, the 1405 and 1433 expeditions by the renowned Chinese Admiral Zheng reached across South East Asia, the Indian Ocean and the Straits of Hormuz, and took place several decades before Christopher Columbus's first voyage in 1492. Moreover, acceptance of a Chinese-centric order appears to have led to a stable East Asia, and notably from 1492 to 1904 the region had only 11 major wars and conflicts versus 53 in Europe across the same period.

In addition, from 1200 onward the number of political units in the region also remained relatively constant (at around 20), compared to Europe where they were large (over 500 in 1500) and ever-shifting. China's overriding primacy aided such stability as 'other nations did not wish to challenge China, and China had no need to fight'.[13] As per Sun Tzu (544–496 BC), author of *The Art of War*, Chinese leaders were cautious in their use of offensive force, which was seen as being unharmonious and too costly. Markedly, China 'had a policy of non-interference toward its tributary states, as long as its sovereignty was acknowledged and not threatened'[14] and thus would not condone others' territorial expansion or provide military security. This concept of international order within East Asia, as constructed around a narrative of peacefulness and harmony, also relied heavily on 'hegemonic benevolence providing global public goods such as trade, security, and multilateral cooperation',[15] making it similar – besides the absence of military protection – to the liberal international order centred on US hegemony.

More significantly, the *Pax Sinicas* all rested on recognition of China's pre-eminence. Based on a self-perception of having a manifest cultural superiority vis-à-vis other countries, as the Middle Kingdom China's civilizational superiority contrasted with other countries' inferiority as uncivilized barbarians. Maintaining this hierarchical superiority rested on a reciprocal tribute system, whereby 'as long as the barbarian states were willing to kowtow to the Chinese emperor and show formal acceptance of their lower position in the hierarchy, the Chinese had neither the need to invade these countries nor the desire to do so'.[16] In exchange for such recognition, China's emperors would bestow economic and other benefits on these vassal countries through a relationship based on suzerainty, which gave the tributary country internal autonomy. Such interactions resulted in a vibrant regional economy that stretched across East and South East Asia, and which closely bound together China's various tributary countries. They would also bequeath new rulers with legitimacy through a process of investiture whereby they would come to China to seek validity. In turn, although the rulers of tributary countries could be emperors in their own entities, they would refer to themselves as kings when visiting China, thus subordinating themselves to the higher position of the Chinese emperor.

Even though *tian xia* was hierarchical, it was also instinctively assimilative as it also involved the adoption of Confucian principles by tributary countries, such as having centrally administered bureaucratic systems, using an examination system to select government bureaucrats (and thus an emphasis on the importance of education) and the use of Chinese characters and vocabulary in their languages (as is common in Japan, Korea and Vietnam). This permeation of China-derived values and practices helped to inculcate regional stability and meant that China was the economic, political, cultural and diplomatic heart of East Asia. Emblematic of this status, in 1750 China had a per capita level of industrialization comparable to that of Western Europe,[17] and accounted for a third of all world trade.[18] Confucian values were intrinsic in determining the success and extent of such dominance, as were China's domestic authoritarian political system and its supremacy in the region.

Rise of modern China and neo-*tian xia*

Despite its prevalence for over 2,000 years, a series of external and internal crises throughout the 19th century resulted in the demise of China's imperial system. These included the military defeats to the British during the Opium Wars of 1839–42 and 1856–60, partial defeat in the Sino-French War of 1884–85 and defeat in the first Sino-Japanese War of 1894–95, all of which inflicted an 'irrevocable break in China's trajectory'[19] as per *tian xia*. Such setbacks were frequently accompanied by what became known as the 'unequal treaties' with Britain, Russia, the US, France, Germany and Japan, whose one-sided terms resulted in China having to give these other countries territory, open up trade ports, pay financial reparations or be forced to grant extraterritorial – including legal – privileges to foreign citizens (such as missionaries). As a result of these treaties, China ceded or leased control of substantial parts of its landmass, including – among others – Hong Kong (to Britain in 1841), Outer Manchuria (to Russia in 1858), Taiwan (to Japan in 1895) and Jiaozhou Bay (to Germany in 1898), and lost its suzerainty over Vietnam (to France from 1885), and thus influence over the Indochina peninsula, which significantly undercut the *tian xia* focus on tributary relations. During this period, a third of China's territory was lost due to foreign intervention.[20]

These incidents coupled with widespread instability within China, including the Āfāq Khoja Holy War from 1759 to 1866 (centred on latter-day Xinjiang), the anti-Qing Miao Rebellion of 1795–1806, the Taiping Rebellion of 1850–64, the Red Turban Rebellion of 1854–56 (initially led by organized crime families in southern Guangdong), the Da Cheng Rebellion of 1855–64 (which claimed independence over part of southern China) and the inter-ethnic Dungan Revolt of 1862–77 (which led to 20 million deaths). Numerous famines across the same period also resulted in many tens of million deaths within China.

Collectively, such events debased both China's regional status – as external powers refused to recognize its natural pre-eminence (as was central to *tian xia*) – and tainted China's internal legitimacy (and hence the emperor's mandate of heaven), leading to the Xinhai Revolution of 1911 that precipitated the downfall of the Qing Dynasty. The collapse of the imperial system led to decades of chaos, instability and uncertainty as a new Chinese Republican Nationalist government led by Sun Yat-sen and then Chiang Kai-Shek struggled to control a China fractured by warlordism and corruption. Despite the new regime, China's woes continued, as the Treaty of Versailles in June 1919 transferred German-occupied portions of Shandong to Japanese control rather than back to China. This event in particular led to the anti-imperialist 1919 May Fourth Movement, which inspired the formation of the CCP in 1921. Although Chiang Kai-Shek's Kuomintang government sought to bring stability to China by modernizing and industrializing the country, these efforts brought them into conflict with the CCP and led to the Chinese civil war from 1927. While both sides united in 1937 to counter Japan's invasion of the same year, this ceased with the end of the Second World War, and the civil war resumed until Republican China's eventual defeat (and retreat to Taiwan) in 1949.

Under the aegis of Mao Zedong, the CCP established the People's Republic of China (PRC) and sought to restore China's stature internally, in the region and on the global stage. After their success in 1949, Mao proclaimed that 'the Chinese people, comprising one quarter of humanity, have now stood up. The Chinese have always been a great, courageous and industrious nation; it is only in modern times that they have fallen behind.'[21] Underpinning this aim was a desire to restore harmony within Chinese affairs so as to avoid the internal and external instabilities of the Century of Humiliation. It also included China's reassertion as the region's pre-eminent country and a need to gain recognition from other countries of the CCP and the PRC as the legitimate embodiments of modern China. China's experience informed key principles structuring this restoration, including anti-imperialism (against the *yang guize* – foreign devils), anti-colonialism and self-reliance (*zili gengsheng*) in order to emancipate China from foreign influence. These views became encapsulated in the Five Principles of Peaceful Co-Existence: respect for territorial integrity and sovereignty; non-aggression; non-interference in each other's internal affairs; equality and shared benefit; and peaceful coexistence. Harking back to the benign underpinnings of *tian xia*, they aimed to create a conducive global atmosphere for China to rebuild its 'comprehensive national strength' (*zonghe guoli*) across interconnected economic, military, diplomatic and institutional parameters.

Although the means to amalgamate this strength would evolve over the ensuing decades, the overarching goal of restoring China's status and vision of international order has been consistent. The relentless focus on communist ideology and totalitarian rule under Mao switched to an emphasis on economic growth and liberalization under his successor Deng Xiaoping; this prowess gradually translated into military, institutional and diplomatic power under Jiang Zemin, Hu Jintao and Xi Jinping, the present incumbent. Underpinning that aim is the pre-eminence of the CCP as China's dominant actor within an authoritarian political, social and (certainly under Mao) economic system. Mao in particular sought to use the collective energy of the Chinese people to reinvigorate China – be it through 'people's war' (*renmin zhanzheng*) during the Chinese civil war or through mass events such as the Great Leap Forward (1958–62) or the Cultural Revolution (1966–76). Such an emphasis would continue to inform China's deep-seated nationalism – as typified by the second of Jiang Zemin's Three Represents (*san ge dabiao*), which concerns protecting and enhancing China's superior cultural (including Confucian) basis. In combination with Mao's leadership style – and arguably Xi's – as the undisputed paramount leader, there would be clear parallels with the emperors and dynastic rulers of China's long imperial period. Different generations of CCP leaders would also all seek ruling legitimacy from their people, which most clearly from the late 1970s was done via economic prosperity. To this end, the '"New China" [the PRC] ... was in fact a leap backward, a new "son-of-heaven plus meritocratic bureaucracy" or a reincarnation of Qin-Han Empire with new trappings of imported Marxism'.[22]

As modern China rose to ever-greater prominence and influence in contemporary geopolitics, and as the hard ideological edge of the CCP reduced in the decades after Mao's death in 1976, reference to new realizations of a *tian xia*-informed international order increased. These narratives flowed into the CCP's aim to restore China's past status, which rested as much on China's traditional cultural Confucian basis as it did on economic and military strength. Part of this resurgence centred on the usage of the concept of *da tong* in order to underscore the cultural nationalism promoted by Jiang. It was also concerned, as Qian noted in 2000, with how the CCP's 'struggle in the 21st century for the great tasks of peace and development takes energy and inspiration from Confucianism's social ideal of Great Harmony'.[23]

These debates emerged at a time when China had been somewhat assimilated into elements of the current international order – most prominently liberal economic growth – as a means to facilitate its re-emergence as a great power. Such a process meant that China was positioned between a deep attachment to the existing liberal international order and more ancient Chinese concepts including *tian xia*, the tributary system and harmony, which broke with several elements of the liberal international order.

Within this context, *tian xia* was resurrected in the 21st century by the Chinese intellectual Zhao Tingyang and revisited by several other scholars such as Qin Yaqing and Wang Yiwei. They aimed to present a vision of international order that serves as a more suitable alternative to the current Western Westphalian-centred model, which is losing much of its explanatory value in a globalized world that is progressively more intertwined across borders. At the same time, China remains an ardent defender of sovereignty and national autonomy so as to protect itself from external criticism.

To its clear advantage in the contemporary era, and by working above the level of states and surpassing the inter-*national* basis of global politics, such neo-*tian xia* is able to construct a sense of *world-ness*. From this basis, 'the conceptually defined Empire of all-under-heaven does not mean a country at all but an institutional world, ... and it expects a world/society instead of nation/states'.[24] For China, such an international order would be premised on an empire with its corresponding emperor, and would be facilitated and accompanied by traditional concepts of the tributary system and harmony (so as to achieve an extra-China Great Harmony). Apart from highlighting the organic nature of international order, and its ability to harness both ancient precepts and present-day structural influences, giving China such a pre-eminent role is not only a historical harking back to previous *Pax Sinicas* but also marries contemporary realities. Such a synthesis opens up 'the possibility of a "hierarchical" system around China, which could provide stability in Asia given its potential as one of the most critical arenas in the world for great power rivalry in the twenty first century'.[25]

This neo-*tian xia* realization also points to a China-centric and non-democratic form of order, as while 'coexisting and competing with Westphalian notions of state sovereignty and liberal ideas of globalization, ... *tian xia* nonetheless largely speaks to a vision of world order in which an authoritarian governor (China) presides over other nations, and projects authority and leadership within a hierarchical setting, precluding international competition'.[26] This vision includes a belief in *para bellum*, which is derived from the fuller phrase '*si vis pacem, para bellum*' ('if you want peace, prepare for war'), whereby China holds both defensive and offensive approaches regarding the use of force against opponents.[27]

Strategic vision and priorities

Evidence of seeking some form of neo-*tian xia* is apparent across Chinese foreign policy and thinking, especially after the end of the Cold War in the late 1980s and early 1990s. Such understandings directly underpin China's grand strategy – that is, the predominant vision of how it approaches the conduct of its international affairs. For China, such a strategy proactively combines the country's military and non-military components together in order to successfully attain its national interests within the international system. Within this strategy, the creation of a harmonious and stable regional and global environment is of primary importance for Beijing, so as to allow its pursuit of economic, social and political modernization. This setting is required in order to augment the country's international standing and 'peaceful development' (*heping fazhan*) – a policy that emerged in 2003 under Hu Jintao which was designed to present China's rapid economic, military and political rise as not being a threat to global peace and security. This policy also reflected China's 'new security concept' (*xin anquan guan*), which emerged in the mid-1990s and reinforced a peaceful approach to China's foreign policy that sought to reform multilateral institutions to make them more representative and cognizant of Chinese power, and explicitly vowed to avoid military alliances. To these perspectives can be added 'charm offensive' – a strategy used in Chinese diplomacy to proactively project an image abroad of China as a trustworthy, benevolent and benign partner – that aimed to augment the country's non-coercive, aspirational and peaceful soft power as a benevolent rising great power that attracts others to it and does not seek hegemony.

From China becoming a pre-eminent power atop the international hierarchy of countries, to behaving in a benevolent and benign manner (including avoiding military competition and pacts) and pulling others towards its vision through its cultural and economic cachet, these policies are a collective modern-day reflection – and realization – of *tian xia*. They also underline a sense of Chinese exceptionalism, built on a perception that China is inherently different from other countries (and must be treated and recognized as such by its peers) – a belief that stems from having (and wishing to reacquire) a historical role of superiority as per the legacy of the Middle Kingdom. In addition, the country's current unprecedented contemporary economic rise, along with the acquisition of ever-increasing military, cultural and diplomatic capabilities, all underscore this return and – by extension – core characteristics of previous *Pax Sinicas*. China is also inclined towards a preference for multipolarity, whereby a number of different major powers compete for influence in the global sphere rather than the world being dominated by one country (as is the mainstay of the current international order under the US). In these ways, a Chinese international order would be less assertive, less coercive and more regional – itself a historical memory of the dangers and unsustainability associated with global hegemons.

As a result, China's leaders have spoken of a 'new international order' (*guoji xin zhixu*), which contrasts with Western conceptions of order consisting of a hegemon presiding over a cooperative system built on shared values, and which asserts the primacy of each country's independent nature. Instead, China's vision of international order rests on a transactional relationship system (*guanxi wang*) within which mutual interests drive relations. In such an order, 'China categorizes states based on their national power and importance to China, ... [and] does not pay overt attention to the domestic political systems of these countries or their international behavior. China's assessment rests on whether or not the country is willing to maintain good relations ... and engage in mutually beneficial cooperation'.[28] Such relations encompass the role of recognition and prestige, as well as maintaining face (*mianzi*) on the regional and global stage. It is from this basis that one of China's modern-day premiers, Wen Jiabao, argued that *tian xia* has the universalizing capacity to signify a world order in which countries could be 'harmonious but different' or achieve 'harmony without uniformity'.[29]

The importance of harmony is also apparent within China's internal affairs and reveals an ongoing harking back to Confucian values and principles. Much of these values also interplay with particular territorial goals, which are often vital to China's restoration as a great power – itself a core pillar of its *tian xia*-focused vision of international order. At the core of these policies is the notion of 'harmonious society' which acts as a social, political and economic vision for the PRC. Dating from Confucianism, it 'aims to overcome inequalities from unchecked economic growth so as to engender social balance and stability, … [and] to do so in a socially and environmentally sustainable manner'.[30] As we saw in Chapter 1, it also involves the use of state oppression as a means to stabilize society and to allow for the continued political dominance of the CCP, which together indicate a form of state-coerced harmony in modern-day China. Accompanying this concept was that of 'great national unity' (*da yi tong*), which underpins the need for peace and stability in China and which can be achieved via its cultural, territorial and political consolidation and unison. It stems from aforementioned ideas of *da tong* (great harmony) that regards division as antagonistic, deviant and temporary. For the CCP, it most firmly refers to restoring the territorial integrity of the PRC, whereby 'lost territories' such as Taiwan, islands in the South and East China Seas, and Arunachal Pradesh (Southern Tibet, and under dispute with India) are all to be reclaimed (as is detailed in Chapter 5). It is also central to protecting its territory vis-à-vis Xinjiang, Tibet, Hong Kong and Macau, and explains the CCP's proscriptive and assertive attitude towards these regions.

Influence of Xi Jinping

Coming to power in 2013, Xi Jinping heads the fifth generation of leadership of the CCP, succeeding Hu Jintao. In his inaugural speech as CCP General Secretary, he asserted that he was 'accepting the baton of history and continuing to work for realizing the great revival of the Chinese nation, in order to let the Chinese nation stand more firmly and powerfully among all nations around the world and make a greater contribution to mankind'.[31] As part of this vision – and reinforcing a Chinese vision of the world – were the phrases 'China Renaissance' (*minzude weida fuxing*) and the 'Chinese Dream' (also called 'China Dream') (*zhongguo meng*). The former concerns the desire to restore China to its former great power status, while augmenting the country's increasing economic and military power, reasserting its cultural heritage and enhancing international stature, leadership and overall stability – all of which pay homage to Confucianism and *tian xia*. The latter is the defining slogan of Xi's period in power and is a call to arms for China's population to work together to collectively help achieve this renaissance and the pursuit of national (and individual) prosperity, collective effort and glory. Actively creating harmony – including the suppression of internal political and social dissent (such as concerning minorities in Xinjiang and elsewhere) – is also a necessary component to realize a strong, peaceful, powerful and ultimately socialist state. Such refrains connect China's glorious past to its glorious future, showing how historical memory is an essential raw material that has comprised and formed China's national identity.

In line with his CCP predecessors, and itself reflective of longer-standing cultural values, Xi has also reiterated the PRC's apparent commitment to widespread harmony and the rejection of global domination, whereby 'in the interest of peace, China will remain committed to peaceful development. We Chinese love peace. No matter how much stronger it may become, China will never seek hegemony or expansion.'[32] In his book, *The Governance of China*, Xi also states the ostensible necessity of spreading the Chinese worldview: 'we should disseminate the values of modern China ... so as to make our culture known through international communication and dissemination'.[33] Moreover, he is also reasserting China's great power status within East Asia (and globally) – itself an integral part of a China-centric international order – via policies such as the Belt and Road Initiative, the Asian Infrastructure Investment Bank, and actively pursuing its various territorial claims (as will be further analyzed in Chapters 3, 4 and 5 respectively). In these ways, Xi is seen to be creating 'a new network that is centred on China, organized according to Chinese interests, and guided by Chinese values'.[34] Through this neo-*tian xia* approach, the CCP's fundamental aim is that China will become the world's leading country in terms of 'national power and international influence'.[35]

Acting in a way reminiscent of Mao but also of the many dynasties of Chinese emperors before the incarnation of the PRC, Xi's removal of any term limit for China's president from China's Constitution in 2018 set him up as president-for-life. This move overturned the two-term limit that had endured under Deng, Jiang and Hu. Xi's status as a princeling – the offspring of a former high-ranking CCP official – only reinforced this sense of emperor-esque rule. In line with his forebears, Xi has also sought to develop his own political theory and thinking concerning how best to manage and achieve China's interests. Known as Xi Jinping Thought, it is based on 14 major points, including a people-centred approach; continued reform; scientific innovation; introducing rule of law; practising socialism; improving development and living standards; protecting the environment; strengthening national security; promoting 'one country, two systems' (which allows for the reabsorption of previously colonized territories such as Hong Kong and Macau); improving Party discipline; and combating corruption.[36] Xi Jinping Thought was adopted into the preamble of China's Constitution in 2018, and joined other leaders' contributions, which now reads as 'Marxism-Leninism, Mao Zedong Thought, Deng Xiaoping Theory, the Theory of Three Represents, the Scientific Outlook on Development and Xi Jinping Thought on Socialism with Chinese Characteristics for a New Era'.

More tellingly, in terms of creating a new China-centric international order, Xi also invoked other phrases that point to the purposeful and proactive creation of a *tian xia*-inspired vision. These include creating a 'community with a shared future for mankind' (*renlei mingyun gongtongti*), as influenced by Confucian concepts of benevolent paternalism equally applied to all people all under heaven. In turn, 'striving for achievement' (*fenfayouwei*) concerns deploying Chinese leadership to fulfil its great power responsibility to spread its domestic economic success (and associated values) abroad. To these can be added Xi's 'two guidances' in regard to how Beijing ought to actively 'guide the international community to jointly build a more just and reasonable new world order' and 'guide the international community to jointly maintain international security'.[37] As ways of assertively shaping the global system and presenting China as a positive force within such dynamics, these mantras are concerted attempts 'to try to elevate China as the new moral authority that can guide (*yindao*) the world'.[38] Finally, and overarching all of these concerns, is that of *he*. Also drawn from Chinese classical philosophy, *he* has two meanings: 'not only peace, but also a harmonious balance with nature ... [that] does not disallow all forms of military force but justifies a defensive use of force because survival is a natural goal of a state' or alternatively as a broad 'desire for positive outcomes'.[39]

Precedence, volition and transition

Assertions of a new China-centric international order do not come out of a cultural, political or social vacuum but are instead premised on deep-seated precedents that were crucial to the construction, maintenance and reiteration of generations of previous *Pax Sinicas*. Central to Chinese society and internal dynamics for well over 2,000 years and straddling the demise of the emperor-based system and the emergence of the PRC under the leadership of the CCP from 1949, the principles and outlooks of such international orders have been remarkably consistent and durable. Such *normalization* and underlying *longevity* are themselves key hallmarks of international order, and major analytical touchstones for this volume. Central to such continuities has been particular Confucian values centred on the domination of a paramount leader and dynasty based on patriarchal hierarchy, benevolence, trust, performance and responsibility, whereby their proper moral conduct leads to the harmony – that is to say, stability – of state and society. The notion of *tian xia* (or all under heaven) encapsulated this graded harmony as a specific *social* – and frequently political, cultural and economic – *order* dependent on (and *facilitated* by) widespread tribute, respect, recognition and reciprocity. At the core of such beliefs has been China's experience of its frequently tumultuous, yet ultimately *assimilating*, history.

Through an emergent neo-*tian xia*, we have also been able to witness the contemporary realization of such long-standing tropes and perspectives. China's modern-day return to be a great power of international influence and importance rests on a resurgence not only of its economic, military, diplomatic and cultural prowess but also on the restoration of its preferred vision of itself in the world – that is, of a China-centric international – if largely regional – order. As China's national strength continues to be augmented across the full range of possible power quotients,[40] the value, success and applicability of the country's deep-rooted Confucian heritage – notwithstanding the CCP's ongoing communist revolution – has become ever more apparent. Collectively, the stability, recognition and hierarchical attributes of a new 'all under heaven' (across China's internal and external spheres) bear clear, obvious benefits that allow for Beijing's continued internal modernization and development. In short, achieving great harmony (*da tong*) in the international system will only accelerate China's restoration as a great power and allow Xi's realization of the China Dream. Such success – predominantly in the economic, but also increasingly in the diplomatic and institutional fields – has legitimized the CCP's continued use of authoritarianism as the best (if not most culturally appropriate) means of governing modern China, making it an essential pillar of its international order vision.

This chapter has not only shown that international order is a contested concept within international politics but also that we can expect a China-engendered international order to – at least to some degree – significantly differ from the current Western vision of order. Certainly, in terms of its political basis – centred on an authoritarian system, as was evidenced in Chapter 1 – this contrasts with the current liberal international order premised on democracy and associated political and social rights. A different set of values and principles underpinning China's identity, as informed by a clearly different set of historical experiences and precedents, underpins this difference and volition. This distinction represents a challenge to the continuance of the Western-dominated international order, particularly coming at a time when democracy appears to be in retreat across much of the world. That China is building institutions reflective of its domestic values and of *tian xia* (as we will see in Chapter 4) emphasizes this contestation. In other ways, especially given China's embrace of liberal economic practices and – gradual – acceptance of globalization (as we will witness in Chapter 3), we can also see elements of similarity.

At its heart, this mélange of change and continuity underscores how the international order is in a process of transition, with old and new elements concurrently coalescing and diverging. In turn, and reflecting the permeation of China's domestic authoritarianism into its global interactions – including in the economic (Chapter 3), diplomatic (Chapter 4) and regional (Chapter 5) spheres – US Secretary of State Mike Pompeo argued in July 2020 that 'today China is increasingly authoritarian at home, and more aggressive in its hostility to freedom everywhere else'.[41] Revealing a shifting balance of both power and confidence between the two sides, Chinese officials tersely responded by noting that such comments were akin to an 'ant trying to shake a tree'.[42]

3

Economic Ascent

Economic dominance is the core factor for any country wishing to influence and direct the international order. With China possessing the world's largest economy,[1] it is acquiring a system-determining capacity that allows it to cast its own vision of authority, order and control throughout the contemporary international structure. China is now the omni-influential fulcrum of the global economy, as its ever-increasing demand for resources, markets and energy has made the world's national and regional economies dependent on China as a major import and export market, cheap labour provider and fruitful foreign investment destination. Beijing's gradual embrace of liberal economics – often merged with the specific Chinese characteristics that we saw in Chapter 1 based on state control of politics and society, and the blurring of public and private ownership – has given it this transformative ability. Despite China's acceptance of liberal economics having been *facilitated* by the West as a way to purportedly socialize and absorb China into the existing international order, and based on the assumption that liberal economic reform leads to democratic political reform, this fusion has instead led to an *authoritarian-capitalist* system that diverges from the liberal economic ideal. With financial behaviour playing such a major part of Beijing's social credit system, this amalgamation has gained ever-greater traction.

This phenomenon underscores how 'today's rising powers are each following unique paths toward modernity based on their own political, demographic, topographic, and socioeconomic conditions. Accordingly, they are developing versions of modernity divergent from the West's.'[2] China's Confucian heritage informs

China's deviating economic outlook and practices, and conjoins the country's social and political basis with its economic proclivities, whereby factors such as loyalty, reciprocity and the primacy of the group over the individual are argued to culminate in high economic growth. Close ties between government and business have also led to a hybrid Confucian capitalism that encourages 'a sustained lifestyle of discipline and self-cultivation, respect for authority, frugality, and an over-riding concern for stable family life'.[3] Such values are favourable to rapid economic development and permeate China's management and work practices relating to: competitiveness, ethical leadership and working overtime;[4] negotiating styles based on *ren* (benevolence), *zhi* (wisdom) and *yong* (courage); interpersonal *guanxi* networks;[5] attitudes concerning consumerism, materialism and greater trust in products from government-involved enterprises;[6] and a reluctance to report bad news to senior management.[7] Given that Confucian principles are evident in South Korea, Japan and Singapore, they are crucial for understanding the political economy of East Asia and are a mechanism for China to order the region.

Domestically, China's liberal economic embrace has led to the rapid modernization of the country's infrastructure and the dramatic transformation of the economic fortunes of its population, pulling hundreds of millions out of poverty. It also moved China away from the highly centralized and stark collective equality of the Mao era and, as Deng Xiaoping remarked, signalled to China's people that 'to get rich is no sin. However, what we mean by getting rich is different from what [Westerners] mean, ... to get rich in a socialist society means prosperity for the entire people'.[8] The Chinese Communist Party's (CCP's) acceptance of an altered form of liberal capitalism formed part of the goal to be a 'moderately prosperous society' (*xiaokang shehui*) by 2021, and the long-term strategy for China to become a 'socialist, modern, and powerful country'[9] by 2049. The success of this new approach, combined with Beijing's non-ideological approach to global trade, now acts as an inspirational developmental model for countries across Africa, Asia and South America, especially among authoritarian leaders. In this way, Xi has described China's authoritarian-capitalist system as 'a new option for other countries and nations who want to speed up their development while preserving their independence'.[10]

By doing so, China has delegitimized Western liberalism's declaration that economic growth inevitably leads to democracy, and – by presenting a viable alternative to it – shows that such an international order can be augmented and usurped. With Western democracies heavily reliant on China's continued economic growth and facing significant political upheavals and crises, the basis of the economic international order appears to be increasingly assimilating and normalizing China's preferred authoritarian basis.

The existing order

Highlighting several of the key themes of this volume, China's admission into the liberal economic order represented a strategy of *assimilation* by the leaders of the liberal international order. This aim was underpinned by an element of *facilitation* whereby this admission was sanctioned and openly encouraged, and Beijing benefited from an international economic order buttressed by US hegemony in terms of currency, institutions and market systems. It also reflected an ongoing process of *normalization*, through which it was hoped that China could be absorbed and socialized into existing practices so as to ensure the current international order's *longevity*. Such efforts were informed by a belief in the universality of the core values underpinning the liberal international order, and the synthesis of Western-derived understandings of human rights and democracy with an economic system based on neoliberal free trade, which was seen to be vital in the construction of liberal democracy.

The foundations of the economic pillar of the current Western international order come from the 1944 Bretton Woods Agreement, which was designed to regulate the international monetary system. Initially involving the allied powers during the Second World War – the US, Canada, Western European countries and Australia but also Japan – and formally ratified into force in 1945, it sought to create open global markets and cooperative free trade practices based on collectivism, anti-protectionism and the rule of law. More broadly, the Agreement was built on liberal Keynesian principles relating to governing the market to achieve near-full employment and using taxation to create a welfare state.[11]

Despite these facets, at its core the Agreement was designed to create a highly US-centric financial order that was controlled by the US. The rules, practices and institutions central to the Bretton Woods Agreement were emblematic of such an aim. One of these, the International Monetary Fund (IMF), which was founded in 1945, issues loans in case of an imbalance of payments (between money flowing into a country and the outflow of money to the rest of the world) in member countries, and does so in order to avoid these members having to deflate the size of their economies. Underscoring its control, not only does the US have the highest voting quota in the IMF, the US Congress also determines the voting quotas of all IMF members. Loans from the IMF are issued in US dollars, forcing recipients to effectively hold US debt, making them further dependent on the price of the dollar and the success of the US economy. In response to such US dominance, Soviet delegates at the Bretton Woods meeting saw the IMF as essentially a 'branch of Wall Street'.[12]

Working in tandem with the IMF and also based in Washington, another notable Bretton Woods institution is the World Bank, which was created in 1944 and provides loans and grants to low-income countries that are unable to be financed by mainstream banks. These loans are issued to achieve the World Bank's wider aims to reduce poverty, enhance economic security and support sustainable development. Countries that receive such aid have to fulfil accompanying economic, political and social conditions, such as: adopting democratic practices and the rule of law; reducing their public sectors and limiting state intervention (including selling state-owned enterprises to the private sector); and opening markets to foreign economic competition and liberalizing trade. In turn, the head of the World Bank is always an American citizen, the US has the highest voting quota of any member at 15.85 per cent (versus second-placed Japan on 6.84 per cent), is its largest shareholder and is the only country with a de facto right of veto. The US Congress is also allowed to vote on its funding, thus granting the US total jurisdiction over the institution. This centrality means that the World Bank is an instrument of US foreign policy, giving the US control of the economic pillar of its international order. The World Bank also subjects all participating countries to the US's broad social outlook in order to transform the character of their states and to disproportionately benefit American allies and their corporate clients.[13]

The use of US economic power as a way to realize an international financial order built on its desired economic – and, by extension, social and political – values was also helped by the US's post-Second World War Marshall Plan. The Marshall Plan was a $15 billion aid package (equivalent to $130 billion in 2019) to assist Europe's economic recovery, but also to inculcate liberal trade by insisting on removing trade barriers, reducing regulations, modernizing industry and adopting American business practices.[14] As a result, the European economy was restructured through the US's global vision. This integrated approach was highly fruitful in that it demanded legal and political concessions, rather than the repayment of loans, and was a strategy that tied these countries to US influence. Underpinning this pre-eminence was an implicit security bargain, whereby the US 'agreed to provide security protection and access to American markets, technology, and resources within an open world economy. In return, America's partners agreed to be reliable partners that would provide diplomatic, economic, and logistical support for the US as it led the wider order.'[15] The IMF and the World Bank have reinforced this strategy by providing – or withholding – loans and aid to countries favourable (or adverse) – to the US's geopolitical machinations. With its roots in the rise of industrialized mass-mechanized conflict starting with the First World War, the use of military force was thus intertwined with this economic order as a way to enforce control. It would eventually result in a strategy of 'permanent war'[16] that sustained the US's industrial-military complex and used military intervention as a way to support any government – democratic or not – sympathetic to US market access.

These essential elements persisted after the Second World War but by the 1960s scholars such as Friedrich Hayek and Milton Friedman began to argue for welfare states and government bureaucracies to be reduced in order to maximize their efficiency, and for a focus on the needs of the individual not the collective.[17] This ideology of neoliberalism would be 'characterized by private property rights, individual liberty, unencumbered markets and free trade'[18] and be defined as 'a combination of ideas about the optimal form of market capitalism ... [and] a project of institutional change'[19] in world politics. Via its encouragement of privatization, deregulation and competition, it can also be regarded as a set of legally binding economic constraints that encourage growth within a structure of individual freedoms and rights. The maximization of private profit through commercialization and commodification also drove neoliberalism, underpinned by an overriding belief in the market over the state and arguments against having 'too much democracy'.[20] Suffering from a recession and high inflation, in 1971 US President Nixon severed the ties between the price of gold and the US dollar, ending the Bretton Woods system. These dynamics all presaged a paradigm shift from liberal Keynesian principles to neoliberalism and gained greater traction as the 1970s saw widespread instability in the world economy due to the 1973 oil crisis and extensive stagflation.[21]

Neoliberalism was first implemented in Chile in the mid-1970s during the military junta led by Augusto Pinochet and was then adopted domestically in the 1980s in the US and the UK by President Ronald Reagan and Prime Minister Margaret Thatcher. Through massive pioneering privatizations, widespread deregulation and dismembering the trade union movement, Thatcher would 'replac[e] post-war collectivism with market individualism'[22] and end up proclaiming that 'there is no alternative'[23] to neoliberalism. In turn, Reagan would pronounce that 'government does not solve problems; it subsidizes them',[24] and introduced similar policies that saw the privatization and deregulation of welfare, education, banks, transport, energy, parks, roads, prisons and the military,[25] as well as healthcare, intelligence gathering, counter-terrorism, domestic security and military operations abroad.[26] These reforms in the US led to 'the state play[ing] a minimalist role [in the economy], leaving ample space for private interest groups to influence policies'.[27]

Leaders of the liberal international order then used the World Bank and the IMF (along with the World Trade Organization, as we will see in Chapter 4) to perpetuate these economic norms as essential non-negotiable foundations for the global economy. Creating a newly dominant neoliberal order, such institutions implemented a set of policies that were enshrined in the Washington Consensus of 1989.[28] A critical dimension of this embedding was linking the issuing of loans to particular conditionalities, whereby countries not only had to provide collateral to access funds but had to align their macro-economic policies with those of the World Bank and the IMF. Informed by the belief that developing countries incurred debts due to excessive state interference with the market, such 'structural adjustment programmes' included austerity, resource extraction, devaluing currencies, trade liberalization, opening stock markets, balancing budgets, removing state subsidies, privatizing state-owned enterprises, enhancing foreign investment and fighting corruption. If the policy prescriptions of the Washington Consensus were not met, it would lead to a country's loans being withdrawn.[29] Numerous countries across Latin America, Asia, the Middle East, Europe and Australasia would adopt neoliberal policies, while several – such as Chile in 1975, Bolivia in 1985, New Zealand in the late 1980s and the former Soviet states in the 1990s – were subjected to the sudden forced introduction of these policies, known as 'shock therapy'.[30]

By the 1990s, the pre-eminence of neoliberalism in Western countries resulted in what can be termed 'market democracy', whereby market capitalism became the dominant determinant of society rather than liberal democracy and its associated human rights. By stating its preference for markets over the state, neoliberalism meant that 'depoliticising the economy ... went along with undermining the strength and autonomy of established institutions, parties, trade unions, churches, local governments, professional associations and universities'.[31] Despite improving material wellbeing and lifting the majority of the global population out of poverty, the privileging of self-interest and individualism also resulted in a form of 'market fundamentalism' that 'put competition in the marketplace above government, in an extraordinary anti-democratic exercise that confined liberty to commerce and turned freedom into competition'.[32] It also reduced human rights, especially in relation to freedoms to strike, organize and associate, which in the US marked a continuation of the reduction of these rights dating from the Taft-Hartley Act of 1947. Such a realization echoed the assertion that 'capitalism is a system in which the central institutions of society are in principle under autocratic control'[33] and are thus authoritarian in nature.

Under Bill Clinton and Tony Blair, the dominance of neoliberalism in the West saw a corporate model being applied to government, via which the state was regarded as a company and the public as consumers. Regarded by observers as a form of 'manipulative corporate populism', it 'made a left/right distinction redundant',[34] leading to what can be termed 'post-democracy'.[35] Both these leaders again saw neoliberalism and its associated policies as a natural state of affairs, with Tony Blair arguing that 'I hear people say we have to stop and debate globalization. You might as well debate whether autumn should follow summer',[36] and Bill Clinton stating 'globalization: it's the central reality of our time'.[37] The 1999 repeal of the 1933 Glass–Steagall Act in the US (which had separated commercial and investment banks) formed part of this rationale and was a precursor to the global financial crisis of 2008. Through excessive risk taking by banks together with the bursting of an enormous housing bubble in the US, 'the financial crash destroyed the promise of a "golden age" and a "new world order"', one 'even greater than the industrial revolution'.[38] Despite leading to the worst economic recession since the Great Depression of the 1930s, so pervasive was the belief in neoliberalism that Western countries ploughed vast amounts of money into their economies – via quantitative easing – to alleviate the crisis, followed by imposing severe domestic austerity measures to pay for it.

Recognizing this deep-seated adherence to the orthodoxy of neoliberalism, scholars note that Western democracies now display 'inverted totalitarianism', which represents 'the political coming of age of corporate power and the political demobilisation of the citizenry'.[39] Within this perspective, and in response to the prevalence in the West of lobbying and political donations from the business world, 'corporate power purports … to honour electoral politics, freedom, and the Constitution. But these corporate forces so corrupt and manipulate power as to make democracy impossible.'[40] Emblematic of this argument and as evidence of the US being ruled as a corporatocracy, Joe Biden raised over $1 billion in donations during the 2020 US presidential election (and Donald Trump raised $950 million), while total spending reached $14 billion – more than double that of 2016.[41] Ten donors accounted for over $640 million of these donations, with most contributions coming from the investment, legal, education, real estate, health, electronics and media industries.[42] Linking together these factors, since the 2008 financial crisis, most Western countries have experienced growing inequality, political apathy and mounting crony capitalism, which is reducing the legitimacy of the economic and political realms of the liberal international order.

Chinese-style authoritarian capitalism

As the Western economic system moved away from its liberal democratic moorings towards a 'marketized incarceration of contemporary corporate democracy',[43] over the same period China's economic system went on its own journey as it travelled away from Maoist totalitarianism towards that of authoritarian capitalism. By openly embracing the virtues of free market liberal economics, while maintaining China's one-party state and an emphasis on 'Chinese characteristics', this shift marked an ever-closer convergence between Western and Chinese practices along the political-economic *continuum*. It also confirmed a certain durability within China's identity and underlying (including Confucian) values concerning its authoritarian basis. As such, it highlighted how China willingly allowed the *assimilation* of its economy into the prevailing liberal economic order but managed to preserve its own preferred capitalist style to which other countries are now drawn. Given the clear benefits of economic growth in terms of domestic modernization and development, as well as bolstering its legitimacy, the CCP is quite willing to uphold the liberal international order, if only economically. Beijing's embrace of guided liberal economics also helps to augment its military, diplomatic and institutional power in order to become globally dominant.

When the People's Republic of China (PRC) was formed in 1949, China's economy had been devastated by decades of instability, civil war and invasion. The CCP also came to power harbouring a deep-seated suspicion of the international system, bolstered not only by the legacy of the Century of Humiliation but also because China was shut out of the Bretton Woods institutions (despite China being on the winning allied side during the Second World War). From this basis, and in line with the CCP's ideology being based on Marxist-Leninist thought, China's totalitarian approach typified not only the foundations of its political system (as we saw in Chapter 1) but also those of its economic system. Central to this system was the implementation from 1953 of a highly centralized command economy centred on five-year plans. Such a planned economy reflected China's wider socialist political basis and was regarded as essential to combat its high levels of poverty and hunger, as well as to drive forward the country's modernization and development aims through a policy of self-reliance (*zili gengsheng*). Such an approach also applied strict controls on imports and exports, and minimized foreign commerce, foreign direct investment and any contact with foreigners or overseas business.

Confirming its totalitarian outlook, all agricultural production was collectivized, with land holding and production being aggregated. Through the prevalence of state-owned enterprises (SOEs), all major industries – including manufacturing, mining, transport, banking and foreign trade – were nationalized, and carried out business and public policy activities for the CCP, which also predetermined production rates and prices. Such a controlled system was anti-capitalist, with no sense of a free market, and no space for private wealth or property, while China as a whole was cut off from the international economy and held no debt. This period also witnessed profound failures, such as the 1958–62 Great Leap Forward, as well as the widespread political and economic chaos of the 1966–76 Cultural Revolution.

For reformist-inclined leaders in the CCP, these upheavals demanded a new source of legitimacy for the Party: namely, the embrace of free market economics. The key advocate of such an approach was Deng Xiaoping. A prominent political figure in the foundation of the PRC who had joined the CCP in 1923, he had taken part in many anti-capitalist campaigns in the 1950s and 1960s but was twice purged by Mao during the Cultural Revolution for his reformist attitudes. Coming to power in the late 1970s, Deng instituted the 'open door' policy to allow China's economy to gain access to foreign trade, markets, expertise, modern technology, international cooperation and foreign direct investment. The opening up allowed China to transition to a free market economic system in which the price of goods and services was determined by consumer supply and demand. It also recognized how China's large working population, untapped markets and natural resources were all attractive to other countries and would serve to embolden such a shift.

This change centred on Deng's maxim that 'it doesn't matter whether a cat is black or white, as long as it catches mice' (in other words, any means of economic growth are acceptable), as well as a need 'to cross the river by feeling the stones' (that is, such major changes need to be done slowly and carefully). This latter ethos embodied the approach of developmental economies in East Asia in the 1980s and 1990s as the CCP learnt from the Russian experience that gradual reform was better than destabilizing shock therapy. Deng also initiated the Four Modernizations, targeting China's agriculture, industry, national defence, and science and technology capabilities in order to rejuvenate and transform China's inefficient and overtly autocratic economy, and broadly recognizing the wider benefits of globalization and multilateralism. To consistently bolster these reforms, China has had very high domestic investment rates, which between 2010 and 2017 averaged 35 per cent of GDP (gross domestic product) per year versus 10 per cent per year in countries such as the US and UK.[44]

This selective embrace of liberal economics was done while also emphasizing China's historical and contemporary context.[45] As Deng stated in a 1982 speech, 'we must integrate the universal truths of Marxism with the concrete realities of China, blaze a path of our own, and build a socialism with Chinese characteristics'.[46] This approach combined China's embrace of capitalist free market economics with the CCP's authoritarian one-party rule in order to produce a hybrid economic and development system known as a socialist market economy. This morphing allowed the CCP to continue to control the country's economic direction by encompassing the planning of both the public and private sectors, including the use of five-year plans, and the greater use of government regulations or intervention (in contrast to Western neoliberal economies). It also permitted the CCP to protect local businesses from multinational corporations, as well as its indigenous culture from destabilizing and alien ideas that endangered China's authoritarian basis. While SOEs were incrementally reformed, restructured and privatized, and their centrality to China's economy greatly reduced, some still persisted and blurred the line between ostensibly private Chinese businesses and their control by China's ruling elites. Overall, the overt emphasis on tangible material wealth and consumption was furthermore used by the CCP to quell calls for political reform, and to structure a society in which the accumulation of economic wealth became the sole guiding aim.

The sweeping changes that the CCP inculcated in China's economy ushered in a period of rapid, all-encompassing and transformative change. China's economy experienced a massive and concerted rise in its annual GDP rates, which was quicker than any other country in history, averaging 9.8 per cent in the 1980s, 10.0 per cent in the 1990s, 10.3 per cent in the 2000s and 7.7 per cent in the 2010s.[47] These increases saw China's GDP (in PPP [purchasing power parity], current US dollars) rise from $1.11 trillion in 1990, to $3.69 trillion in 2000, to $12.39 trillion in 2010 and to $23.49 trillion in 2019, overtaking the US in 2017 as the world's largest economy.[48] As a consequence, China's GDP per capita rose from $184 in 1979 to $10,216 in 2019, and life expectancy rose from 66.4 years to 76.9 years.[49] Such a shift in the country's fortunes led one observer to note how for 'the first time in human history China ... has realized that living standards in a man's lifecycle can be increased by more than 100 times, as well as the important effects China brings to people from other countries in the world and to the global economy'.[50] In comparison, average wages in the US and across the West have stagnated since the 1970s,[51] while life expectancy has declined in the US since 2014.[52]

Although it also brought in a series of problems ranging from mounting individualism and income inequality to ever-worsening corruption and environmental degradation, the CCP's economic transformation made China the essential centre of the global economy. Reflecting this criticality, in 2013 China produced essential parts for 91 per cent of all personal computers, 80 per cent of all air conditioners, 74 per cent of all solar cells, 71 per cent of all mobile phones, 63 per cent of all shoes, 60 per cent of all cement and 45 per cent of all shipping capacity,[53] and by 2019 China accounted for 28.7 per cent of the world's manufacturing output.[54] Moreover, China also became the world's top energy consumer in 2010 and in 2017 was the world's largest importer and consumer of raw materials, including 59 per cent of all cement, 56 per cent of all nickel, 50 per cent of all copper, coal and steel, 47 per cent of all aluminium and pork, 33 per cent of all cotton, 31 per cent of all rice, 27 per cent of all gold and 23 per cent of all corn.[55] Such demand created a complex web of interdependence between the global economy and that of China, with the success of the latter irrevocably informing that of the former. Further underscoring this dominance, by 2019, in terms of foreign direct investment, China received $209.6 billion or 13.6 per cent of the global total and invested $176.4 billion or 13.4 per cent of the global total, and on both measures was second only to the US.[56] From 2008 to 2019, China also gave $462 billion in overseas development finance loans, which was only $5 billion less than World Bank lending over the same period.[57] A key part of China's economic success was being lent large sums of money by the World Bank (which China joined in 1980) for domestic projects relating to transportation, urban development, rural development, water resources management, energy and the environment,[58] but also joining the World Trade Organization in 2001 (as will be detailed in Chapter 4). In both these ways, the existing liberal economic international order willingly allowed China – through concessions made by Beijing – to sign up to its major institutions and to then dominate its worldwide economic system.

Such open *facilitation* was driven by the benefits that China brought in terms of cheaper manufacturing costs, lower wages and fewer restrictions in terms of labour rights,[59] which thus greatly benefited the profit margins of foreign corporations and shareholders. The value of this facilitation is clearly shown in a letter that President George H.W. Bush wrote to Deng a month after the events in Tiananmen Square in 1989, noting that 'I explained to the American people that I did not want to unfairly burden the Chinese people with economic sanctions.'[60] This attitude was underpinned by the belief, as Bush later stated, that 'selling Big Macs to Beijing … [would act as] a force for change in China, exposing China to our ideas and our ideals,'[61] whereby economic liberalization was the natural precursor to political liberalization. In this way, the economic benefits of engagement with China unmistakably trumped dealing with a clearly authoritarian country, even after the political and human rights of its population had been so publicly attacked. The long-term acceptance of such a fait accompli – and the economic synergy typifying China–US relations – persists to this day, as trade between the US and China rose from $7.7 billion in 1985 to $75.4 billion in 1997, to $407.5 billion in 2008, to $560 billion in 2020, with a trade surplus in favour of China since 1985.[62]

China's dramatic economic success of the last 40 years and the ability of the CCP to maintain its authoritarian political basis has produced a new developmental paradigm. The resultant political-economic system can be considered as an authoritarian-capitalist or Marxist-capitalist[63] model that results from the 'construction of a particular kind of market economy that increasingly incorporates neoliberal elements interdigitated with authoritarian centralized control'.[64] Such a model 'bypasses democracy',[65] and by giving the population wealth without political freedoms the CCP has successfully sidestepped arguments that there are no 'viable systematic alternatives to Western liberalism'.[66] This success represents a direct challenge to the legitimacy of the current liberal economic order and is one that seeks to actively recraft it along more authoritarian lines, in what some observers have noted represents a 'Beijing Consensus'.[67] It also represents a process of selectivity, whereby China has cherry-picked the elements most useful to it – unfettered economic growth and investment – but mixed them with its own preferences, values and worldview. China's success after the 2008 global financial crisis, when it was able to maintain high growth and avoid the deep recessions affecting Western countries, stressed the validity of its alternative approach by showing that an authoritarian system can help – rather than hinder – economic growth. As we saw in Chapter 1, the CCP's control of the country's legislature and judiciary, and hence trade unions and labour laws, as well as China's natural resources and land, aid this feat, through a belief in 'markets before democracy [and limiting] civil and political rights ... in the name of stability and economic growth'.[68]

At its core, such a 'China Model' is 'open to emulation by others, in which case its relevance transcends the boundaries of Chinese society',[69] and informs Xi Jinping's China Dream with its aim of fostering 'social wealth for the benefit of all members of society'.[70] The model itself is argued to be based on technological innovation, equitable and sustainable export-led growth (which is favoured over GDP) and the preservation of self-determination and state-sovereignty (as opposed to domination by the US and its associated institutions).[71] In this latter regard, countries are argued to need to develop free from foreign interference, via a focus on incremental reforms and policies that are reflective of unique local – not universal – conditions.[72] As such, China's approach promotes the idea of 'harmonious inclusionism', whereby – unlike the neoliberal system – Beijing appears to 'reject the legitimacy of the domination of one ... ideology, or approach in world politics'[73] and embraces plurality. Such an order 'encourage[s] different opinions, norms and models in a civil society'[74] and rests on a conception of power centred on 'harmony with difference', which contrasts with the universalist aims of the Western liberal international order. Such plurality would produce a uniquely – neo-*Tianxiaism*-based – normative order.

Within the China Model the state plays a proactive and interventionist role in many companies even as they compete in global markets. The CCP thus 'safeguard[s] its own policy space as to when, where and how to adopt Western ideas'[75] by selecting which individuals run the country's largest businesses, which further binds the economy to one-party rule. It is also willing to punish high-profile individuals who appear to question CCP policy, as happened with Jack Ma, the founder of Alibaba, who disappeared for three months in 2020 and was ordered by the CCP to divest from certain markets.[76] It is, furthermore, a model based on very tangible, inclusive and visible gains, as personified by the rapid modernization of China's infrastructure and living standards, that provides vital evidence of the China Dream being realized by the CCP. It hence contrasts with more moribund Western societies and an American Dream which has been in decline since the 1970s.[77]

Such gains make the China Model increasingly attractive to developing states, and by 2018 China had provided training programmes to 160,000 government officials, engineers and doctors from Africa,[78] along with those from other regions, which effectively socialized them into China's preferred practices. In a contemporary upgrading of Mao's efforts at 'exporting revolution', such training is regarded as 'less dictatorial compared to Western capacity-building programs in that China does not assume their experience represents the "ultimate truth"'.[79] As part of this process, 492,000 foreign students studied in China in 2018,[80] while statements by officials that 'China will not engage in invasion, plundering, war or expansion that Western powers used to practice'[81] also appear to differentiate and advertise China's divergent approach. Such is the apparent success of this attitude that regional observers note how 'most Africans are switching from the West to China, [which] will be a disaster ... [for] human rights, democracy and free speech'.[82]

Enacting the new order

The export of China's economic model, as the basis of its preferred economic international order, is most visible through its Belt and Road Initiative (BRI). Launched in 2013, it aims to create a China-centric international trading network that will 'promote connectivity of Asian, European and African continents, ... establish and strengthen partnerships ... [and] align and coordinate the development strategies of the countries along the Belt and Road'.[83] The BRI is envisioned to create a 'community of common destiny for mankind' (*renlei mingyun gongtongti*) through the win–win nature of mutual trade gains designed to be adaptable to the needs of each involved country.[84] It thus appears to avoid the zero–sum thinking of the current US-led order based on conditionalities such as promoting democracy or universal human rights, or arming and allying with other countries, aims which are seen by China as hegemonic and conflict inducing. From this basis, the BRI is a vehicle for China to alter the existing international order through the introduction of new norms and preferences,[85] while increasing openness and 'strategic trust'[86] between China and other countries. Moreover, the BRI attests to a confident and proactive China that is actively shaping international conditions and which builds up its global strategic credibility by offering clear economic and developmental benefits to other countries.

The BRI further reflects China's aspiration to refind its Middle Kingdom past as it makes 'China the center of geoeconomics and geopolitics in the region and beyond'.[87] A major aim of the BRI is to inculcate regional stability around China in East Asia that then fans out to other regions in order to guarantee an uninterrupted trade flow between China and the rest of the world. By using trade and investment to reduce poverty, underdevelopment and a reliance on extra-regional influence, Beijing thus projects its wider aims of harmony and tolerance via *tian xia* to Asia and beyond. The BRI further aims to integrate the world with Chinese-led aid, trade and investments[88] by creating deep-seated interdependence between itself and member countries. It also seeks to protect Asia from external interference, whereby Asian affairs and Asian security would be decided by countries in the region. In addition, the BRI helps China to find new markets for its production and capital surpluses, and to secure its growing energy needs, thus providing stability to allow Beijing to pursue its domestic modernization and development agenda, and to maintain the legitimacy and dominant rule of the CCP. More broadly, it encourages these countries to deal with each other *independently* of China,[89] negating comparisons with the Marshall Plan that was dominated by the US. Finally, the BRI aids internal stability through the creation of economic prosperity in China's western regions, and conversely explains why China so actively subdues the populations of Xinjiang and Tibet (as we saw in Chapter 1), as these regions provide the most vital trade routes into Eurasia.

As of January 2022, 140 countries from around the world had joined the BRI, with 40 members in sub-Saharan Africa, 34 in Europe and Central Asia (including 18 members of the European Union), 25 countries in East Asia and the Pacific, 17 countries in the Middle East and North Africa, 18 countries in Latin America and the Caribbean and 6 countries in South East Asia, with several others currently negotiating membership.[90] Notable exceptions from the current order include the US, Canada and the UK. Recreating historical legacies relating to the Silk Road and other ancient trade routes that linked China to the rest of the world, the BRI is primarily based on investment in railway, road and sea route infrastructure, as well as construction, real estate, aviation, telecommunications and power grids.

Different parts of the BRI include the Silk Road Economic Belt, consisting of three belts: a North Belt stretching from China through Central Asia and Russia to Europe, a Central Belt passing through Central Asia and West Asia to the Mediterranean, and a South Belt running through South East Asia and South Asia to the Indian Ocean. In turn, the 21st Century Maritime Silk Road links South East Asia, Oceania and Africa via the South China Sea, the South Pacific and the Indian Ocean, and extends up through the Suez Canal to the Mediterranean, using rail links to then cross Europe to the North Sea, while the Ice Silk Road crosses northern Russia and the Arctic. Allowing goods to be transported more quickly, cheaply and efficiently, such interconnection aims to transform entire supply chain and production models,[91] and is majorly bolstered by China having the world's longest high-speed railway network.

China's sustained economic success, and resultant major economic clout – as well as its civilizational basis – underpins its BRI vision, and from 2013 to 2019 the BRI initiated over 3,100 projects with total investment estimates ranging from $1 trillion to $8 trillion.[92] Such investments are claimed by Beijing to have led to the creation of tens of millions of jobs, significantly boosting the economies and material living standards of the countries involved. And, in contrast with loans issued by the World Bank and the IMF, China does not attach any conditions for internal economic reform to its loans. In general, such loans are structured 'with an interest rate of 2 per cent, a 5–7 year grace period, and a 15–20-year maturity',[93] which are generally in line with global capital markets. Being denominated in *renminbi*, these loans also help to internationalize China's slowly liberalizing currency.

These loans have, however, been criticized for Beijing ignoring debt sustainability standards,[94] leading to accusations of 'debt-trap diplomacy' whereby the terms of these loans often involve China using key ports (such as in Greece, Djibouti and Australia) and other infrastructure (such as gold mines in Tajikistan) as collateral in case of missed payments.[95] Moreover, observers note how the 'sheer scale of Chinese lending and the lack of strong institutional mechanisms to protect the debt sustainability of borrowing countries poses clear risks',[96] especially if a country owes the vast majority of its large amount of debt to China. In turn, China has shown little interest in enforcing compliance by its companies operating overseas,[97] which has increased local corruption, leading to political backlashes and unrest in recipient countries. Furthermore, China does attach some conditionalities to the loans, in the form of recipient countries recognizing key parts of CCP policy. These principally include acknowledging the One China policy, wherein countries must have no diplomatic relations with Taiwan, must not criticize the CCP concerning Xinjiang or Tibet and must align with China in the UN Security Council.[98] Recipients are also expected to use Chinese companies, equipment, technology and workers.[99]

In these ways, and given that it involves a focus on policy coordination, financial integration, liberal trade facilitation, infrastructure construction and people-to-people exchanges, the BRI has an important legal dimension to it. As such, it exports China's attitude concerning rule by law and major parts of its legal system 'as the BRI will demand that countries adopt its own Chinese-based dispute resolution mechanism'.[100] When combined with longer-term ambitions to use greater economic interconnectivity as the basis for removing trade barriers, regulations and tariffs, so as to create new free trade areas, the BRI acts a mechanism to further export key dimensions of the CCP's authoritarian rule, especially when combined with the widespread sale of its surveillance technology. As such, critics of the BRI see it as 'an attempt to establish a comprehensive system for moulding the world in Chinese interests'[101] that is not necessarily in the interests of Western liberal democracy. Beijing can now also use its increasing economic leverage to force countries to ignore human rights violations in Xinjiang or Hong Kong, or to allow China to use critical infrastructure developments to support its possible military expansion overseas. Balancing out these threats with the BRI's economic benefits poses a dilemma for Western countries, especially those suffering severe downturns as a result of COVID-19.

Acquiescence, divergence and usurpation

Over the last 40 years, China has used the existing liberal economic order to rapidly augment its power, standing and influence in the world. It has done so through an acceptance of the fundamentals of such an order and by assimilating itself to its dominant practices. This process was actively facilitated by the West, which was seeking cheaper forms of production, greater profits and new investment markets. Such a *facilitation* was also driven by a belief in the underlying contention of the liberal international order that economic liberalization would lead to political – that is, democratic – liberalization and the realization of universal human rights. In the last decades, China's rise has revealed the fallibility of this contention. In the West, this interlinkage has itself been replaced by a neoliberal economic vision that firmly places the market above politics and downplays the role of democracy. Although China has arrived from a different start point – within Mao's totalitarian outlook – it has now reached a similar place, whereby as long as the pre-eminent position of the CCP is maintained, politics has been removed from the country's economic calculus. In these ways, 'the

China boom has been dependent on the global neoliberal order ... [and] it is in China's vested interest to maintain the status quo'.[102] China has thus defended the merits of globalization, and in the midst of the 2019 US–China trade war Beijing accused Washington of 'deliberately destroying international order ... [via] unilateralism and protectionism'.[103]

Despite this acquiescence, we have also seen how, while China 'might accept and benefit from the current international economic structure, ... [it is] far less likely to conform to the politics and principles of the current liberal hegemonic order when organizing its own domestic politics and international political relations'.[104] Thus, although China has no need to entirely overthrow the existing international order, it has injected its own preferred style – its Chinese characteristics – into how it orders its economic affairs and how it would like to order those of the world. This morphing has led to the creation of a counter-hegemonic alternative that places Beijing in a dominant but not domineering position, whereby it trades with other countries in a largely condition-free, neutral, black-and-white manner, which contrasts with that of US-led neoliberalism through the World Bank and the IMF. Nor does it appear that China wishes to seek hegemony in economic terms (as the US has), and instead seeks to promote a worldview based on 'diversity in harmony'. The deep symbiosis between the Chinese and US economies highlights this position, as does a statement by Chinese Foreign Minister Wang Yi in 2020 that 'there cannot be a "cold war" in the era of globalization, as it is impossible to divide the world into two or three camps when all countries have become an interconnected community of shared interests'.[105]

What we have also witnessed – as China has grown richer, and as the world's countries and their economies have become dependent on Beijing's continued success – is a slow *counter-assimilation* of the world to China's preferred economic outlook. As part of this process, China is actively seeking to export its authoritarian-capitalist model – and the values, outlooks and practices underpinning it – so as to create a more stable, tolerant, harmonious and therefore *ordered* world via which it can achieve its modernization and status ambitions. By drawing other countries towards it through the win-win of economic opportunity, investment and connectivity, as well as promoting the demonstration effect of its own rapid economic success, Beijing seeks to achieve its ultimate goal 'of establishing itself as the preponderant power in Eurasia and a global power second to none, … without provoking a countervailing response or a military conflict'.[106] Given its scale and scope, as well as its clear basis on Chinese-derived values concerning how such an international order would be structured economically – but also, as we have seen, politically and legally – the BRI is the primary vehicle for realizing this goal. It is also one that harks back to the glories of past Chinese dynasties, underpinned by Confucian values relating to stability and benevolence, with China at the fulcrum of such an order.

In this way, the BRI represents a clear hierarchy, with China being pre-eminent over other countries, and also implies a sense of past tributary relations, whereby these countries (implicitly) recognize China's superiority. Emblematic of such motivations, the BRI is seen by Chinese observers as 'an unprecedentedly sweeping and bold vision for humankind. No government – including the Roman Empire, the British Empire, or the US – has ever proposed such a vision. This is nothing less than a Chinese manifesto for its global leadership … [that] will usher in a new era in international politics'.[107]

4

Competing Institutions

The ushering in of a China-centric international order is furthermore being realized through Beijing's construction of competing international institutions. Such regimes aid the creation and maintenance of international orders, as we have already seen with the US-originating World Bank, and do so by binding their members together around particular interests and associated values, rules, practices and understandings. They also demand some form of collective identity and collective action. China is seeking to challenge the existing architecture of international affairs but also to alter its underlying principles and norms through the realization of new groupings such as the Asian Infrastructure Investment Bank – a multilateral development bank founded in 2015 – and the Shanghai Cooperation Organization – a Eurasian security organization initiated in 1996. It also supports – and at times attempts to recraft – established bodies such as the United Nations and the World Trade Organization.

Forming new international institutions provides Beijing with a managerial role through which it can better govern and regulate international affairs. They are also vehicles for Beijing to disseminate an alternative narrative and vision of the world onto the global stage as informed by Chinese characteristics, including its authoritarian-capitalist model. Underscoring this 'system-determining' potential, by consolidating their structural power, institution creators have the capacity to 'increase or decrease the security of others, to exercise control over production of goods and services, to determine the structure of finance and credit, and to have wide-ranging influence over ideas, information flows, and knowledge from many areas'.[1] This chapter will show how China's specific beliefs concerning multipolarity (*duojihua* – a world where a group of countries, not just one, all have influence), global governance, human rights, peaceful development and non-intervention are engendering a new form of international order. This basis challenges the hegemony of rival Western institutions and, by extension, the very liberal political and economic values on which they have been crafted, imagined and legitimized. It rests as much on attracting like-minded countries as it does on contestation with the West, whereby co-option was a key facet in the realization of the current US-led international order and is also key in China's emergent order.

The essential component of this attraction is that of soft power, which can be seen as a form of 'competitive politics of attraction, legitimacy and credibility'.[2] As a non-coercive and socializing form of power that is centred on a country's national and political values, principles and behaviour, it informs a country's cultural diplomacy and international brand. It is successful 'when one country gets other countries to want what it wants, ... in contrast with the hard or command power of ordering others to do what it wants'[3] and is often only effective when backed up by more tangible and harder forms of power (such as economic inducements or the threat of military force). Maintaining a positive image, as well as high peer recognition, is thus essential, which for China means presenting itself as a benevolent and trustworthy rising great power that does not wish to dominate the international system. The creation of positive narratives underscores this process and is achieved via the China Public Diplomacy Association, which seeks to peacefully create an international environment advantageous to China and to promote its national values. Specific policies such as hosting the 2008 Olympic Games inform this process, as does the proliferation of think tanks to craft the rhetoric that reflects Beijing's standpoints.

Beijing's clearest strategy has been its global proliferation of Confucius Institutes, which promote China's culture, language, ideas and image in host countries. Acting in a similar fashion to the British Council, the Goethe Institute and the Maison Française – and thus counteracting the pro-Western narratives emanating from such organizations – there were over 475 Confucius Institutes in 149 countries in 2021, including 85 in the US, 30 in the UK, 19 in Germany and 18 in France.[4] They act as a 'geo-cultural force', while adhering to the Confucius adage that 'if remoter people are not submissive, all the influences of civil culture and virtue are to be cultivated to attract them to be so; and when they have been so attracted, they must be made contented and tranquil'.[5] The Institutes further act as testing grounds for Beijing to adjust its international messaging until it is accepted by external audiences, and which is often linked to aid and investment in developing countries.[6] Confucius Institutes also realize billions of dollars of revenue via language instruction, testing and certification facilities, and increase the legitimacy of Mandarin as the lingua franca for trade.[7] With Institutes seen to be under-delivering, a proactive 'wolf warrior diplomacy' has now also emerged, indicating how 'the days when China can be put in a submissive position are long gone'.[8] As China's then-ambassador to Sweden noted, the Chinese Communist Party (CCP) 'absolutely cannot allow any country, organization or person to harm China's national interests. Of course, we must take countermeasures, ... cultural ... economic and trade relations will [thus] also be affected'.[9]

Creation and crisis

China's assertive promotion of its own narratives is being used to counteract many of the multilateral regimes that are characteristic of the current US-led international order. These institutions have allowed the US to shape the international system in its own image, and to propagate its domestic values and interests across the world. They also rest on a prevailing neoliberal economic vision whose underlying interests often supersede the wider promotion of democracy (even if such a political vision of the world is habitually voiced by US leaders). The US's creation of international institutions reflected this ethos, based on the belief that their in-built 'incentives and opportunities ... influence state choices and global outcomes, ... leading to a political convergence on liberal democracy'.[10] As we saw in Chapter 3, this (neo)liberal basis directly mapped onto the Bretton Woods institutions, such as the World Bank and the International Monetary Fund (IMF), and also free trade agreements, like the General Agreement on Tariffs and Trade (GATT) – the precursor to the World Trade

Organization (WTO). These groupings – alongside others such as the Asian Development Bank – were used after the Second World War to construct the global economy according to the US's economic interests, and to establish international norms that sought to maintain US hegemony. To stabilize this system (and protect US interests), global and regional security institutions – such as the United Nations (UN) and to a lesser degree the North Atlantic Treaty Organization (NATO) – also crafted the US's preferred security architecture, with the latter being directly used to contain the expansion of communism during the Cold War.

At its heart, the values of the US and other liberal democracies enabled the construction of this liberal hegemonic order organized around 'multilateralism, alliance partnership, strategic restraint, cooperative security, and institutional and rule-based relationships'.[11] It was underpinned by a political bargain, whereby its less developed members accepted American hegemony so as to interact in this system, which made it clearly hierarchical in nature. Such 'buy-in', and the much-needed economic development that it brought after 1945, was used to counteract differing norms and values emanating from the communist bloc and showcased apparent US benevolence and restraint (at least in the European context).[12]

As we also saw in Chapter 3, that developing countries needed to fulfil certain conditions – such as adopting democratic practices, the rule of law, privatization and liberalization – only served to further embed these values across the international sphere. The World Bank and IMF's focus on 'developed' and 'developing' countries also maintained the perceived superiority of the US and Western economies within such a dynamic. It is also shown by the West 'kicking away the ladder' as wealthy countries actively hinder developing and rising countries from reaching their full economic potential.[13] Such factors would influence China's creation of its own regimes based on its own values and worldview.

Beyond the economic domain, the US strategy of cooperative security aimed to make countries constrain – and thus stabilize – each other. Such a tactic can be seen through the 1948 Marshall Plan, which actively 'create[d] economic interdependencies that crossed over the traditional lines of hostility between European states'.[14] The UN was also forged on such a principle, which was integral to the negotiations that took place at the Dumbarton

Oaks Conference in the summer of 1944 between the Allied Big Four powers of the US, the UK, the Soviet Union and China. Stemming from the 1941 Atlantic Charter that set out US and UK global goals after the Second World War, and coming into being on 24 October 1945, Article 1 of the UN Charter mandates member countries to 'maintain international peace and security and to that end: to take effective collective measures for the prevention and removal of threats to the peace ... in conformity with the principles of justice and international law', while 'promoting and encouraging respect for human rights and for fundamental freedoms for all without distinction as to race, sex, language, or religion'.[15] Overarching these goals, the UN is authorized to carry out economic, diplomatic and military sanctions (including military force) to resolve disputes. These obligations are mandatory and supersede all other international treaties. Of note here is that the UN seeks to guarantee rights on an individual level, itself a key neoliberal norm, which often supersedes norms of sovereignty, as shown by the UN's Responsibility to Protect norm to defend populations from human rights violations such as genocide, war crimes, crimes against humanity and ethnic cleansing.[16]

While being highly assimilative in nature – in that it aims to pull member countries towards a standardized US-centric vision of international politics – the formation of the UN also gave its key architects permanent membership of its Security Council, the body which determines threats to international peace. Under Article 27 of the UN Charter, such guaranteed pre-eminence was assumed by the victorious allies in the Second World War – the US, the UK, France, the Soviet Union and China (the so-called Permanent Five or P5) – and gives them the ability to veto any Security Council resolution, and thus an inviolable ability to shape the contours of international politics for their own interests and allies. Until the end of 2020, Russia had used its veto 117 times, the US 82 times, and the UK, China and France, 29, 17 and 16 times respectively. Notably, in the post-Cold War period, Russia has vetoed UN Resolutions 27 times, followed by the US on 17 and an arguably more proactive China on 15.

The other major security organization created by the US as part of the liberal international order was NATO, which was effective from 4 April 1949. Based on the military pre-eminence of the

US, NATO intended to dissuade armed attacks by the Soviet Union against Europe and to counteract Moscow's Warsaw Pact (a collective defence treaty formed in 1955 between the Soviet Union, Poland and assorted Eastern European countries). Signatories from across Western Europe and North America agreed 'to safeguard the freedom, common heritage and civilization of the peoples, founded on the principles of democracy, individual liberty and the rule of law, ... [and] to promote stability and well-being'.[17] Central to NATO is its mutual self-defence clause, which was never invoked during the Cold War but was carried out once after 9/11. NATO forces have carried out regular inter-military exercises, and numerous 'crisis management operations'[18] in Iraq, Russia and Central Asia, Libya, off the coast of Somalia and the Horn of Africa, Sudan, Pakistan, Afghanistan, the US, Greece and the Balkans and is currently active in Kosovo and the Mediterranean. As with the UN, these actions allow the US to propagate its preferred hegemonic world vision and associated norms.

With the advent of the 21st century, the core pillars of this US-led international order were being openly questioned. The 2003 invasion of Iraq by the US and its allies bypassed the authority and processes of the UN and led the then-Secretary-General of the UN Kofi Annan to declare 'from our point of view and from the charter point of view it [the invasion] was illegal'.[19] Such an observation undercut the legitimacy of the UN as a force for maintaining international security and the sanctity of sovereignty in global affairs. The US's subsequent human rights violations through its widespread use of rendition, torture and detention facilities – such as at Guantanamo Bay and Abu Ghraib – further weakened the US's credibility as a bastion of liberal international values and by extension its integrity as the leader and architect of the wider Western-centric liberal international order. Notably, the US also does not regularly pay its membership fees to the UN and in 2019 owed over $1 billion in outstanding contributions,[20] while in December 2021 it was one of the lowest contributors to UN Peacekeeping Operations, giving only 31 uniformed personnel versus 6,358 by top-ranking Bangladesh.[21]

In turn, the 2008 global financial crisis can be seen as an economic 9/11 that irrevocably shook the IMF and the World Bank's assertions that they could guarantee a stable, global free trade economy and questioned why the US should still set the rules for international trade. As Barnett attests, 'the core ideology of neoliberalism imploded with the great financial crash of 2008. The market, which was supposed to know best, had failed. Governments, which were supposed to be the problem, had to rescue the rich.'[22] It also discredited elites from across the West – and indeed across the political spectrum – who had perpetuated such policies for decades. Together, these events led to a major 'crisis of authority, a crisis over the way liberal international order is governed, ... [which] generat[ed] pressures and incentives for a reorganization in the way sovereignty, rules, institutions, hierarchy, and authority are arrayed in the international system'.[23]

China asserts itself

It is within this context that China has grown increasingly proactive in its involvement with, and creation of, international institutions. This behaviour is based on a greater global confidence that has overcome China's historical misgivings that multilateral institutions were merely another tool of Western domination. However, after utilizing the advantages of multilateral regimes since the late 1970s, China now perceives the current system to be inadequate in terms of its effectiveness and representativeness, which combines with Beijing's mounting aspiration to propagate its own global vision. Within such dynamics is a persistent tension between the extent to which China is embedded within the current system – primarily through the trade and diplomatic benefits that this brings – and how China seeks to progressively shape it towards its own norms and worldview.

The first side of this dynamic relates to how the neoliberal international order is 'easy to join [yet] hard to overturn'[24] via a process of 'institutional lock-in' that socializes new entrants to existing practices. Exemplifying this embrace was Deng's mantra of keeping 'a low profile' (*taoguang yanghui*), and by 2000 China had joined over 50 intergovernmental organizations and nearly 1,250 international nongovernmental organizations.[25] As part of this strategy, China was frequently keen to broadly maintain the current system, as shown by its adherence to the liberal market pillars of the economic domain by quickly assimilating itself into the IMF after the enactment of market reforms in 1978 and joining the World Bank in 1980, both of which aided its advantageous transition and integration into the global economy. China also joined the WTO in 2001 (after concerted opposition from Western countries over its economic immaturity and it being perceived as an economic threat) and revised over 2,300 national laws in order to meet the organization's demands.[26] Membership brought China (and for WTO members, via the outsourcing and offshoring of production and services to lower-paid Chinese workers) major trade, technological and investment benefits.

In the security domain, China is also supportive of the UN's 'system-maintaining' nature.[27] It signed the Nuclear Non-Proliferation Treaty in 1992 that prevents the spread of nuclear weapons and aims to achieve universal nuclear disarmament, and the Comprehensive Nuclear Test Ban Treaty in 1996 that bans all nuclear detonations for either military or civilian purposes (although Beijing has yet to domestically ratify the Treaty). Through such steps, China could be seen to have been successfully co-opted into the current order, which would mitigate any desire by Beijing to change or challenge it, and would mean that 'while America may be in decline, the liberal order or liberal hegemonic order it created will persist and might even co-opt its potential challengers, including China'.[28]

In contrast, the other side of this dynamic is that China 'is seeking to increase its status and authority within the existing system rather than laying the foundation for exerting leadership in an alternative world order'.[29] Here, China challenges the liberal order's *exclusivity* by promoting its own particular characteristics that over time will reimagine and implicitly *reorient* the international order along more China-centric lines. Such a process replicates in much the same way how its authoritarian-capitalist model acts as an evolution not a wholesale replacement of the current economic system (as shown in Chapter 3). In turn, by 'building and operating within layers of regional and global economic, political, and security institutions – [China is] thereby making itself more predictable and approachable'.[30] As part of this integration and peaceful reorientation, China wishes to build a 'harmonious world' based on a strong and effective role for the UN, the development of collective security, mutually beneficial cooperation that enables prosperity for all, and tolerance and deepening dialogue among diverse countries.[31]

The core values that China asserts within its robust diplomacy appear to seek to provide stability for its society and economy, and to defend sovereignty, openness and multipolarity. Accompanying norms relating to self-determination and non-intervention inform this worldview, especially in relation to not dictating how other countries ought to manage their internal political or economic affairs. In this way, 'China takes a highly conservative, pluralist view of sovereignty and non-intervention'[32] that is anti-hegemonic and supports a diverse international order, which is antithetical to the US-led liberal international order. Also underpinning this vision are principles of hierarchy, paternalism and harmony (as per *tian xia*), which are centred on China's natural primacy over other countries. Additional virtues such as benevolence, justice, equality, fairness and righteousness – whereby 'one's behavior must be upright, reasonable and necessary'[33] – are further argued to complement such a China-centric positioning, as is that of *minben* ('people as the foundation') in which elite rule must be legitimated by popular consent. Notably, all of these elements are present in China's domestic politics, as we saw in Chapter 1. These notions, conjoined with China's civilizational basis and its ever-greater share of global power, makes Beijing willing to form a new international order that is more representative of current power balances, in contrast to the liberal international order that reflects a bygone era when the US could establish its unquestioned dominance.

A new economic vision

Beijing's pursuit of new institutions partially stemmed from the realization, as shown by the formation of the BRICS (Brazil, Russia, India, China, South Africa) grouping in 2010, that 'the world is undergoing major and swift changes that highlight the need for corresponding transformations in global governance in all relevant areas'.[34] In this new paradigm, the world's emergent great powers – China being foremost among them – demanded more recognition and influence commensurate with their growing economic and diplomatic clout. They also argued that their collective command of major portions of the world's population and economic production necessitated such a renovation, and – for the BRICS – a shared focus on values relating to non-interference, multipolarity, development, equality and opposition to hegemony. Such values were reflective of those permeating a China-centric international order and by extension were diametrically opposed to those supporting the US-led liberal international order. The BRICS, along with their New Development Bank (which sought to gradually reform the architecture of global finance in favour of the developing world), thus showed Beijing the potential for creating a major new global economic institution. Such a regime would be more exemplary of its own values, which were also broadly shared across the wider developing world and much of Asia, as well as it being time for a rising China 'to make a difference' (*you suo zuo wei*).[35]

China's creation of the Asian Infrastructure Investment Bank (AIIB) in 2014 was precipitated by the failure of the US Congress to reform IMF governance and its voting quotas, which according to former US President Barack Obama created 'an opportunity for China to assert itself'.[36] As Ben Bernanke, then chair of the Federal Reserve Board, further noted, 'the US Congress refused to allow the governance system ... to appropriately reflect the changing economic weights',[37] which emboldened Beijing's growing dissatisfaction with existing global multilateral financial frameworks that clearly underrepresented China as the world's soon-to-be largest economy. As such, the structural forces of the liberal international order appeared to be constraining China and preventing the optimum realization of its 'institutional voice' (*zhiduxing huayuquan*). Growing dissent after the 2008 global financial crisis, and a perception that the World Bank contributes to 'growing numbers of the destitute as well [as] ... the growing privilege of the world's rich',[38] opened up the viability of a new Chinese narrative that was as attractive to those in the West as it was to those outside it. Reflecting this narrative as based on Chinese values and Chinese goals for a new international order, the first AIIB President, Jin Liqun, stated that as 'we set forth on the historical journey ... towards building a new type [of] multilateral financial institution, ... [the] AIIB offers a fresh platform for enriched cooperation and enhanced regional connectivity and integration'.[39] In turn, Xi Jinping further noted that 'the founding and opening of the AIIB ... means a great deal to the reform of the global economic governance system'.[40]

Holding its inaugural meeting in January 2016, the AIIB drew together 57 Asian and Western countries, including France, Germany, Italy and the UK, which was crucial for 'establishing the AIIB as a credible institution in the global financial architecture and on international capital markets'.[41] Notably, the US and Japan did not join, citing human rights and labour condition issues. By the end of 2020, the AIIB had 103 approved members representing 79 per cent of the global population and 65 per cent of global GDP.[42] With an initial capital stock of $100 billion, as of 2021 the AIIB had plans to invest $24.66 billion in 123 projects in 28 member countries.[43] Such a level of capital stock seeks to rival that of the World Bank and the IMF. Operational power in the AIIB is centred on a board of 12 governors led by the AIIB president, currently Jin Liqun, a Chinese national and former staff member of both the World Bank and the Asian Development Bank (ADB). In contrast to the World Bank, which has always been governed by a US citizen appointed by the US president, the statutes of the AIIB clearly state that a non-Chinese citizen is eligible to become president of the AIIB, leading the AIIB president to remark that while the AIIB was 'born with the birthmark of China ... its upbringing is international'.[44] Primarily based on the fluctuating number of shares of the capital stock of the AIIB held by that member, in 2021 China had the most overall voting power with 26.57 per cent, followed by India (7.60 per cent), Russia (5.98 per cent), Korea (3.50 per cent), Australia (3.46 per cent) and Indonesia (3.17 per cent).[45]

The AIIB specializes in 'green infrastructure with sustainability, innovation, and connectivity at its core',[46] with the aim of stimulating economic development, reducing poverty, creating prosperity and increasing economic relations among members. Such loans also directly aid China's Belt and Road Initiative, especially in terms of augmenting the quality of infrastructure across Asia, which is regarded as 'a serious bottleneck region-wide'[47] in terms of its development potential. In line with how China conducts its bilateral trade – and in stark contrast to the neoliberal conditionalities associated with World Bank loans – AIIB loans are issued with 'no strings attached'[48] based on mutual benefit, self-determination, respect for sovereignty and non-interference in the internal affairs of member states. In the latter regard, recipient countries are also not required to deregulate or privatize their domestic enterprises but must be legally transparent. The likelihood that loans can be repaid is therefore the AIIB's most decisive criteria and eschews political considerations in contrast to the influence of hegemonic US interests concerning the terms of IMF loans (as shown in Chapter 3). Together these norms result in a non-confrontational and 'positive discourse about mutual development and mutual respect'[49] based on 'value-neutral cooperation' regardless of a country's ideological orientation. Rather than insisting that other countries follow its own political proclivities and using military force to back up such demands, Beijing's non-violent pursuit of its aims directly contrasts with most of Western imperialist history.

In these ways, the AIIB is an 'instrument for China to lend legitimacy to its international forays and to extend its sphere of economic and political influence, ... while changing the rules of the game ... [and giving] the existing institutions a kick in the pants'.[50] This challenge to the economic institutions of the liberal international order rests on how the AIIB is based on a different set of values, which result in an amalgam of 'state-led development' and 'social-welfare' models, both of which differ from the US's laissez-faire model.[51] They also seek to majorly restructure the architecture of global development finance in favour of rising, developing countries such as China and those across the global South. More fundamentally, the AIIB can be regarded as an 'economic vehicle' used to pursue China's wider geopolitical interests in East Asia and across the world. It is thus no wonder that Larry Summers, a former chief economist of the World Bank, saw the creation of the AIIB as marking the 'moment the US lost its role as the underwriter of the global economic system'.[52]

Notably too, the AIIB acts to indirectly challenge the ADB, which was established in 1966 to promote regional economic cooperation. Pursuing similar neoliberal values and practices to those of the World Bank and IMF, as well as issuing loans with economic and political conditionalities,[53] the ADB is likewise dominated by the US and its key regional ally, Japan, whose parallel voting quotas of 15.57 per cent at the end of 2021 greatly exceeded those of China (6.43 per cent), India (6.32 per cent) and Australia (5.77 per cent), and whose president has always been a Japanese citizen. In 2020, the ADB distributed loans worth $31.6 billion among its 68 members,[54] and has also worked with the AIIB on some infrastructure projects.

Supporters of the Western liberal international order maintain that while the AIIB can advance Chinese interests and international influence, it will not threaten the liberal economic order as the AIIB will work along similar lines. The AIIB and the associated Chinese-derived norms underpinning it henceforth 'complements existing funders, rather than [being] a revolutionary one that replaces them'.[55] Central to such observations is the argument that in order to create a new international order, a country must create an original and fundamentally fresh vision of the world. Yet by being able to create new institutions that are attractive to other countries and are based on differing values and conceptions of the international system, the very existence of the AIIB bolsters a perception of US decline and the end of unquestioned US fiscal dominance concerning how geopolitics ought to function.

Through the AIIB, China thus challenges who rules the existing order and opens up the beginnings of a new form of geo-economics, revealing the deeper *counter-assimilative* dimension of a coming China-centric international order. Emblematic of this threat, as former US President Obama remarked in 2015 in relation to the US not joining the AIIB, 'we can't let countries like China write the rules of the global economy'.[56] His successor President Donald Trump's protectionist trade policies also seemingly signalled a withdrawal from previous tenets of globalized liberal free trade.[57] This retreat by the US led to an effective global leadership vacuum that allowed China to further occupy that void, with Xi Jinping proclaiming in 2015 that China 'work[s] as an active promoter of economic globalization and regional integration'.[58]

Reimagining international security

Beijing's concurrent creation of new institutions – while working within existing multilateral institutions and simultaneously injecting them with favourable Chinese values – can also be seen increasingly in the security domain of international relations. In line with its reinterpretation of economic groupings, China's interactions with regional and global security regimes again reflect the country's domestic principles and interests. China also promotes them as a means to draw other countries towards Beijing's influence and uses them as a tool to be legitimized by the peer recognition of others. Although currently still highly regional in nature, as more members join China-backed groupings they challenge the security groupings of the US-led liberal international order and are thus heralding a viable alternative anti-hegemonic and multipolar vision of how the world ought to be structured.

Illustrative of these arguments is the Shanghai Cooperation Organization (SCO), which was originally founded in 1996 as the Shanghai Five with China, Russia, Kazakhstan, Kyrgyzstan and Tajikistan as its members. Subsequently renamed and expanded in 2001 to also include Uzbekistan, it has slowly grown in size with India and Pakistan joining as full members in 2017. In 2021 it additionally had four observer countries (often a stepping-stone to full membership) – Afghanistan, Belarus, Iran and Mongolia – and six dialogue partners – Azerbaijan, Armenia, Cambodia, Nepal, Sri Lanka and Turkey. By late 2021, the formal process for Iran's accession to the SCO as a full member had also started. All members, as based on the so-called Shanghai Spirit, adhere to the SCO's 'internal policy based on the principles of mutual trust, mutual benefit, equality, mutual consultations, respect for cultural diversity, and a desire for common development, while its external policy is conducted in accordance with the principles of non-alignment, non-targeting any third country, and openness'.[59] These principles stem from Beijing's 'new security concept' (*xin anquan guan*) (see Chapter 2), and are seen to be a 'new international political, economic, and security order responsive to the needs of our times',[60] one that is based on territorial integrity, non-aggression and non-interference, as well as avoiding nuclear anti-proliferation and shunning military alliances. The vast majority of these creeds run counter to those propagated by the US-created NATO.

Reflecting China's domestic national security concerns (as detailed in Chapter 1), the SCO also aims to combat the 'three evil forces' (*san gu shili*) of terrorism, ethnic separatism and religious extremism, which are threats shared across all members. These provisos show the direct extension of China's authoritarian proclivities into the international and regional realm and their attractiveness to SCO members that face similar threats. From this basis, the SCO is concerned with preserving regional harmony through 'joint efforts to maintain and ensure peace, security and stability in the region',[61] principally via mutual economic development achieved by promoting cooperation in politics, trade, the economy, research, technology and culture. Underpinning these goals is Beijing's vision of harmonizing its surrounding region through mutual trust, disarmament and cooperative security.[62] This latter aspect is also referred to as 'collaborative security', which emphasizes military and policy coordination and includes Asian peace-building efforts, the coordination of joint military operations and dissuading external influence in the region. In direct contrast with NATO, there is no commitment to mutual defence or collective security, which further bolsters the perception that the SCO functions as a 'geopolitical counter-weight'[63] to the US. It is also notable that there is no commitment to democratic values within the SCO's charter, again indicating Beijing's preference for a pluralistic international order that does not privilege one set of political arrangements over another. Implicitly, however, while not openly promoted (notwithstanding the political basis of the vast majority of SCO members), authoritarian regimes are permitted and not vilified by the SCO.

In all these ways, the SCO can be regarded as a 'new type of inter-state relationship ... and a new model of regional cooperation'.[64] It also clearly evidences Beijing's repeated ability and determination to build novel multilateral regimes that are independent of the West and based on non-Western principles. The conscious distinctiveness of the SCO – and Chinese multilateralism in general – therefore provides an 'in built dual function: the inward-looking one of providing a basis for members to work together productively, and the outward-looking one of challenging what at least some of these states see as the threat of both strategic and philosophical unipolarity in international relations'.[65] As such, the SCO can be considered to have a clear counter-hegemonic purpose versus the prevailing political basis of the existing liberal international order.[66] In turn, the SCO has a significant 'demonstration effect' in the formation of new groupings and new thinking in Chinese diplomacy, which flows into the organization's overarching goal of 'moving towards the establishment of a democratic, fair and rational new international political and economic order'.[67] In league with the AIIB, the SCO is a vehicle to first reconstitute the international order on a Eurasian scale, and to use multilateralism to reimagine its core architectures to better reflect China's global interests, values and worldview. Backing up this ambition, in terms of the percentage of the world's population that it now covers, at 41.25 per cent the SCO is clearly the world's largest regional organization, outstripping the Commonwealth (30.72 per cent), the African Union (16.21 per cent), NATO (11.19 per cent) and the European Union (6.52 per cent).

Beyond creating new institutions, China is using its already powerful position in existing regimes to further amalgamate its influence but also to reorient the contours of the international order. Nowhere is this presence more obvious than in the UN, wherein Beijing already exerts significant power through its permanent (P5) status, which it gained in October 1971 when the People's Republic of China (PRC) replaced Taiwan as the only legal representative of China. This positional strength was given to it through the peer recognition of the other P5 members, which legitimized both the PRC and the Chinese Communist Party. It also served to counter extant narratives from the time of Mao – when China was shut out of the organization – that the UN was a form of Western imperialism and great power neocolonialism, which had reached its nadir during the Korean War of 1950–53 when Chinese troops fought US-led UN forces. It is concerning its involvement with UN Peacekeeping Operations (UNPKOs) that China has been the most active, and whose missions are based on 'a central mandate of the UN Charter that demands that its members collectively act to maintain international peace and stability'.[68] Beijing has contributed PKO personnel since 1981 and since 2012 has yearly sent more personnel overseas than the other P5 powers combined.

In recent years, China has also significantly increased its budget contributions from 3.00 per cent of the total in 2013 to 10.25 per cent in 2018 and pledged to provide $1 billion in funding from 2018 to 2023,[69] and now leads several of the key organizations within the UN. China's participation seeks to uphold UN norms of sovereignty, non-intervention and economic development within international relations (as opposed to global affairs being based on universal norms, primarily concerning human rights as espoused by the US, or a common extranational legal basis). Thus, by frequently contributing to selective UNPKOs that often chime with its wider energy, trade or specific security interests in a particular region, China seeks 'to defend a pluralist world order based on cultural and political diversity while the West works hard to make a solidarist world order built on liberal democratic values'.[70]

Such contentions are evident within the context of Responsibility to Protect (R2P), which China has rejected as being a cover for intervention by external powers, instead stating that military force with humanitarian objectives should be labelled as 'assistance'.[71] While China was initially supportive of the first use of R2P (in Darfur in 2006), its attitude changed during its implementation in Libya in 2011. As such, while Beijing voted in favour of UN Resolution 1970, which imposed sanctions and referred Libya to the International Criminal Court, it abstained on the vote that authorized intervention and opposed the eventual UN-sanctioned regime change that deposed Muammar Gaddafi.[72] As a result, when R2P was raised again in relation to the Syrian civil war in 2011, China strongly advocated the need to respect sovereignty and for the UN to gain the consent of a country prior to any intervention within it.[73] China then used its P5 veto seven times (along with six abstentions) to both promote its position and to prevent the Libya precedent becoming a new UN norm,[74] a stance that reflected its own desired geopolitical norms and interests, and its own fears of invasion. Beijing also endorsed its own doctrine of 'Responsible Protection' that sought to monitor authorized UN actions and to reduce the chance of R2P being used for regime change, actions that showed China's 'growing willingness to assert its own normative preferences in defining and shaping international law and global governance'.[75]

Beijing is also increasingly proactive and dominant within the UN concerning discussions relating to human rights and has promoted Resolutions in the Human Rights Council 'call[ing] for quiet dialogue and cooperation rather than investigations and international calls to action, and pushed the Chinese model of state-led development as the path to improving their vision of collective human rights and social stability'.[76] In this regard, observers note how China has asked for UN budgets relating to human rights to be cut, has argued that NGO observer status and external funding need to be reduced and has requested that the phrase 'human rights defender' be excised from the UN lexicon.[77] Such actions serve to shield both China and its major diplomatic partners from criticism concerning their domestic human rights violations, and to 'change norms surrounding transparency and accountability in dealing with human rights violations'[78] – primarily through an emphasis on sovereignty and non-interference that effectively provides cover for countries not to be obliged to disclose information relating to possible abuses.

At their core, such actions are undermining one of the three core pillars of the UN (the others being peace and security, and development), and China has acted in concert with Russia to undercut human rights investigations relating to Sri Lanka and Syria. In these ways, and to the consternation of international observers, 'China and Russia and others have launched a war on things that have human rights in their name.'[79] Observers have further noted how Beijing is 'also pushing its own agenda – with an emphasis on "harmony" rather than individual rights in UN forums. And [tellingly] a lot of countries like what they hear'.[80] Such actions are not limited to the UN. The most severe example of an alternative vision for core values relating to peace concerns the Confucius Peace Prize set up in 2010 by a Chinese businessman. Explicitly done in response to the 2010 Nobel Peace Prize being given to Chinese dissident Liu Xiaobo, it was awarded for the 'promotion of peace from an Eastern/Confucian perspective' and before being disbanded in 2018 its winners included Vladimir Putin, Fidel Castro, Robert Mugabe and Hun Sen.

Creation, competition and subversion

Through its explicit creation of institutions such as the AIIB and the SCO, China is directly threatening the economic and security realms of the existing liberal international order, which have – until now – been dependent on Washington's unquestioned control and dominance. Such a challenge seeks to present a viable and competing alternative to the values and interests perpetuated by the US and its allies, as well as to draw other countries towards Beijing's global vision. While not presenting an entirely new basis for the international system – in either economic or security terms – China's actions do constitute a significant reorientation and subversion of how the global system's multilateral regimes function. The explicit injection into international politics of China's core domestic values pertaining to authoritarianism (as analyzed in Chapter 1) and authoritarian-capitalism (as elucidated in Chapter 3), as well as other norms intended to protect such penchants – most notably an insistence on sovereignty, non-intervention, plurality and multipolarity – have all galvanized the realization of this emergent new order. Beijing's use of global and regional institutions also mirrors the US's realization of its liberal international order, accentuating the rationale of creating institutions as an active and calculated strategic choice in international relations.

As per this volume's key analytical assertions, we have also seen how China's rise has been – in part – openly *facilitated* by the US and its belief that China's greater involvement in the liberal international order and its dominant institutions would eventually *assimilate* and socialize it to its major contentions and conventions. In a similar fashion to what we saw in Chapter 3, and in the face of an ever-more influential and openly assertive China, this approach instead empowered Beijing and can be seen as a case of extraordinary strategic naivety. More tellingly, it has been the West's refusal to better represent China within existing structures, such as the IMF and the World Bank, that also acted as a catalyst for Beijing to proactively reshape geopolitics and geo-economics to its own interests. This reimaging has formed the basis of an emergent China-centric international order, which is successfully attracting numerous illiberal and liberal – as well as non-Western and Western countries – to it, especially when Beijing presents itself as an alternative anti-hegemonic power. Even if China's new institutions exist '*within* the liberal framework which challenge the West as a sole power centre but [are] not a *fundamental* challenge to liberal order itself',[81] the very fact of their existence and increasing succour indicates the end of US global dominance, which itself has been the fundamental basis of its current liberal international order. As such, although 'America's substantial economic, military and research power still guarantees it a major role in the inevitable transformation of the international order',[82] it will no longer be an international order that solely caters towards US interests.

That China is also undermining the current liberal international order's emphasis on neoliberalism (as it does through the AIIB), mutual self-defence (as it does through the SCO) and universal human rights (as it does at the UN), at the very least legitimizes – if not *facilitates* – global authoritarianism. By perpetuating narratives concerning liberal democracy's failure as a governance system,[83] China's success is also delegitimizing liberal democracy as the most viable, appropriate or singularly possible political basis of international order. Instead, a hybrid model that fuses Chinese values and a China-centric worldview within Western-created – but no longer Western-dominated – institutions and global financial markets has come into being. Such questioning, undermining and promotion of an alternative order point to a more representative realization of current political, economic and diplomatic power balances in contemporary international affairs, for both China and others. More fundamentally, such profound *normalization* also includes the potential for replacing 'Western dominance and principles, known for centuries as "Westphalian" and "post-Westphalian" concepts, with a new "Eastphalian" alternative'.[84]

5

Asian Behemoth

The fulcrum of China's authoritarian century rests on East Asia, which the country dominates physically and – as we have seen in the last two chapters – economically. This superiority appears to be a direct realization of China's Middle Kingdom self-image of being at the centre of its desired international order according to core principles concerning *tian xia* ('all under heaven'), hierarchy, benevolence and respect in its relations with the region. Such principles aim to create the core of Beijing's 'harmonious' international order, which (at times) is proactively pursued, especially through the projection of military power. The construction of such relations seeks to reassert a regional hierarchy with China at the top and to recreate China's historical domination of East Asia. Such a reassertion signals to China's neighbours a potential return to a previous era that has been noted by historians to have been more stable from 1300 to 1900 than during the same period in Europe.[1] Of note too is a resolute focus on consolidating power with East Asia, as opposed to seeking a wider global empire. This observation is evidenced by Chinese explorers who had been active since the 2nd century BC, such as Zhang Qian who reached Central Asia, Persia, India and the Middle East during this period, as well as those who reached the east coast of Africa in the 9th century but who returned to China rather than taking over any territory overseas. That China had so many neighbours – and still currently does – influenced this decision to focus on its region.

As noted in previous chapters, this China-centric ruling system was based on the win-win dynamics of tributary relations and mutual trade, which have a direct correlation to the potential gains to be made from both the Belt and Road Initiative (BRI) and the Asian Infrastructure Bank (AIIB). The inbuilt asymmetry of these relations, as determined by China's unquestioned dominance, can also be regarded as a way to enable China's need for deference and recognition from smaller countries that wish to secure their own prosperity and autonomy. It is also through mutual cooperation that greater regional stability is assured without the need for competition. This combination of familiarity and understanding contrasts with the more historically fractious relations among Western countries and explains why the region is more open to a China-centric regional system, which is often only regarded as threatening by observers *outside* Asia. In East Asia, we can thus see how previous and future China-centric regional orders coalesce.

Confirming the contemporary foundations of a China-centric international order, it is notable that – with the exception of Japan, Bhutan, North Korea and Turkmenistan (as of 2021) – all Asian countries are members of the AIIB.[2] The BRI has also been broadly embraced across the region, with the exception of India and Australia (within the wider Indo-Pacific) along with the four countries not included in the AIIB.[3] Of note too is that for the last decade China has been one of the top three importers and top five export destinations for all of its immediate neighbours,[4] and in 2016 was the leading import source in the region for Japan, India, Russia and Australia, among others.[5] These institutional and economic ties all create very deep-seated interdependencies between China and the region.

Moreover, Confucianism is also highly present across the region. It influences the conduct of China's regional relations, to be based on values of 'humane authority', justice, meritocracy, 'leading by example' and benevolence toward its neighbours, which juxtaposes with US and Western hegemonic strategies of deterrence, balancing and containment. Given this manifestation, and its emanation from China – albeit with a significant communist component – the 'pan-Asian phenomenon of Confucianism offers alternative values, ... [it] celebrates the relational values of deference and interdependence ... [and] contrasts starkly with the discrete, self-determining individual ... [so] closely associated with liberal democracy'.[6] As such, China's international order is different from that of the West, one premised on a *shared* cultural basis that flows from its domestic basis into its economic, diplomatic and regional dealings. It also adds extra credence to China's claims to create a 'harmonious global society' and a 'community of common destiny', as we saw in Chapter 2 concerning the realization of its neo-*tian xia* vision.

Further reflecting China's Confucian roots, scholars note the crucial role played by face, status and hierarchy concerning regional conflicts, whereby China's neighbours can 'assuage Chinese behaviour on the ground by signalling recognition and respect of China's overall self-role and world-order conceptions'.[7] If China's superiority is not respected Beijing will, however, 'assert the natural order of things and, if necessary, punish those who step out of line'.[8] This stance is apparent concerning territorial disputes in the South China Sea but also within status disputes with Japan, as well as concerning China's ongoing need for control and subservience.

A Confucian presence is most explicit in South Korea and Japan, but also – through so-called Asian values – present across South East Asia, much of which adheres to principles of paternalism, hierarchical rule and communities based on the collective rather than the individual.[9] The term 'Asian values' explains the 'combination of rapid economic growth and high social stability, extraordinary individual effort and persistent group effort'[10] present in the region. Underscoring conspicuous differences between values found in the East and those in the West, this presence also shows a common authoritarian impulse – even in the region's democracies – whereby individual freedoms are restricted for the purpose of maintaining strong state control.[11] Notably, according to Freedom House, of China's 14 neighbours only one (Mongolia) is considered to be 'free' in terms of political rights and civil rights with all others being classed as either 'not free' (Russia, North Korea, Vietnam, Laos, Myanmar, Afghanistan, Tajikistan, Kyrgyzstan and Kazakhstan) or 'partly free' (India, Pakistan, Bhutan and Nepal).[12] This commonality indicates a clear overlap – and a regional fit – with China's political basis. As explained by former Singaporean Prime Minister Lee Kuan Yew, 'with few exceptions, democracy has not brought good government to new developing countries, … Asian values may not necessarily be what Americans or Europeans value, … as an Asian of Chinese cultural background, my values are for a government which is honest, effective and efficient'.[13] In the context of centuries of Confucian-based rule, Western-centric liberal democracy is thus an alien cultural concept for Asia, and we can see how a Sino-centric perspective 'persists in the mentality'[14] of China's leaders and its neighbours.

Confucianism also serves to help the CCP to 're-legitimize its rule in China by using nationalism to strengthen traditional legitimacy and political, economic, and diplomatic development to increase its performance legitimacy'.[15] As part of this process, China actively aims to overturn the perceived injustices of the Century of Humiliation and to transform the country into a modern, prosperous and developed entity. It also seeks to restore lost territories in the South and East China Seas, including Taiwan, in the hope of consolidating China's cultural, social and political basis. These goals play into notions of a new 'Asian century' – that is, the expected political and cultural dominance of global affairs in the 21st century by countries situated in Asia – a process intrinsically led by China, and which echoes the American century. Nationalism in China also includes the affirmation of the country's majority Han Chinese population as well as anti-Western characteristics,[16] so as to emphasize the country's unique nature. It is achieved through the use of public propaganda, school textbooks and other practices,[17] as well as using the internet to exploit citizens as active nationalist agents.

Military force and the US-led international order

In addition to its liberal political and economic values (as we saw in Chapters 1 and 3), as well as the various institutions instituted by the US (as shown in Chapter 4), the US-centric liberal international order is heavily premised on the use of military force. Military power projection acts as the key tactic to stabilize and strengthen the US's desired international order, which intrinsically does not tolerate any peer competitors in Washington's quest for global hegemony. Such a strategy – in much the same way as the US's unquestioning international imposition of liberal political values, a neoliberal economic model and US-dominated institutions – is *intrinsically authoritarian* in that it rejects political and economic plurality, desires absolute control and will not allow any rivals to emerge that could possibly challenge its supremacy.[18]

The US has deployed such a mindset since 1801 until the present day and politically has been involved in myriad attempts at regime change.[19] Some of these efforts targeted democratic regimes and replaced them with authoritarian ones (such as across Central and South America during the Cold War). US force has also been used to gain territory to expand its regional sphere of influence, most notably from Mexico (1845, when Texas declared independence), Samoa (1889), Hawaii (1893) and Panama (1903, securing the land for the Panama Canal). Actions in Ottoman Tripolitania in 1801 ('the first US attempt to replace a hostile foreign government'[20]), Spain (1898), Germany (1941) and Japan (1941), Korea (1945, 1950) and Vietnam (1954) were also all intended to create extra-regional – and wider global – stability in order to favour US interests, in particular concerning economics and trade, and most clearly concerning accessing oil (Iran, 1953; Cuba, 1961; Iraq, 2003, among others), fruit (Guatemala, 1954) and sugar (Cuba, 1961).

Generations of US political leaders have used military force as a foreign policy tool to enable and protect a US-led liberal international order. In 1823, via the Monroe Doctrine, President James Monroe claimed hegemony over the Western hemisphere, stating (in reference to European powers) 'any attempt on their part to extend their system to any portion of this hemisphere [i]s dangerous to our peace and safety'.[21] In 1947, President Harry Truman then declared the aim of containing the Soviet Union in Europe based on the premise that the 'free peoples of the world look to us for support in maintaining their freedoms. If we falter in our leadership, we may endanger the peace of the world – and we shall surely endanger the welfare of our own nation'.[22] The NSC-68 document of 1950 formally called for the US to pursue the 'intensification of affirmative and timely measures and operations by covert means in the fields of economic warfare and political and psychological warfare, with a view to fomenting and supporting unrest and revolt in selected strategic satellite countries'.[23] In 1957, President Eisenhower used his eponymous doctrine to deploy armed force 'to secure and protect the territorial integrity and political independence'[24] of Middle Eastern countries from Soviet aggression. Most recently, under President George W. Bush, the 2002 National Security Strategy outlined the doctrine of preventive war, whereby the US 'as a matter of common sense … will act against such emerging threats before they are fully formed'.[25]

Consistently high expenditure levels have underscored the US's focus on the use of military force to preserve and stabilize its liberal international order. This vast spending has outstripped that of all other countries, and averaged $336.05 billion per year in the 1990s, $500.77 billion in the 2000s and $687.98 billion in the 2010s, representing per-decade increases of 49 per cent and 37 per cent.[26] In 2020, US spending stood at $778.23 billion (40.37 per cent of the global total) or 7.9 per cent of all government expenditure, while total US spending from 1949 to 2020 was $20.23 trillion.[27] In comparison, China's annual military spending was estimated to be $252.30 billion in 2020 (13.09 per cent of the global total) or 4.7 per cent of all government expenditure.[28] China's military spending averaged $13.41 billion per year in the 1990s, $48.19 billion in the 2000s and $180.05 billion in the 2010s.[29] Although these averages are considerably lower than those of the US, they indicate per-decade increases of 259 per cent and 273 per cent,[30] which evidence growing global threat perceptions regarding China's rapid international rise. In 2021, the US had 170,000 troops stationed in over 150 countries abroad (not including where it is engaged in active combat operations), with the vast majority of these being in Asia, including 55,297 in Japan, 24,870 in South Korea and 6,125 in Guam, ostensibly to contain China.[31] Besides its involvement in UN Peacekeeping Operations (see Chapter 4), China has no significant troop numbers deployed overseas. Overall, US military campaigns from 1945 to 2007 are estimated to have resulted in 20–30 million military and civilian deaths worldwide.[32]

Apart from deeply normalizing the use of military force as an essential realm of the US-led liberal international order, military interventions have also been used against China. These include during the Qing Dynasty in 1900 to contain the Boxer Rebellion in Beijing, in 1946 to support the nationalist Kuomintang (KMT) in the civil war against the CCP and using the CIA to covertly support anti-communist forces from 1949 to 1954.[33] More contemporarily, the US has endeavoured to use its military force to restrict China's rise as a great power and Beijing's current challenge to the liberal international order. As a leading US strategist has noted 'if China continues to grow economically, it will attempt to dominate Asia the way the US dominated the Western Hemisphere. The US, however, will go to enormous lengths to prevent China from achieving regional hegemony.'[34] Building on Washington's attempts to positively *engage* and effectively *socialize* Beijing into the existing liberal international order (especially economically and institutionally, as we saw in Chapters 3 and 4), military power is used to *contain* China within East Asia. The US pursues such an aim by deepening its formal military alliances in the region to limit China's power acquisition by deterring its regional or international expansion in any form.

Such approaches are personified by the Obama administration's 2012 Pivot to Asia strategy, which aimed at 'strengthening bilateral security alliances; deepening our working relationships with emerging powers; ... engaging with regional multilateral institutions; expanding trade and investment; forging a broad-based military presence; and advancing democracy and human rights'.[35] However, and similarly to its strategic naivety concerning enveloping China within the major institutions of the Western-conceived (neo)liberal international order, 'Washington ... put too much faith in its power to shape China's trajectory',[36] as is now shown by Beijing's proactive regional assertion.

A further dimension of US military spending concerns the export of weapons systems to other countries. Such sales allow an exporting country to influence the foreign policies of recipient countries, and the wider regional and proxy conflicts that they may be involved in. Between 1950 and 2020, the US consistently dominated the global export of weapons, selling a total value of $703.48 billion (versus $600.25 billion by Russia/the Soviet Union, $143.01 billion by the UK and $57.03 billion by China).[37] In 2020, the US was the top arms exporter (at $9.37 billion) followed by Russia ($3.20 billion), France ($1.99 billion) and Germany ($1.23 billion), while China ranked eighth globally on $0.76 billion.[38] From 2011 to 2020, the top five buyers of US military equipment were Saudi Arabia ($17.25 billion), Australia ($77.40 billion), the United Arab Emirates ($69.51 billion), South Korea ($65.87 billion) and India ($41.66 billion).[39] The top five export destinations for Chinese weapons across the same period were Pakistan ($57.11 billion), Bangladesh ($25.93 billion), Myanmar ($14.34 billion), Algeria ($9.10 billion) and Thailand

($4.15 billion). In these ways, both the US and China openly sold weapons to many other authoritarian countries, with few sales by Beijing to democratic regimes.[40]

Achieving China's regional order

Just as has been apparent in its political, economic and diplomatic dealings, which indicated a newly emergent China-centric international order, Beijing's attitude and dealings with its immediate region also differ from the US's approach. Again, China's historical experience as the Middle Kingdom (see Chapter 2) – which from 900 to 1900 included an 'integrated, extensive, and organized [trading system] ... from Japan through Korea to China and ... from Siam through Vietnam and the Philippines'[41] – has influenced the formation of Beijing's *zhoubian* (peripheral) diplomacy. At the very heart of this policy is the desire to preserve the regional stability that aids China's continued economic growth and modernization, as do its undergirding principles of being 'amicable, tranquil, and prosperous' (*mulin, anlin, fulin*). From this basis, for former Premier Wen Jiabao, China aims to present itself as 'a good neighbour and a good partner, to strengthen good neighbourly ties, to intensify regional cooperation, and to push China's exchanges and cooperation with its neighbours to a new high'.[42] From its inception in the mid-1990s, *zhoubian* diplomacy also emphasized 'a restrained, non-confrontational mode of competition'[43] that sought to enhance China's status, power, security and respect. The Confucian tradition of seeking *da tong* ('great harmony') further informs such an attitude in order to allow for China's peaceful rise and development, as part of its wider diplomatic charm offensive (*meili gongshi*).

China's peripheral relations also encompass aspects vital to the fulfilment of the China Renaissance and China Dream, most clearly in terms of restoring territory lost during the Century of Humiliation, including Taiwan and islands in the South and East China Seas. Regaining these areas is critical to consolidating China's territorial integrity but also fully returning it to its past basis as per previous *Pax Sinicas* and previous China-led regional orders. These aims supersede those of other non-negotiable interests, such as ensuring domestic political stability and economic development and modernization, and are underpinned by differing attitudes in its conduct of regional relations. In these ways, we can see two conjoined, interest-specific approaches, wherein 'one is a tougher and more uncompromising approach toward issues that China regards as concerning its core interests. The other is a more flexible and cooperative position toward interests that, while significant, are of secondary importance.'[44] To the former approach, we can add Xi Jinping's assertion that 'no one should expect China to swallow anything that undermines its interests'[45] and that in its ideal regional – *but not its international* – order, China must be the unquestioned hegemon.

Such nuances are magnified by China's acquisition of enhanced military capabilities, including the development of asymmetric capabilities such as anti-satellite weapons and anti-ship ballistic missiles, as well as other stealth and hypersonic technologies. Through its revolution in military affairs, such advances aim to enhance its regional security through strategies such as 'area denial', which seeks to fashion a protective buffer around a country's continental and maritime periphery so as to deter military attacks against its mainland. They also underscore a 'blue-water strategy' (*lanshui zhanlue*) for China's naval capabilities, to give Beijing the ability to operate in all of the world's oceans and to protect the country's trade routes and energy supplies.[46] To achieve this latter aim, China is acquiring longer-range air defences, aircraft carriers and larger ships that allow greater power projection overseas. These, in turn, create a need for access to naval ports for resupply and maintenance support across the Indo-Pacific region, which in the future could include in Myanmar, Pakistan, Sri Lanka and Cambodia. Beijing currently has one overseas base in Djibouti. As part of such a need, China's 'string of pearls' strategy already includes facilities in Thailand, Bangladesh, Yemen, Somalia and the Maldives, which can also be viewed as an essential part and by-product of the maritime dimension of the BRI. In combination, these abilities are all part of China's ambition to control the near seas (*zhihaiquan*) and Hu Jintao's wider concept of a 'harmonious ocean'.[47]

Such elements all produce tensions within the region and within China's establishment of its preferred regional order, with Beijing at its centre and zenith. Much of these frictions stem from the dual-use essence of China's military expansion. On the one hand, better military capabilities allow for the protection of key sea routes vital to the import and export of raw commodities, gas and oil supplies, and manufactured goods essential for sustaining the Chinese economy. They can also be used to prevent these trade and energy routes being blocked, perhaps by China's regional competitors, further underscoring their strategic logic. On the other hand, such strengths can be used to affirm particular territorial claims – as in the South China Sea and vis-à-vis Taiwan – either by compelling regional competitors to withdraw or actively domineering portions of disputed land or water. All of these factors are intertwined, whereby positively resolving China's territorial issues helps to protect its trade and economic interests, and thus amplify their joint significance.

They also complicate Beijing's desire to present itself as an alternative to US hegemony in the region, which has explicitly used military power to enforce its regional interests through the use of force, alliances and arms racing. Presenting China as a more benign and benevolent order is thus crucial, especially when compared with the Mao era when China actively tried to export the communist revolution across the region (primarily in Cambodia, Indonesia and Vietnam) and invaded Vietnam in 1979 (its last foreign military foray). Beijing also wishes to overcome any reference to its repression of protesters in Tiananmen Square in 1989 and seeks to present itself as a cooperative and non-ideological partner that is naturally – rather than forcefully – dominant in the region. It was for these reasons that Beijing actively helped South East Asia following the 1997 Asian financial crisis, which occurred when large amounts of mainly Western investment were suddenly extracted from several countries in the region that had introduced rapid neoliberal economic programmes, causing their economies to implode. Such programmes had been introduced on the guidance of the International Monetary Fund, and China helped the region's subsequent recovery by not devaluing its currency during the crisis and also offering favourable loans to aid recovery.

Active reintegration in the South China Sea

It is accurate to conclude that China's current attitude towards – and use of – military force is certainly far more non-threatening and much less global in scope when compared with how the US views and uses such capabilities in the current liberal international order. There is no evidence of China using its military prowess to acquire territory beyond its region or of it blockading trade routes, as has been a hallmark of US foreign policy since 1801. Military force should thus not be regarded as an essential realm of a China-centric international order but more as a growing and evermore utilized tool that helps its accomplishment. Tellingly, many Western views on China's rapid military modernization oppose this view, primarily because China is seen as a competitor to US hegemony (in East Asia and on the world stage) and due to a belief that China will try to achieve global domination and will try to do so in the same way that the US has. Within such a 'China Threat' school of thought, observers contend that 'China is a rising power and that, as such, it is unlikely to behave differently than others of its type throughout history'.[48] This volume's core argument, that the divergent values and principles of different countries will inherently produce different realizations of international order, contrasts with this view. That stated – and as we have seen earlier concerning the cultural precedents of its former regional orders – Beijing is willing to use its military capacity to *regain* territory that it regards as part of its natural landmass, and which it does not see as being an expansionist policy (much to the consternation and confusion of mainly Western and US-based observers and policy makers).

Encompassing this perspective, and as part of China's ongoing search for *tian xia* that respects China's regional superiority combined with the region's economic significance, is the South China Sea dispute. The dispute concerns a vast area of around 3,500,000 km^2 – incorporating the myriad islands which pepper the area – that is variously claimed by China and Vietnam, while Brunei, Indonesia, Malaysia and the Philippines all have competing and overlapping claims to its adjoining areas and their associated exclusive economic zones.[49] Declarations of China's apparent control of the region have appeared on Chinese maps for many centuries, and rest on claims from Beijing that it can trace back Chinese authority over the region since before the third century,[50] as supposedly evidenced by its previous well-established and regionally recognized orders. Beijing's claims also encompass the 'nine-dash line' (*jiuduan xian*) that was declared in 1947, which establishes China's territorial claims in the South China Sea, amounting to about 80 per cent of its total area. Beijing's other major territorial claims include assorted groups of small islands and atolls across the South China Sea, such as Scarborough Shoal, as well as Subi Reef, Mischief Reef and the Fiery Cross Reef, all of which serve to collectively extend China's strategic scope deep into the southern end of the region.

China formally declared sovereignty over the Paracel and Spratly Islands in 1951 during the Allies' peace treaty negotiations with Japan. These claims would, however, conflict with the United Nations Convention on the Law of the Sea (UNCLOS) of 1982, which came into effect in 1994. In particular, Article 57 of the Convention declares that 'the exclusive economic zone (EEZ) [of a country] shall not extend beyond 200 nautical miles from the baselines from which the breadth of the territorial sea is measured'.[51] In line with its approach to the region that rests on a benign, cooperative and non-threatening approach wherever possible, in the early 2000s China signed various agreements with the Association of South East Asian Nations (ASEAN), whose members include all the other countries that have competing claims in the South China Sea.

These agreements included the Declaration on the Conduct of Parties in the South China Sea (DOC) of 2002, in which China agreed to 'undertake to resolve their territorial and jurisdictional disputes by peaceful means, without resorting to the threat or use of force'.[52] These agreements were designed to 'formally commit China to enforcing the principles of non-aggression and non-interference'.[53] As we saw in Chapter 2, such principles are reflective of China's Five Principles of Peaceful Coexistence. ASEAN and China then signed a further agreement in 2011 that restated China's obedience to the DOC, which signposted to onlookers that this Declaration could not be regarded as a mandatory agreement and therefore could not entirely restrain China's behaviour concerning the dispute. This factor is more apparent when taken together with China's deep-seated belief regarding the need for all countries to respect territorial integrity and sovereignty, of which the South China Sea – at least from Beijing's perspective – is a key part of China's, and which is the core principle concerning a China-centric international order.

Regional and international attention became fully focused on the dispute in 2016 when the United Nations Permanent Court of Arbitration in The Hague ruled that China (and indeed all the other countries with competing claims) had no legal prerogative to the South China Sea.[54] At the heart of this judgment, China's claims were seen to contravene the UNCLOS as they comprised China attempting to appropriate territory that fell within the 200 nautical mile EEZs of five South East Asian countries. Beijing quickly repudiated this decision, and then combined with a growing assertiveness and confidence in its regional diplomacy, China's 2019 Defense White Paper explicitly avowed that 'the South China Sea islands ... [are an] inalienable part of the Chinese territory. China exercises its national sovereignty to build infrastructure and deploy necessary defensive capabilities on the islands and reefs in the South China Sea, ... it firmly upholds freedom of navigation and overflight by all countries in accordance with international law and safeguards the security of sea lines of communication'.[55] This opinion from Beijing inherently reflected the trade, energy, territorial and status elements intrinsic to China's *zhoubian* diplomacy.

As a consequence of this position, China then built infrastructure on Mischief Reef, Subi Reef and Fiery Cross Reef. These three islands have been reclaimed from the sea and built into small man-made atolls, each of which are one to two square miles in size. China then placed infrastructure on them including administration and service buildings, military landing strips, naval port facilities, fuel storage depots, missile launch capabilities, heliports and electronic listening arrays.[56] In these ways, the islands can now effectively act as military staging areas, especially as they have defensive capabilities such as air-defence guns, antennas for satellite communication, anti-submarine defences and full radar capabilities.[57] Collectively dubbed the 'Great Wall of Sand' in 2015 by the then-commander of the US Pacific Fleet,[58] China's actions are seen as another affront to liberal and Western-originating conceptions of international law and its associated norms. Such developments have been accompanied by more frequent sea and air patrols by Chinese vessels in the region that have led to scores of skirmishes with vessels from other countries, as well as cutting off access to islands claimed by other countries.[59]

Controlling the South China Sea also rests on several elements that are critical to China's continued international ascent and thus to the realization of its preferred international order. First among these is the perception that the South China Sea, along with the Strait of Malacca, is at the fulcrum of the Indo-Pacific region in that it interconnects Asia to India, Africa, the Middle East and Europe to the west, and also to North, Central and South America to the east. Underpinning this centrality is the amount of international trade that passes through the area, which the United Nations Conference on Trade and Development has estimated amounts to 70 per cent of the total value of world trade, as well as one third of all world trade by volume, which is valued at $3.37 trillion annually.[60] Underlying its centrality to China's economy, more than 60 per cent of all China's trade transits the South China Sea,[61] as does 58 per cent to 86 per cent of all trade for the countries that are geographically within it.[62] The South China Sea is also a vital route for Beijing to have much-needed oil and gas supplies transported to China from the Middle East, further underpinning its strategic necessity.

In turn, the South China Sea and its myriad small islands are claimed to have vast energy resources. In this regard, the US Energy Information Administration has estimated that there is approximately '11 billion barrels of oil reserves and 190 trillion cubic feet of natural gas reserves'[63] in the region. While the actual amount of hydrocarbons is disputed, the potential benefits to Beijing in terms of fulfilling its ever-growing energy needs – as well as the much lower costs that such resources would provide in terms of transport and protection, along with reducing its dependence on volatile regions such as the Middle East and Central Asia – are clear. Securing such resources are thus seen as crucial to securing China's long-term prosperity and stability and its continued dominance of East Asia, and are thus vital to the foundations of a China-centric international order. To these factors can be added the South China Sea's significant fishing stocks, which are vital to all its constituent countries. Furthermore, as part of the Maritime Silk Road, the South China Sea is an integral part of the BRI, and thus needs to be controlled and ordered by Beijing.

China's behaviour in the South China Sea also contains a significant symbolic element whereby China uses the territorial dispute as a 'diplomatic instrument to send signals to other states and to test their commitments and responses'.[64] Such a strategy influences China's other major territorial disputes in the region, most obviously with India concerning the 83,700 square kilometres of Arunachal Pradesh, which Beijing regards as being Southern Tibet. Underlying such a tactic is the deeper aim of asserting China's pre-eminent regional position in economic, military and even diplomatic terms, while attempting to limit the presence of the US in the wider Indo-Pacific region. In this way, the building of critical military infrastructure aims to deter US naval vessels from entering the area, leading regional rulers such as the Philippines' President Rodrigo Duterte to remark 'ignore the missiles there [on Scarborough Shoal]. They are not for us.'[65] Overarching these elements is the further motivation of using the dispute to evidence China's growing power projection capabilities as part of the modernization of the country's military proficiency. Such shows of strength play to the domestic nationalist audience as evidence of China 'standing up' and asserting its historical civilizational rights, whereby China's true 'natural position lies at the epicentre of East Asia'.[66]

Fulfilling China's 'sacred commitments'

The reassertion of China's natural position also involves overcoming the effects of the Century of Humiliation, primarily in terms of other lost territories – in the shape of Taiwan, as well as several islands in the East China Sea – and concerning lost status when Beijing's regional pre-eminence was usurped by Japan. All of these issues are intertwined, as Japan's occupation of parts of China from the 1930s until the end of the Second World War included Taiwan (then known as Formosa). Japan's occupation also contributed to China's general instability during this period that ultimately culminated in the Chinese civil war of 1945–49, and which ended with the nationalist Kuomintang fleeing to Taiwan. Before its occupation by Japan after the Sino-Japanese War of 1894–95, Taiwan had been part of China since 1683 under the Qing Dynasty.[67] Such possession was later recognized by the international community via the Cairo Declaration in 1943 and upheld in the Potsdam Proclamation of 1945, which promised to return the territory to China. From this basis, Beijing has attempted to regain Taiwan since 1949, which is its foremost 'sacred commitment' that is integral to restoring China's great national unity (*da yi tong*) in territorial, political and cultural terms, and which is seen by Xi and the CCP as an 'unshakeable commitment'.[68] In turn, China's sovereignty claims on islands in the East China Sea also rest on ownership of Taiwan.

With the Taiwan Strait – itself a part of South China Sea, between mainland China and Taiwan – being only 110 miles wide, in 1954–55, 1958 and 1995–96 Beijing used the People's Liberation Army either to try to regain the island by force or to dissuade secessionism. The Strait has thus been the scene of several military confrontations between China, Taiwan and the US, which the latter periodically supports as a democratic bulwark in East Asia. The US has also regularly sold weapons to Taiwan (including – under President Donald Trump from 2017 to 2020 – missiles, torpedoes, destroyers, tanks, communications and aircraft parts worth $18 billion), which heightens the military threat that Taiwan poses to China. It also underscores how for Beijing the '"Taiwan independence" separatist forces and their activities are still the biggest threat to [China's] peaceful development'.[69] In unison, these factors indicate how reincorporating Taiwan into China is not only about nationalism but also about opposing US hegemony. With reference to Taiwan, China's 1998 Defense White Paper furthermore stated that 'the Chinese government seeks to achieve the reunification of the country by peaceful means but will not commit itself not to resort to force'.[70] Relatedly, the 2005 Anti-Secession Law legally commits China to use force should any part of its territory secede, which explicitly includes Taiwan, and is intended to deter any Taiwanese leaders from openly declaring independence. In line with Beijing's hard-line policy concerning separatists in Hong Kong, Xi Jinping has aggressively specified that 'anyone who attempts to split any region from China will perish, with their bodies smashed and bones ground to powder'.[71]

Central to these perspectives is the desire to ensure that '[t]here is but one China in the world, and the government of the People's Republic of China is the sole legal government that represents the whole of China.'[72] Xi Jinping has also sought to stress how people on Taiwan and people on the mainland are 'brothers and sisters of the same blood, ... [whose future reunification will be the] cause of the great rejuvenation of the Chinese nation'.[73] Moreover, in 2017 he proclaimed that 'we have sufficient abilities to thwart any form of Taiwan independence attempts'.[74] These measures have included China using its diplomatic, economic and military power to dissuade other countries from recognizing Taiwan as an independent sovereign entity. As such, Beijing has used significant amounts of aid, investment and other incentives to convince countries not to recognize Taiwan, or conversely has threatened to cut off diplomatic ties with any country that seeks relations with Taipei. By the end of 2021, only 13 of the UN's 193 member countries – Belize, Eswatini, Guatemala, Haiti, Honduras, the Marshall Islands, Nauru, Palau, Paraguay, Saint Kitts and Nevis, Saint Lucia, Saint Vincent and the Grenadines and Tuvalu (plus the Holy See) – recognized Taiwan, all of which lack enough major diplomatic or economic clout to significantly threaten China's interests.[75]

The wider territorial dispute emanating from Taiwan concerns the Diaoyu (for China)/Senkaku (for Japan) islands dispute. Both sides claim the islands under international maritime law and as part of their respective and overlapping EEZs, and in a similar fashion to those in the South China Sea, the islands potentially contain plentiful oil and natural gas deposits. Tokyo's claim dates from the late 1800s, when the islands' fishing grounds were incorporated into the Japanese province of Okinawa in 1895.[76] This incorporation was not opposed by China, most likely due to Beijing traditionally seeing the boundaries between countries and cultures in East Asia as being fluid and permeable, rather than static and fixed, as per Confucianism. Japan's claims were later reinforced by the 1952 San Francisco Treaty, which formalized peace between Japan and the allied powers after the Second World War (but which neither China nor Taiwan signed), as well as the US–Japan Okinawa Reversion Agreement of 1971 that specified the return of the islands to Japan. For Beijing, the islands are regarded as being part of Taiwan, and thus part of China's natural landmass. Sporadic crises have erupted over who owns the islands, resulting in Chinese and Japanese civil and naval vessels skirmishing in the region, and periodic nationalist outbursts such as the 2012 anti-Japanese protests in over 100 cities across China and Taiwan that involved the vandalism of Japanese businesses and cars, boycotting Japanese products and the forced closure of many Japanese factories.

The islands dispute in the East China Sea is representative of a deeper tension between China and Japan concerning which country is pre-eminent in East Asia. Japan's occupation at the end of the 19th century signified the low point of the Century of Humiliation that debased not only China's regional superiority but also its national standing, as personified by the 1937–38 Rape of Nanjing during which Japanese troops killed between 40,000 and 300,000 civilians on the orders of senior military commanders. Apart from sowing a deep level of mutual suspicion and antagonism, these events served to catalyze the end of Imperial China and millennia-old dynasties, which had overseen several China-centric international orders. It thus marked the end of Chinese hegemony in East Asia and ushered in a period of mass internal upheaval in China, as well as Japan's eventual ascent as a leading Asian economic powerhouse by the 1980s. Hence, Tokyo remains as a rival to Beijing, including in military terms and through its close security relationship with the US, which has persisted and only deepened since the end of the Second World War. As a result, in recent decades, as their economic and military competition has persisted, both sides have vied for hegemony over East Asia, although by the 2020s Beijing's prowess in these areas, along with its ever-increasing diplomatic strengths, now resolutely outshine Tokyo's.

Consolidation, restoration and confrontation

Through its growing economic, diplomatic and military strength China has succeeded in successfully consolidating its position as the foremost country in East Asia. By creating ever-deeper interdependencies between itself and its immediate neighbours, these ties are resulting in a contemporary re-realization of China as the Middle Kingdom on which other countries are reliant and – due to Beijing's overwhelming superiority in all domains – increasingly subservient to. Such relations have, implicitly at least, recreated the foundations of previous China-centric international orders based on Confucian-oriented principles of hierarchy, recognition and respect, as well as benevolence and harmony, accompanied by the threat of force if China's neighbours do not subscribe to Beijing's worldview. Part of this consolidation has been to restore China's territorial integrity through the absorption of the islands in the South China Sea, a process which will not be completed until control over Taiwan and related islands in the East China Sea is achieved. China's restoration has also been in terms of status, both compared with its regional rival in the guise of Japan but also the US, whose military and economic presence make it a regional competitor per se. Indeed, in many ways the ongoing US presence since the end of the Second World War has helped to *facilitate* the stabilization of the region – now principally to China's benefit – by dampening down the vitriolic antagonisms between Beijing and Tokyo, which have yet to be fully resolved by the two sides. What is also clear is that China is now willing – primarily as a result of the vast economic, diplomatic and military power amassed over the last 40 years – to actively assert its regional standing and, by extension, Beijing's vision of its preferred international order.

While China's position as an Asian behemoth clearly indicates some of the key themes of this volume, especially in terms of the *assimilation* of other countries towards a form of regional order that is *facilitated* by Beijing, and whose *longevity* is increasing *normalized*, China's dominance of East Asia is not entirely unquestioned by all of the region's actors. This applies to Japan and also to Vietnam but in particular the limits of Chinese power have been shown in Beijing's relations with Pyongyang. Despite having very close relations, whereby China remains one of North Korea's few allies, Beijing has been unable to completely quell the instability caused by the hermit kingdom's frequent testing of nuclear weapons. Desiring a buffer state, and wishing to avoid North Korea's political and economic collapse, which would threaten regional stability and China's trade security, Beijing has tried to broker talks with Japan, North Korea, Russia, South Korea and the US (the so-called Six Party Talks) since 2003 to resolve their various tensions but these have been unsuccessful. China has also urged North Korea to implement free market economic reforms but to no avail, which has added to Beijing's frustration.

In a similar fashion to the US liberal international order that had a solid but not unquestioned basis in the West, it appears that the legitimacy of a China-centric international order will rest on a broad adherence to it by the majority – but not all – of the world's countries. Farther afield, countries that had benefited from deep economic ties with China – such as Australia and New Zealand – are also re-evaluating their relations as they have become increasingly politicized and beset by perceptions of Beijing asserting its dominance but also its preferred authoritarian political basis,[77] which is threatening investments relating to the BRI and Chinese telecommunications.[78] Such interludes suggest frictions concerning the realization of a China-centric international order but also show the complex – especially economic – synergies that now bind countries to Beijing, and which are difficult to untangle. These ties have precipitated China's dominant regional position, further making Beijing's authoritarian-capitalist mélange into a now legitimate political-economic force.

6

The Global Stage

The previous chapters of this book have revealed the overwhelming authoritarian nature of China, which is evident within the country's domestic politics and social basis but also influences the conduct of its economic and diplomatic relations, globally and regionally. Confucianism has given a China-specific flavour to this authoritarianism and has imbued Beijing's relations with other countries – and especially those in its region – with deep-seated hierarchical, paternalistic and harmony-seeking foundations, whereby China's superiority must be recognized and respected by others. China's economic prowess – and its conversion of this power into Asia-centric yet globally minded institutions – has in many ways reasserted this hierarchy and with it Beijing's preferred way of ordering the international system, whereby other countries have simultaneously interdependent yet implicitly subservient relations with China as per *tian xia* ('all under heaven').

But it is not only China's behaviour and actions that are helping to form this China-centric international order. So too are the simultaneous behaviours and actions of other countries – in particular the other major great powers – that are now frequently echoing this ever-more evident and influential authoritarian-driven order. The unique dynamics of these other countries, which are also concurrently experiencing a growing disillusionment regarding globalization, have been seized on by their more populist-minded politicians to advance clearly illiberal agendas. Such a coalescence around authoritarian practices by other major countries, harnessed through their, albeit indirect, recognition and emulation of – and

121

passive *assimilation* towards – China's worldview, is what will eventually accomplish the authoritarian century.

In the last decade, authoritarian-populist leaders have become increasingly evident across the world. From Hungary's Viktor Orbán and Turkey's Recep Erdoğan to Brazil's Jair Bolsonaro and the Philippines' Rodrigo Duterte, such leaders seek to debilitate their domestic democratic political systems, weaken internal human rights and accompanying civil societies, and reject the rule of law, all of which are sustained by attacking minorities and displaying increasing xenophobia. This, in turn, serves to effectively supplement China's own authoritarian success. Populist rhetoric has also surged and normalized in global politics and is evident in authoritarian parties such as Germany's Alternative für Deutschland, the Sweden Democrats, France's National Rally and Italy's Northern League. The widespread use of social media to convey such messaging is a common technique among all these leaders and parties.[1] In total, across the world, the number of liberal democracies contracted over the past decade from 41 countries to 32, with a population share of only 14 per cent, while 87 closed autocracies and elected autocracies expanded across the rest of the world.[2] China's undoubted economic success – while clearly keeping its autocratic political system – has legitimized and advertised the efficacy of authoritarianism and has concurrently delegitimized liberal democracy.

Coupled with Beijing's modernization and development achievements, China has become the global cheerleader for authoritarian-capitalism that other countries cannot ignore. A deepening global divide has accompanied this role, whereby 'the attitude of many emerging markets to China is very, very different to rich industrialized nations. They want to learn from and aspire to the China model.'[3] This divide is underscored by China now lending more than the International Monetary Fund and the World Bank *combined*,[4] which underlines China's centrality to global geopolitics and geo-economics that has – for example, in Africa – transformed the continent's road, bridge, railway, port and internet infrastructures. There, leaders note how countries in the region do not wish to antagonize China as 'developing countries – many that are also highly indebted to Beijing and depend on China for the bulk of their trade – ... are not in a position to withstand the immediate blowback that would result from upsetting China'.[5] This dominance has further led many of the region's authoritarian-minded countries to support China concerning its human rights abuses in Xinjiang. More significantly, and as recognized by Ai Weiwei, 'all the companies in the West, they have the same conclusion. You know, this is not about China for them, just profit-seeking. Why should they upset China?'[6] China's economic strength thus eclipses and masks its authoritarian political basis and is another device via which its global pre-eminence and international order can be achieved. Notably, in 2020 China was the top trading partner of the US ($560.10 billion[7]), Russia ($103.97 billion[8]) and India ($77.70 billion[9]).

From this basis, this chapter demonstrates how China's underlying authoritarian values and characteristics are increasingly present in the politics of the world's major powers – most overtly in Russia but also in the democracies of the US and India. Given the world-leading influence of these countries to dynamically shape international affairs, the presence of such authoritarian traits acts as an actively *enabling* and legitimizing mechanism for China's worldview. Highlighting such similarities also underscores how the political principles and behaviours of these countries' ruling regimes are fundamentally interrelated on one *continuum*, and are currently and increasingly clustered towards the authoritarian zone of its spectrum. Such a convergence, accompanied by the weakening of the Western-led liberal international order (as we have consistently seen in all the preceding chapters of this book) and the numerous challenges that China poses to it, illustrates how an authoritarian international order is both feasible and highly achievable.

As shown in Chapter 4, China's belief in multipolarity (*duojihua*) and its continued repudiation of global hegemony – either by consent or by force, as sought by the US in its international order – means a China-reflective authoritarian century will come about not solely because Beijing is clearly authoritarian but also because *the majority of the world and the majority of its most powerful countries* increasingly demonstrate such an inclination. As we shall see, this inclination is evident in the declining political and social freedoms of the world's pre-eminent countries, as well as in their ever-increasing use of technology-driven methods of domestic surveillance and control.

Creeping great power authoritarianism

The liberal international order is currently not only under question but is being virulently contested. Typifying this viewpoint, Russia's Vladimir Putin stated in 2019 that liberals 'cannot simply dictate anything to anyone, just like they have been attempting to do over the recent decades, ... the liberal idea has become obsolete'.[10] This contestation now reaches into and affects the political basis of all countries, which are susceptible to being pulled towards the authoritarian zone of the political continuum. As discussed in the Introduction of this volume, authoritarianism can be defined as: lacking political plurality (including limiting the civil liberties of opponents, as well as the media); using a legal system to advantage those in power (resulting in rule by – not of – law); having a weak civil society (that is not independent from business or government); and not allowing universal suffrage in democratic elections. A high degree of control and surveillance (that limits the political, economic and social lives of the population) can be added to these factors, which we will discuss in the next section. As per Schedler's 'chain of democratic choice',[11] a country is regarded as authoritarian if it violates *even one of these elements*, a criterion we use here to look at the US, Russia and India, which as the world's largest and most powerful countries are most able to influence global politics. This criterion is also essential to hold democracies to the highest possible political standards, and which actively warns against any degree of democratic backsliding.

In the last decade, all these countries have seen an ever-greater restriction of freedom of speech and expression, in particular concerning within their domestic media. In the US, the Republican Party and former President Donald Trump have rejected the role of a free press in American democracy, frequently besmirching some journalists as members of the 'fake news' media or as the 'enemy of the people', with police targeting and attacking journalists covering protests in the US.[12] This led to the annual *World Press Freedom Index* classifying the US as a 'problematic' country for journalists to work in[13] and to the UN's special rapporteur on freedom of expression to remark that such attacks were 'a repudiation of fundamental rights enjoyed by all Americans, under the constitution and human rights law'.[14] Attacks on the media are polarizing debate in the US, leading to there now being 'two different senses of reality, with two different sets of actors ... who are not open to listening to the other side – that's not how democracy functions'.[15] The corporatization of the US media has also highly narrowed opinion, reducing freedom of expression and speech, as has an increasing 'cancel culture' whose 'intolerance of opposing views [and] vogue for public shaming and ostracism, ... [leads to] the restriction of debate ... mak[ing] everyone less capable of democratic participation'.[16] Although Joe Biden defeated Trump in the 2020 presidential election, these inclinations – along with many of those noted below – continue to permeate and deeply influence US politics, including the country's vast electorate.

India has further experienced a gradual deterioration of the freedom of the media, with Prime Minister Narendra Modi only giving a handful of press conferences since coming to power in 2014 and abusing journalists as 'presstitutes', '*dalals*' (pimps) or '*bazaru*' (for sale).[17] Defamation laws have also been used to silence journalists and news outlets that oppose the policies of the Bharatiya Janata Party (BJP) government.[18] Frequently denied bail, by January 2021, of the 154 journalists in India who were arrested, detained or interrogated since 2010, 40 per cent of these instances happened in 2020.[19] A number of journalists have also been murdered or threatened with violence or rape.[20] Together, these developments are seen to signify an anti-democratic shift, whereby 'all the authoritarian impulses evident before are more pronounced today – intolerance of the media and free speech, tolerance of hate speech and religious polarisation, secrecy, lack of transparency and lack of communication'.[21]

Similarly, Russia seeks to counteract critical and independent journalism, and the state has asserted its control through 'the threat of commercial writs, libel cases, ... telephoned menaces and close news management by the Kremlin'.[22] In 2020, the Russian Duma passed new laws 'to block foreign social media and punish media who made "slanderous" comments, including accusations of major crimes like embezzlement'.[23] In turn, from 1992 to 2018, over 200 reporters, correspondents, editors and directors were murdered in Russia,[24] leading one editor to remark that 'to be a journalist in Russia is suicide. It's suicide if you talk about truth.'[25] In all three countries, such measures have resulted in increased self-censorship, a reduction in freedoms of speech and expression, and the suppression of fact.

There has also been increasing evidence of what can be termed strongman politics in these countries, whereby power is focused on a single omnipotent individual in a way that is reminiscent of Xi Jinping's position in China. In reference to Xi removing China's presidential term limit in 2018, Donald Trump remarked to Republican donors, 'He's now president for life ... I think it's great. Maybe we'll give that a shot someday.'[26] In July 2020, Vladimir Putin (one of many authoritarian leaders admired by Trump[27]) won a vote to amend the Russian Constitution, allowing him to rule until 2036, which effectively ushered in a 'politics of eternity'.[28] Elsewhere, Narendra Modi, who won the last Indian election in 2019 with a majority, looks likely to rule until at least 2029. Mimicking Putin's media appearances, Modi has attempted to project himself as 'a symbol of masculinity [and] strength', as 'the alpha-male ... [who] wants to have iconic status globally'.[29] Trump's mass rallies (a frequent occurrence in Indian politics) and his 2019 US Independence Day celebrations, which co-opted a military-style rally (akin to such annual events in Russia and India), also helped to promote a similar self-image.

Complementing such muscular politics, attacks on minority groups are becoming more frequent in the other great power countries. Under President Trump, there was a significant upswing in reported hate crimes across the US, as his administration discriminated against minority ethnic groups, LGBTQ individuals, those with disabilities and immigrants.[30] Trump also set up detention centres along the US–Mexico border to detain illegal immigrants, which were derided by opponents as 'concentration camps'.[31] The US carried out analogous practices during the Second World War when it interned 120,000 Japanese-Americans in similar camps. Since 2014, violence and discrimination against India's 200 million Muslims has also significantly increased under Modi's Hindu nationalist BJP. The National Register of Citizens and the Citizenship Amendment Act of 2019 excluded Muslims from the same rights enjoyed by the Hindu majority. Other BJP policies have included the construction of vast concentration camps for undocumented Muslim migrants in Assam, which are seen by researchers as 'the stage just before genocide',[32] as well as legislation to prevent marriages between Muslim men and Hindu women (in order to prevent 'love jihad', according to BJP leaders). In Russia, attacks against minorities – in particular from the Caucasus – and foreigners are also very common, with racism in the country being seen as broadly 'out of control'.[33]

Weaknesses in the voting systems in the US, India and Russia also indicate how political plurality is threatened in these countries. In the US, despite being a democracy premised on each citizen being treated equally and fairly, policies concerning voter suppression (such as voter purges, reducing polling places, preventing mail-in ballots and voter ID laws), redistricting (also known as gerrymandering), the politicization of judges and the ambiguity of the electoral college result in a flawed democracy wherein true universal suffrage is not possible. These policies particularly discriminate against minority groups and include the structure of the Senate, which 'is an outdated, racist ... relic meant to enshrine white landowner power in our government, by prioritizing land over people'.[34] So deep-seated are these issues that Freedom House's vice-president for research and analysis noted that 'a change of president is not gonna [sic] make them go away'[35] and that they indicate a fragile democratic system. In mid-2021, the US had over 400 bills pending on voter suppression[36] and over 230 bills pending on criminalizing protest,[37] while corporate campaign donations also significantly skew electoral integrity towards private interests (see Chapter 3).

Such frailties were evident in January 2021 when thousands of Trump supporters stormed the US Capitol seeking to overturn the result of the 2020 election, which was regarded as an 'all-out assault on our institutions of democracy'[38] by incoming President Joe Biden. It was abetted by at least 1,000 Americans in positions of public trust (including elected officials), as well as over 400 organizations.[39] The attack also debased the standing of American democracy worldwide, and as a pillar of its liberal international order, as observers declared that 'if the post-American era has a start date, it is almost certainly today'.[40] In Russia, elections are widely seen as non-competitive, with opposition parties being stifled by those in power through their destruction of civil liberties, control of the media, use of police brutality and financial inducements. International observers are also routinely prevented from monitoring elections. In India, the integrity of the electoral system is being weakened by the widespread existence of inter-generational political dynasties, the presence of vote-banks (a bloc of voters from a single community), the use of financial inducements by candidates during election campaigns and the giving of over $7 billion in – often undisclosed – corporate donations during the 2019 election.[41]

The subversion of democratic processes in the US also involves the politicization of the judiciary, not only in terms of appointments but also in terms of injecting ideological biases into judicial processes and judgments.[42] This contention most clearly applies to the life-long appointment of judges on the Supreme Court, which is done by a sitting president whenever a serving judge dies but also applies to the nomination of federal judges in district or circuit courts. The last four US presidents – Bill Clinton, George W. Bush, Barack Obama and Donald Trump – appointed 387, 340, 334 and 245 judges respectively.[43] Such politicization undercuts the legitimacy of the courts and its rulings, but also challenges the authenticity of the US justice system being completely based on rule of law, whereby 'Democrats and Republicans implicitly assume that they have a right to control the outcomes of the court'.[44] The 2020 impeachment of Trump reflected these instincts, which was seen to represent a 'hollow pretence of justice, without testimony or an ounce of impartiality'[45] and seemed to reveal that 'intelligence agencies, advisers, the whole government apparatus is justified only as long as it supports the truths of power'.[46] President Trump had earlier turbo-charged this logic with his firing of FBI Director James Comey who was investigating whether Trump had colluded with a foreign power during the 2016 presidential election. Such an action was regarded by observers as 'a grotesque abuse of power … this is the kind of thing that goes on in non-democracies'.[47] After the failed 2020 impeachment, Trump also purged the US civil service, widely installing his loyalists in key positions.[48]

The first year of the Trump presidency saw the introduction of 30 separate anti-protest bills, which for the American Civil Liberties Union indicated 'an unprecedented level of hostility towards protesters in the 21st century'.[49] These curbs further reduced freedoms of speech, association and expression in the US, and were the latest realizations of using legal means to control protest. At their most extreme – and authoritarian – the US's Insurrection Act of 1807 empowers the president to deploy the US military and other personnel in the event of civil disorder, insurrection or rebellion, which has been invoked on dozens of occasions, most recently during the 1992 Los Angeles riots. Elsewhere, Article 352 of the Indian Constitution allows for the declaration of a national emergency resulting from war, external aggression or armed rebellion, and allows for restrictions on freedom of movement, freedom of assembly and the suspension of many judicial procedures. Article 352 was enacted from 1962 to 1968 and from 1971 to 1977. This latter period encompassed Indira Gandhi's 1975–77 Emergency, during which 'India's democratic process was suspended, over 110,000 individuals were detained, press freedom was curtailed and judicial powers were diminished'.[50] In Russia, martial law can be introduced by presidential decree against an external threat, and other laws also permit the declaration of a national emergency against internal threats. It is of note that governments in virtually all countries in the world will have access to such authoritarian-invoking laws and can use them during times of national emergency.

In India, similar processes of politicizing the judiciary are also palpable, with new governments controlling appointments. Moreover, India is seen to suffer from a form of 'judicial barbarism', whereby the 'application of law becomes so dependent on the arbitrary whims of individual judges that the rule of law or constitutional terms no longer have any meaning. The law becomes an instrument of oppression; or, at the very least, it aids and abets oppression.'[51] This barbarism has weakened civil liberties and general dissent, demonizing sections of Indian citizenry as 'enemies of the people'. We have already seen such coercion towards India's Muslim population but it also includes the amending of the Unlawful Activities (Prevention) Act (UAPA) in 2019, which is 'being used to harass, intimidate, and imprison political opponents ... [and] silence dissent in academia'.[52] Under the UAPA, individuals can be held for up to six months in jail without bail. Civil society organizations that are not favourable to the BJP are also being restricted in their actions via the Foreign Contributions Regulation Act (FCRA). Revamped laws on defamation aid this repression, and since 2014 over 7,000 people have been charged with sedition

– under the wide-ranging Section 124A of the Indian Penal Code of 1870 – most of whom were critics of the BJP.[53] Since early 2020, during the coronavirus pandemic, the vast majority of public gatherings and protests have also been banned and most courts suspended.[54] In sum, these factors are all 'contributing to the descent into electoral authoritarianism in what used to be the world's largest democracy'.[55] Such factors are increasingly routine in Russia, whereby the country's administrative regime 'subverts the rule of law'[56] and whose repression is reinforced by underlying power structures based on patronage and nepotism.

Apart from these political factors, it is notable that all of these countries – and indeed the vast majority of countries globally, with perhaps the exception of North Korea – now have similar capitalist-driven economic systems. In contemporary global affairs there is thus no longer a deep-seated competition between different economic approaches as there was during the Cold War and, as observers note, countries are being increasingly instrumentalized by 'economic interest groups that seek to manipulate its activities on the international scene for their own purposes'.[57] As its most free-wheeling form, neoliberalism seeks – as we saw in Chapter 3 – to supersede a country's political basis and to become the dominant ideology of global trade, which at its heart is authoritarian-minded in its scope and ambition. From the 1980s, neoliberalism has declared that 'the global market knows best, that government is the problem, … that individuals must compete against each other rather than cooperate for the common good … [and] that money govern[s] politics'.[58] Significantly – and in line with China – Russia and India now broadly subscribe to such a model but supplement it with elements of centralized control that allow for greater regulation over their economies, and which places government above the market.

Common architecture of Big Tech

Further drawing together the converging political and economic natures of the US, Russia and India towards that of China is the high degree of political, economic and social control of their populations that each reinforces through widespread surveillance technology. In all three countries, and as is now commonplace throughout the world, such technologies are facilitated and abetted by companies in the form of Big Tech, in particular those that create the algorithms that underpin these systems. When coupled with neoliberal business models that harvest and monetize personal data, the dominance of companies such as Facebook and Google are incompatible with the right to privacy and 'pose a serious risk to a range of other rights, from freedom of expression and opinion, to freedom of thought and the right to non-discrimination'.[59] Further undermining the current liberal international order, in April 2021 investigators revealed that Facebook officials 'repeatedly allowed world leaders and politicians to use its platform to deceive the public or harass opponents despite being alerted to evidence of the wrongdoing'.[60] This practice included in India, where fake accounts were allowed to inflate the popularity of BJP leaders (months after Facebook was alerted to the problem), as well as across Europe, Asia and the Americas.[61]

Accompanying this restriction of liberal human rights has been a concurrent upsurge in countries restricting their populations' access to the internet through sophisticated censorship technologies, often – as we saw in Chapter 1 – facilitated by China. Such moves act in tandem with the business models of Big Tech to assist authoritarian regimes, at the expense of more democratically-minded ones, leading the US non-governmental organization Freedom House to record consistent declines in internet freedom from 2010 to 2018 amid the rise of 'digital authoritarianism'.[62] In many ways, China and the West are increasingly mirror images of each other, whereby 'the collaboration between state actors and non-state organizations is becoming a main feature not only of China's governance but also of Western politics'.[63] As such, these technologies are able to exert authoritarian control via 'computational propaganda' that uses 'algorithms, automation and human curation to purposefully manage and distribute misleading information over social media networks'.[64]

Such methods were used by Russia to interfere in the UK's 2016 referendum on European Union membership[65] and during the 2016 US presidential election.[66] In both these cases, domestic political groups also used data harvesting companies, most notoriously Cambridge Analytica, to influence opinion – and the ultimate outcomes – of these democratic events.[67] Commonalities with China's social credit system can also be seen concerning the ubiquity of algorithms in Western countries to determine everything from getting credit, insurance and a job, to university entrance requirements, predicting crime and dating compatibility.[68] The widespread presence of CCTV cameras, often with facial recognition technology, further underscores this similarity. In 2020, while China had the most installed CCTV cameras in the world (at least 200 million), the US ranked highest in the world for every 100 individuals (at 15.28), followed by China (14.36), the UK (7.50) and Germany (6.27).[69] At the most extreme end, in 2020, 29 countries carried out a total 155 internal internet shutdowns, 109 of which were done by India, including for the whole year in the Kashmir region.[70]

In the US, domestic surveillance can be traced back to the 1861–65 American Civil War when President Lincoln ordered the tapping of telegraph lines. Later in the 1930s, President Franklin D. Roosevelt authorized the Federal Bureau of Intelligence (FBI) to intercept 'any communications, either domestic or abroad, of persons suspected of engaging in subversive actions against the US'.[71] In the 1960s, FBI Director J. Edgar Hoover launched the Counterintelligence Program (COINTELPRO) that consisted of illegal covert projects to monitor and disrupt various supposedly 'subversive' organizations and persons, including communists and broader left-wing groups, the civil rights movement, the Black Power movement, and anti-Vietnam War organizations and activists. After the programme was later exposed to the public, the Reverend Jesse Jackson – who had been targeted by COINTELPRO – remarked that 'when you have this feeling that the government really is watching you ... it has a chilling effect. It takes away your freedom ... it neutralizes people'.[72]

This erosion continued under Presidents Bush and Obama, who significantly accelerated the US's domestic electronic surveillance capacity after the terrorist attacks of 11 September 2001 (9/11). After 9/11, the Bush administration systematically eroded the 1978 Foreign Intelligence Surveillance Act (FISA) and the 1986 Electronic Communications Privacy Act (ECPA), with the effect of curtailing the First and Fourth Amendment rights of US citizens (primarily, freedoms of speech, the press, assembly and petition; and the right to be secure in their persons, houses, papers and effects). FISA had been enacted in response to abuses under COINTELPRO and all warrants for wiretaps, listening devices and mail interceptions required proof of probable cause that the target was a foreign agent or acting on behalf of a foreign power to conduct surveillance. ECPA had decreed that browser histories, transactions or 'non-content customer records' could only be obtained with a court order or search warrant, while the FBI could compel service providers to produce billing and transaction records provided that they pertained to a foreign counterintelligence investigation or were linked to a foreign power.

The 2001 Patriot Act then majorly lowered the oversight mechanisms of both FISA and ECPA and 'granted the Bush Administration ... the right to use these tools with only minimal judicial and congressional oversight'.[73] Under the wartime powers granted after 9/11, the Bush administration dramatically expanded the scope of surveillance, which allowed the National Security Agency (NSA) to intercept phone calls and emails in and out of the US where one party had suspected ties to Al-Qaeda. Another NSA unit, Special Source Operations, allowed warrantless eavesdropping on Americans' international communications. The 2007 Protect America Act, and the later 2008 FISA Amendments Act, circumvented the FISA warrant process and replaced it with a self-certification process by senior government officials, which critics regarded as resulting in 'a massive surveillance dragnet'.[74] Both measures resulted in a 'chilling effect' on civil rights that increased self-censorship,[75] led to the 'repression of political dissent'[76] and furthermore allowed 'a resurgence of domestic spying by the CIA [Central Intelligence Agency] ... [signalling] the death-knell of privacy'.[77]

The revelations in 2013 by Edward Snowden, a former CIA and NSA subcontractor, revealed several ongoing NSA projects and surveillance programmes.[78] These included the collection of metadata on bulk telephone records (comprising the numbers in each call, the duration and the time of each call but not the content), which were stored for five years and involved tens of millions of contacts.[79] A computer program, called EvilOlive, collects 'all web surfing data, including all internet addresses a consumer visits'.[80] Another NSA program, PRISM, collects massive amounts of communications directly from the servers of major US service providers including Microsoft, Google, Facebook and Apple, and covers 'the vast majority of online email, search, video and communications networks',[81] as well as email, video and voice chats including Voice over Internet Protocol (as is used by Skype, FaceTime and Zoom), file transfers and social media details. XKeyscore is also a NSA program focused on retrieving the collected data, which 'gives analysts the ability to search through the entire database of your information without any prior authorization – no warrant, no court clearance, no signature on a dotted line'.[82]

This program is integrated with the intelligence agencies of other countries – notably the UK, Germany, Australia, New Zealand and Japan, among others – which contribute data and are given access to the program, which parses data from all these sources together.[83] This includes the UK's Tempora program, whose scope was so vast that the number of people targeted was argued to 'be an infinite list which we couldn't manage'.[84] Combined, these programs form a massive system of data collection, storage, processing and retrieval which the NSA and allied agencies may use to monitor any person in the world, including their own citizens, and collectively undermine the entire spectrum of human rights central to the liberal international order.

Pre-dating these activities, in 1970 the CIA and its German counterpart the BND bought the firm Crypto AG and added encryption weaknesses to its products, allowing them to eavesdrop on adversaries and allies alike. In the words of a CIA report, 'it was the intelligence coup of the century. Foreign governments were paying good money ... for the privilege of having their most secret communications read'[85] by the US and its allies. Initially codenamed Thesaurus and then Rubicon in the 1980s, Crypto AG encryption devices were sold to more than 100 other countries (but not to China or Russia, which were suspicious of the company's origins), before the US sold its share of the company in 2018.[86] In addition, during the Cold War, CIA sources asserted that the US had active operatives in 'at least one newspaper in any foreign capital at any one time'.[87] Together with the capabilities of the NSA, these surveillance mechanisms are clearly analogous to, and appear to vastly outstrip, China's well-honed domestic – and possibly international – capabilities. They also have a rather hypocritical edge when compared with current Western allegations towards Huawei concerning apparent fraud, theft and spying.[88]

Of significant note too is that a number of US companies sell surveillance technology to at least 32 countries across the world, including authoritarian governments in Saudi Arabia, Sudan, Egypt, Turkey, the Philippines, Myanmar, Russia and even China.[89] These sales include technology that captures video, audio and biometrics, and carries out electronic monitoring, licence plate recognition, thermal sensing and content filtering. Notably, IBM has helped to build parts of China's surveillance architecture in Xinjiang,[90] Zoom has blocked online meetings among activists in China at the behest of Beijing,[91] and from 2006 to 2010 Google ran a censored search engine in China.[92] Overall, in 2019, '51% of advanced democracies deploy[ed] AI [artificial intelligence] surveillance systems'[93] resulting in so-called 'networked authoritarianism'. Much of this technology is also used within the US, especially by police departments and federal agencies which routinely collect biometric information, using facial recognition technology, constructing large databases to trace the population's online activities and tracking the movement of citizens.[94] These practices often feature in the building of ultra-networked 'smart cities'. An array of US companies aid these exercises, such as Clearview AI which has a database of three billion labelled faces that it sells to law enforcement agencies across the world.[95]

In Russia, Moscow's control of RuNet (the internet within Russia) initially focused – in line with Beijing – more on censorship rather than the blanket surveillance approach of Western countries. Few laws restricted its users during the 2000s and early 2010s but the Lugovoi Law of 2012 granted Roskomnadzor, a government agency linked to the Ministry of Communications and Mass Media, the right to block and censor websites deemed to contain extremist content that might pose a threat to public order.[96] Then in 2014, two anti-terrorism laws were passed that severely increased the scope of surveillance by requiring websites, as well as Russian internet companies with servers in Russia, to store extensive amounts of user data without a court order (which was extended by the 2017 Yarovaya Law). A further law banned the anonymous use of public Wi-Fi.[97] As a result, Russia became a 'total surveillance' state as the Kremlin implemented scan software to review all content posted on the internet and criminalized the dissemination and redissemination of 'extremist materials'.[98]

In 2019, Russia's Federal Security Service (FSB) required internet companies 'to install special equipment giving the FSB automatic access to their information systems and encryption keys, and to decrypt user communications without authorization through any judicial process'.[99] Moscow's surveillance regime is now frequently dominated by the FSB in conjunction with 'cultural norms and practices grounded in centuries of authoritarianism, and deliberate framing of the internet as dangerous',[100] which results in at least tacit public support for such controls. Underpinning these approaches is the Kremlin's perception that the internet is a danger to regime security, public safety and social cohesion, especially concerning political freedoms, civil rights and criticism of the Putin regime.

All of these measures represent a clear continuation of deep-seated old Soviet surveillance practices, including the use of intimidation and uncertainty to encourage self-censorship by internet companies and individuals alike.[101] As such, and when compared to other countries' surveillance practices, 'in RuNet control strategies tend to be more subtle and sophisticated and designed to shape and affect when and how information is received by users, rather than denying access outright'.[102] The blurred ownership of infrastructure by companies with the government, in a similar way to China, heightens this sense of ambiguity and insecurity. Although less advanced technologically compared with China or the US, the Russian authorities are now able to carry out the automatic collection of data from mobile calls, emails, social networks, passenger lists, drones and roadside cameras, in order to create an all-encompassing surveillance system. These measures are backed up by strict penalties, including imprisonment if any of Russia's legal restrictions are broken, and thus 'severely undermine the ability of people in Russia to exercise their human rights online, including freedom of expression and freedom of access to information'.[103] In 2019, the Sovereign Internet Law transferred full control of online communication networks to a government agency. Further, it contained provisos to be able to shut down internet networks in certain areas of Russia and to entirely cut off the RuNet from the World Wide Web (which Moscow successfully tested in 2019). No online communication in Russia is safe from government surveillance.[104]

In India, the internet also exists under heavy state surveillance, threatening the privacy of citizens and associated freedoms of speech, thought and expression. Underpinning this control is a long historical relationship of judicial power being used to regulate media usage in India, which dates from the time of the British Raj when information and communication were used as tools of control.[105] Such a legacy has been maintained in modern India and contributes to broader ambivalence towards freedom of expression by the Indian government.[106] In addition, Indian leaders have consistently used periods of political and economic crisis in India's history to justify increases in the censorship of dissent,[107] as we have already seen by the Modi government, which has used the coronavirus pandemic to limit freedoms of speech, expression and association. At other times, Indian politicians have requested Google, Zoom and WhatsApp to restrict search terms and to hand over information on online gatherings relating to the farmers' protests of 2020–21 and others.[108]

As the primary form of control, the Central Monitoring System (CMS) launched in 2011 is a centralized system for monitoring mobile phone, landline and internet communications that is conducted without the intervention of telecom service providers, and thus grants the government direct access to user information. The 'central' aspect of the system lies in the ability of the CMS to accumulate all of India's communications onto servers, which will then intercept, store and forward the data to government agencies. As part of this capacity, the CMS allows the Indian government to access personal information without a court order. Such power is accompanied by an absence of government accountability for misusing surveillance frameworks, which leaves it open to abuse and is a negative portent for the future of Indian democracy.[109] The CMS is a significant upgrade from the Information Technology (IT) Act of 2008 and has resulted in 'a tectonic shift from targeted surveillance regime under the IT [A]ct, to blanket surveillance through the CMS'.[110] In turn, Section 66a of the IT Act makes sending any offensive information or messages online a crime. However, by lacking a definition of what constitutes 'offensive', it effectively allows the CMS to examine private communications and prosecute with minimal legal restraint and is often justified on the obscure grounds of national security, as is common practice in the US, China and Russia, and elsewhere.

India's surveillance powers are so wide that they result in the 'arbitrary monitoring and the subsequent prosecution of citizens'[111] that, while not directly censoring free speech, have a psychological impact that causes self-censorship among citizens. The lack of information given to the public about the CMS plays a significant role in this self-censorship, meaning that 'an oppressive surveillance regime is taking hold in India, and yet its citizens have little to no power to fight it'.[112] The government launched the Digital India programme in 2014, which aimed to use digital technology to spur the country's development; it also arguably 'brought about drastic changes in the policy framework of governance as it circumscribed privacy and made surveillance ubiquitous in India'.[113]

Data collection has not only become big business for India's largest tech firms but has also permeated political campaigning. In 2018, the default permission settings of Narendra Modi's NaMo app gave it 'almost full access to the data stored on users' phones, including audio, photos and videos, contacts and location services'.[114] In 2019, the Modi government issued a tender for automated nationwide facial recognition systems even though there is no clear legal framework concerning the use of such technology,[115] while India also built 'the world's largest biometric database, with few checks on information processing and data mining'.[116] Reflective of these collective surveillance and collection capabilities, mixed with an authoritarian-minded regime by the Bharatiya Janata Party and an opaque legal environment, Arundhati Roy remarked in 2020 that 'the coronavirus is a gift to authoritarian states including India, … pre-corona, if we were sleepwalking into the surveillance state, now we are panic-running into a super-surveillance state'.[117]

Commonality, convergence and confirmation

Despite being seemingly counterintuitive, authoritarian tendencies that we have shown to be present in China in Chapters 1, 2, 3, 4 and 5 of this book are also extremely evident in the world's other most powerful countries. These commonalities include the increasing limitation of freedom of speech and expression within domestic media, which has frequently involved attacks on journalists and anyone viewed as opponents of these countries' ruling governments. In Russia and India, they also encompass leaders using legal mechanisms to stifle dissent. Such actions are resulting in a narrowing and constraining of opinion, especially when backed up by bombastic, divisive and confrontational strongman politics. As another threat towards plurality in these great power countries, discrimination and attacks on minority groups are also increasing, particularly against Muslims – most obviously in India where the Modi government's actions chime with China's actions in Xinjiang.

We have also seen glaring weaknesses in the ostensibly democratic systems of the US, India and Russia, which are undercutting claims of equality, fairness and plurality in these countries. While not as blatantly authoritarian as China, elections in Russia are essentially non-competitive and at best maintain a façade of democracy, while in the US universal suffrage is arguably non-existent due to voter suppression, gerrymandering and the influence of vast corporate donations that appreciably twist the political landscape towards particular interests. Much the same is true of India's democracy that has shifted towards a form of electoral authoritarianism and is also weakened by the widespread existence of intergenerational political dynasties. Furthermore, in all three countries, there is evidence of the consistent politicization of the judiciary and, by extension, of the rule of law, which – certainly in Russia and at times in India and the US – today resembles rule by law and is essentially becoming a tool of elite control. The use of legal measures to suppress protest has also reduced freedoms of speech, association and expression in the US, Russia and India, which are now threatening the influence and very existence of each of their civil societies.

At their core, all of these factors – on some level – are validating for China in that they echo the forms of control and monitoring that we have seen deployed by Beijing. That stated, when directly compared with China, the scale and scope of these authoritarian tendencies does vary between the US, Russia and India, as does the volition behind them, which is more direct and deliberate when carried out by Beijing and Moscow, and perhaps New Delhi, than by Washington. Regardless of such nuances, these behaviours mark a significant convergence around the authoritarian segment of the political *continuum*, with all of these countries moving closer to – and therefore *assimilating* towards – China in terms of their policies, actions and deep-seated dispositions. More fundamentally, according to Schedler's 'chain of democratic choice', we can therefore classify each of these countries as being somewhat authoritarian in nature. As such, they act as a form of implicit and explicit confirmation of China's authoritarian basis, and hence by extension of an emergent authoritarian international order. These practices not only *facilitate* this coming order but also serve to *normalize* it and suggest a latent viability and *longevity* to such a global ordering in the decades ahead. They also show how this international order can come about without Beijing needing to achieve outright hegemony, whereby the live-and-let-live attitude underlying China's conception of a multipolar world (as we saw in Chapter 4) can thrive so long as the world respects the country's (regional) pre-eminence.

Nowhere is this convergence more evident than in these countries' construction of massive surveillance structures, which are directed inwards as much as outwards and pervade all aspects of everyday life, and as such restrict the thoughts and actions, the expression and choices of their populations. Based on entrenched instincts of control, these structures are eroding freedoms of speech, the press, assembly and petition in these three countries and beyond, in particular when they are actively exported – as is the case with the US. Such 'digital authoritarianism', and the monitoring and surveillance capabilities driving it, is now a commonplace phenomenon in the US, Russia and India and much of the world, and involves – willingly or not – the major Big Tech companies in these countries, which can thus be seen as 'sleepwalking' towards a variant of China's social credit system.[118] Using such technology, coupled with other anti-democratic tendencies, points to a hypocrisy between what countries representing the liberal international order say and do, especially when it involves – notwithstanding again issues of scale, scope and volition – clear overlaps with practices present in China. This inconsistency and open pretence has been evident throughout this book, across the political and social, economic, diplomatic and military realms, and is only further confirmed here.

China's ongoing pursuit of advanced technology based on AI, and the competition that this is engendering with the West, appears to only further underline an increasingly technology-infused and authoritarian-oriented future. This competition is demonstrated by the US's $250 billion investment in AI in 2021 to challenge China and its severing of any Chinese ties with US companies selling defence or surveillance technology.[119] Such actions have bolstered a discourse in China that 'emphasizes the *limits* of free markets and the dangers of reliance on foreign technologies ... [and the need] to protect technologies, companies, and networks'.[120] This search for autonomy to protect China's political and social – authoritarian – basis, has resulted in Beijing pushing for the concept of 'cyber sovereignty' that seeks to recognize the right of every country to control the internet within their borders. In marked contrast to the US's model of continuing an open, worldwide internet, Xi Jinping has stated that 'we should respect the right of individual countries to independently choose their own path of cyber development and model of cyber regulation, and participate in international cyberspace governance on an equal footing'.[121]

As part of this vision, China is building a separate internet structure that uses blockchain technology to track and store data,[122] resulting in 'a completely different digital architecture, complete with its own ideological governance and values'.[123] Related to this project, Beijing is laying undersea cables along Africa's eastern and western coasts to increase connectivity and to provide free internet access, but it will also mean that countries using this infrastructure will need to agree to Chinese control and subjugation, which will be attractive to authoritarian-minded leaders in the region. Countries already using Chinese technology and associated methods would be further integrated and *assimilated* into such a project, further *normalizing* Beijing's authoritarian approach.

Also apparent in these dynamics is a much more meta-level convergence between China and the West in terms of the way that their economic systems function. This conjunction does not mean neoliberalism being accepted by Beijing, which it does not (see Chapter 3), but is more in terms of the mechanisms through which capitalism is conducted. Central to these debates is

Zuboff's 'surveillance capitalism', which 'unilaterally claims human experience as free raw material for translation into behavioural data ... [which is] fabricated into *prediction products* that anticipate what you will do now, soon, ... [and then] traded in a new kind of marketplace ... call[ed] *behavioural futures markets*'.[124] Such a concept has spread across all sectors of the global economy and – via its ability to shape behaviour – subverts freedom of thought and action, leading to power asymmetries that undermine democratic practices.

When compared with China's authoritarian-capitalism and China's social credit system (see Chapter 1), and then interlinked with the rapid spread of surveillance technology in the US, Russia and India, we can see a fundamental unifying nexus of three distinctive elements – surveillance, capitalism and authoritarianism – across all these great powers and beyond. It remains to be seen if 'Europe and North America [can] pull together to construct the legal and technological frameworks for a democratic alternative'[125] to this nexus or if an ultimate convergence with a China-esque, authoritarian-centric system will prevail. Reflective of these debates, in a 2021 survey carried out across 53 countries, 48 per cent of respondents considered Big Tech to be a threat to democracy in their country, followed by the US (44 per cent), China (38 per cent) and Russia (28 per cent), while economic inequality ranked highest on 64 per cent.[126]

Conclusion:
Realities and Eventualities

China's return to global pre-eminence over the last 40 years has resulted in a direct and resolute challenge to the liberal international order premised on US and Western dominance. With a political, social, cultural and (to a degree) economic system built on core authoritarian values and practices, that are – at their most severe – significantly divergent from those within the world's democracies, this book has shown how the essential nature of global politics, and the international order on which it is premised, is undergoing a profound shift. Central to this shift is China's deep-seated Confucian and authoritarian basis that has shaped the country's internal politics for the last 2,000 years, and which has been selectively resuscitated and sustained by the Chinese Communist Party (CCP). Giving its leaders near total control of China's political, social and legal basis, as well as significant influence over its economic foundations, the CCP seeks to use this power to stabilize and harmonize the country based on its unquestioned authority and power. Such a monopoly is undoubtedly authoritarian – *even totalitarian* – in its vision, its practices and its execution. With its ascendant geo-economic and geopolitical power, China is aiming to harmonize the international order towards its preferred hierarchy, with itself pre-eminent.

This volume began in the Introduction by examining the nature of the liberal international order and highlighted its three essential realms: the social and political, the economic and the military. In its most idealized sense, the social and political realm promoted a form of order based on universal, democratic and individual human rights, which was then carried over into the economic realm via global free market capitalism and its neoliberal realization resting on privatization, deregulation and globalization. The military realm then utilized armed force as a means to enforce the other realms and was similarly bolstered by the construction of institutions, through which US and Western values could be codified and normalized within the conduct of international politics.

Chapter 1 investigated the social and political realm of a China-centric international order and evidenced its clearly authoritarian basis. Here we saw that Beijing actively curtails democratic representation, including an active civil society, and constrains associated rights relating to freedom of speech, expression and association. In all areas, including the media, academia and non-governmental organizations, the behaviour of China's citizens is sanctioned and controlled, often via legal means, resulting in a society governed by rule by law rather than rule of law. This control is backed up by an extensive security and surveillance apparatus that seeks to actively subjugate opponents and minorities (most glaringly in Xinjiang), and which led to China's – nationwide and highly exportable – social credit system that monitors, regulates and now *harmonizes* its entire population.

In Chapter 2, we pinpointed the very different set of values and identities that influence China's conception of international order, primarily Confucianism's hierarchical, paternalistic and benevolent values used to harmonize Chinese society since around 202 BC. Principles of *tian xia* ('all under heaven') and *da tong* ('great harmony') sought to create an *internal order* overseen by a single ruling group (presenting the CCP), and an *external order* with China at its centre, whose superiority must be recognized by all other countries. Such an order is *China-centric* and multipolar in that Beijing is willing to allow other political forms to exist so long as China's supremacy as the Middle Kingdom is recognized by others, and it would only use force if such a ranking was not respected. This outlook typified 1,150 years of *Pax Sinicas* across five different Chinese dynasties and is the historical touchstone that links Beijing's past status to its current and future ambitions. It is the foundation of the narratives that the CCP has deployed to pursue and maintain power in modern China.

Beyond these historical roots, in Chapter 3 we saw how China's centrality to the global economy is allowing it to export its authoritarian values – and their legal basis – across the international system. By successfully morphing the social, political and economic realms of its international order into an *authoritarian-capitalist* basis, Beijing has completely and publicly broken the supposed bond and dependency between liberal democracy and liberal trade, and thus brought into question entire areas of the liberal international order. Notably, China has been able to synthesize its own authoritarian values with those of global free trade, showing a clear resilience in its authoritarian basis, which other countries can replicate. This 'China Model' of economic development allows the state to be interventionist, binds the economy to one-party rule and resists a complete integration of neoliberalism. Beijing is now exporting this approach via its Belt and Road Initiative (BRI), the largest infrastructure funding project in history, which aims to create in-built interdependences between China and member countries, and to sustain its economic growth and authority. The BRI has also successfully pulled democratic countries into its ever-increasing orbit and is being used as a diplomatic mechanism to dissuade criticism of its internal politics, especially in Xinjiang.

Beyond these two realms, Chapter 4 showed how China is injecting the different values, practices and – overall – identity underpinning its vision of international order into international affairs. Beijing is doing this through the construction of new multilateral institutions built on these different principles, and is primarily using its economic clout (especially compared with a weakening US) to attract other countries to them. Such an undertaking is most evident concerning the ever-expanding Asian Infrastructure Investment Bank (AIIB) but also carries over into the security domain with the Shanghai Cooperation Organization (SCO). These regimes challenge the exclusivity of Western-created international organizations and are reorienting the international order along more China-centric lines, especially in terms of its 'state-led development' and 'social-welfare' economic models. Within these dynamics, notions of *tian xia* are also prominent with Beijing seeking to realize a more representative and equitable (certainly for Asia and developing world regions) global power structure that features China at its highest echelons.

In Chapter 5, we witnessed the active fulfilment of a China-centric international order, in which the region is ever-more dependent on China's economic success and is expected to recognize Beijing's superiority. This chapter also displayed how

China is proactively re-realizing its Middle Kingdom heritage by using all founts of its power – including military – to claim islands in the South China Sea and the East China Sea. These areas are crucial to its vital trade and energy routes but also to its self-conception and integrity, most clearly concerning Taiwan, and are the only regions where Beijing forcefully deploys its military capabilities. To date, there is little evidence to suggest that China will use its military power in the same way as the US has done – that is, to coerce regime change in countries whose interests are antithetical to its own. Thus, when combined with a desire for multipolarity which is anti-hegemonic, a military realm is less prominent and seemingly less important in a China-centric international order.

Last, Chapter 6 underscored the social aspect of international order that has pervaded this volume. Going beyond how a country's values, practices and identity inform its vision of international order, here we evidenced how social peer recognition from other countries – not just concerning status but also reflecting and replicating certain principles and behaviours – also confers legitimacy on it. Across the US, Russia and India we evidenced an entire spectrum of policies and behaviours that are clearly authoritarian in nature and which – especially in the case of Washington and New Delhi – undermine their democratic foundations. These factors imply a greater *global convergence* around authoritarianism, deep-seated among these great powers, that is being validated by their actions and is then filtering out into the international sphere, reinforcing its pervasiveness and primacy. Apart from indicating a general weakness infusing the liberal international order, this assertion underscores the current order's lack of sufficient resilience to resist a China-centric international order and henceforth the long-term realization of the authoritarian century. The presence of systematic hypocrisies and disconnects between the purported values of the liberal order and its eventual enactment, as argued below, reinforces this fragility.

All of these chapters verified the five themes of *continuum*, *facilitation*, *assimilation*, *normalization* and *longevity*, which I laid out in the volume's Introduction, as being central to the definition, identification and achievement of international order. These themes were evident both in my discussion of the liberal international order and the emergent China-centric international order. A political *continuum* was observable concerning China's own shift from being totalitarian under Mao to becoming authoritarian under his successors (and arguably shifting back towards totalitarianism under Xi Jinping). Equally, throughout the chapters we also saw how the US (and India in Chapter 6) have shifted from the opposing democratic end of this continuum towards its authoritarian zone. In terms of *facilitation*, China's active pursuit of autocratic politics domestically and its transmission of such policies internationally through its economic, institution-building and diplomatic activities is abetting the creation of its desired international order. We also saw how the US in part facilitated this creation by supporting (and benefiting from) China's inclusion into the economic and institutional basis of the liberal international order. This support came despite Beijing's clear authoritarian basis and is an excellent example of how US strategic and economic interests have taken primacy over its purported political values.

In turn, this backing was an act of *assimilation* that attempted to socialize China into the values and practices of the liberal international order but which was eventually superseded by China's own power and agency. Beijing is now also carrying out its own process of assimilation by attracting other countries to it through China's vast economic power, massive global investments and clearly benefit-driven institutions. Although not actively promoting authoritarianism around the world in the same way that the US ostensibly encourages democracy, the very tangible demonstration effect of China's successful authoritarian–capitalist model acts as an appealing assimilative tool. At its core, this continued success essentially legitimizes authoritarian practices in global politics. It also – along with China's continued expansion of its power capabilities in all spheres – underpins a process of *normalization* that is entrenching Beijing's influence and strengthens the foundations and eventual full realization of its international order. Finally, *longevity* is being evidenced by the CCP's vision of achieving a durable international order akin to previous Chinese dynasties that prevailed over many centuries, and which the CCP will now oversee, revealing its raw ambition to accomplish such an importance as part of the nascent authoritarian century.

Harking back to the Preface, global responses to the coronavirus pandemic have also served to accentuate the utility, and even proclivity, for authoritarianism in international politics. In attempting to deal with a deadly threat to their populations, COVID-19 is a hyper-crisis that is also an incredible opportunity for realizing any authoritarian impulses. According to the UN Secretary-General António Guterres, the world has consequently witnessed a 'pandemic of human rights abuses',[1] reversing decades of progress in this area. As such, authoritarian (and to a degree, democratic) regimes have used the virus as a reason to curb rights and freedoms and to suppress dissent, including cracking down on opposition activists, attacking journalists and censoring the media, as well as using invasive tracking apps and extreme real-world and online surveillance measures to restrict populations in as many ways as possible.[2] Such developments clearly reflect and resonate with the authoritarian shifts that we saw in Chapter 6 of this volume, as well as the use of technology to achieve these new realities, and which together facilitate, assimilate and normalize authoritarianism in global affairs.

To counter COVID-19 in China, people's movements are constantly tracked by telecom firms; entering one's home or workplace requires scanning a QR code, while facial recognition technology is being used to sense elevated temperatures in a crowd or to identify citizens not wearing a face mask.[3] From late 2020, a system called Health Code also allocated individuals one of three colour codes based on their travel history, their time in virus hotspots and exposure to potential virus carriers.[4] Mirroring other countries, these measures are done under the official refrain of this being an 'extraordinary time' (*feichang shiqi*) that requires extraordinary measures, and clearly reinforces and expands existing powers under the social credit system. China's relatively early success in controlling the internal spread of the virus also signalled a diplomatic victory for Beijing, which in turn legitimized its authoritarian basis globally (resulting in its measures being openly discussed and then being widely deployed across the world), as did its early successes in vaccine diplomacy.[5] This success was most apparent when compared with the US, where former President Trump initially denied the existence of COVID-19, which helped result in 400,000 deaths by the end of his presidency.[6] Such actions damaged the US's democratic credentials and was an 'epic policy failure [that] will further tarnish [its] reputation as a country that knows how to do things effectively'.[7] It is unclear who will eventually win the narrative battle regarding which country has been more successful in handling the pandemic but it is one that Beijing is currently winning.[8]

From these analytical findings, some decidedly palpable realities are apparent.

An illiberal international order

Our investigation into a China-centric international order has highlighted the consistent authoritarian underbelly of the current liberal international order. Contemporarily, as per Chapter 6, this assertion relates to the many ways in which democratic human and civil rights are being systematically reduced in the US and India, as well as in numerous other middle- and lower-ranking countries. It is also evidenced historically by how the main fulcrum of this order – that of US hegemony – is essentially an authoritarian outlook in that it seeks to remove plurality from, and enforce subjugation within, international politics. This baseline is apparent regardless of whether other countries willingly acquiesce to such hegemony or if they are forced to accept it by whatever means. Notions of 'universal' human rights or the unquestioned implementation of neoliberal economics also exemplifies such an outlook, as does the US's habitual use of military force to actively coerce any dissenters towards its worldview. Beyond its hypocrisy – in that the very values on which the liberal international order is supposed to rest have been frequently superseded by its architects' interests – the US's political, economic, diplomatic and military activities have substantiated this authoritarian instinct in international affairs.

The US has therefore – *to a degree* – enabled and facilitated authoritarian politics in international affairs, especially when its economic or strategic goals have taken precedence. Washington's overt and covert manipulation of scores of democratic elections, as well as its use of 'permanent war' to pursue its interests by force, have also – *often knowingly* – led to the continuance or creation of authoritarian regimes. There is no better example of this facilitation than China, whereby Beijing was invited into liberal economic structures as a way for the US economy (and US corporations) to benefit from cheap labour and manufacturing and vast new markets, and which masked stagnating wages and living standards across Western countries. Further premised on the hoped-for eventual socializing of Beijing into liberal practices, which was not entirely successful, it can be regarded as an act of great strategic naivety that revealed the true limits of the liberal international order – particularly in terms of its assimilative and attractive power. This shortcoming – albeit observed with considerable hindsight – is also the case with many other US bilateral relations, and is true of contemporary US-India relations in that the greater goal of balancing Beijing in global affairs now outweighs criticizing India's internal record concerning myriad human rights abuses, most obviously in Kashmir and also increasingly in Assam.

Accompanying this sublimation of the ostensibly liberal international order into its present illiberal incarnation has been a presumed 'politics of inevitability' in the West. Premised on the West's victory in the Cold War, itself then sustained by Fukuyama's assertion of the 'end of history' and narratives of US exceptionalism and unipolarity, this has resulted in 'a sense that the future is just more of the present, that the laws of progress are known, that there are no alternatives, and therefore nothing really to be done'.[9] As such, neoliberal capitalism and democracy were so unquestionable that they became an unchallenged and 'natural' element of international politics that frequently rejects historical perspectives. Underlying this contention is that US and Western leaders (and their populations) are notably ignorant of the history of their own countries, and that of other countries, and hence lack the capacity to learn from the past, not least in terms of contextualizing their actions. As such, Western leaders would do well to note Thucydides' observation that 'the events of future history ... will be of the same nature – or nearly so – as the history of the past, so long as men are men'.[10] Applying such wisdom could have assuaged the strategic myopia – and resultant mis-steps – that has now come to wholly typify the US-led liberal international order. The contrast with China, where the CCP actively learns from its and others' histories, is stark, as its leaders argue that 'we hope that the world will view China in an objective, historical and multi-dimensional light, and see the true and full picture of a dynamic China'.[11]

Reflective of these dynamics, the concept of modern democracy has been falsely regarded as the inevitable basis of global politics despite universal suffrage only being technically achieved in Australia in 1967, the US in 1965, India in 1950, Japan in 1947, France in 1945 and the UK in 1928. When compared with authoritarianism, which (in some form or other) has dominated the rest of human history, and which remained prevalent in international politics *irrespective* of the existence of the liberal international order, indicates – at worst – that democracy may simply be a historical aberration, a mere grain of sand in time. If past behaviour and actions are regarded as a historical repository, as is the case in China concerning the very engrained nature of its authoritarian political and social basis, the even more uncomfortable observation is that authoritarianism is also an undeniable part of the histories – and thus the values and identities – of all (including Western) countries, which may explain its continued presence in present-day politics.

Moreover, claims as to the universality of liberal democracy are not only historically misrepresentative but sustain suspicions from China and elsewhere that democracy is simply being deployed by Western countries as a veneer to justify the pursuit of their core interests. This volume's revealing of the contradictions and hypocrisies, as well as the mythologized nature, of the liberal international order only further underscores such a position. It also points to a diffident West that is now unsure of its global relevance, as evidenced by the 2020 discussion at Davos concerning apparent 'Westlessness',[12] and also a West whose criticism of China – particularly when couched in terms of the ideological simplicity of Western liberty versus Chinese tyranny – runs ever-more hollow.

China's dawning order

As the chapters of this book attest, the international system is currently experiencing a period of transition and rebalancing as more economic, institutional and military power is being amassed by China. This shift is depleting the relative influence and stature of Western countries, their associated values and worldviews and, by extension, the Western-centric liberal international order. Furthermore, Beijing is now able to articulate an alternative vision of international order that is frequently premised on different economic, institutional and normative conditions and is becoming increasingly legitimate in the eyes of many world leaders. Growing authoritarian and populist traits across the world – and its dominant great powers – accelerate this trend, and show that the period of US hegemony, and the legitimacy of US exceptionalism as underpinning this omnipotence, is over. As Chinese observers note, 'history has never set any precedent that an empire is capable of governing the world forever',[13] and the US's denouement is reflective of the wider historical rise and fall, and ebb and flow, of international orders across time. In its place, the coming China-centric international order will be more multipolar – and potentially less unified and certainly more disjointed in nature – and will be characterized not so much by a hegemonic country but by the hegemonic governing philosophy of authoritarianism.

One debate concerning this apparent shift has been whether or not Beijing can truly realize its preferred international order. Here, critics note that China does not contest the liberal trade aspects of the current order and has openly embraced the benefits of free markets and globalization. Such an embrace would imply that Beijing has been successfully assimilated into the existing order and effectively negates Mao Zedong's mantra that 'the only way of building a new world is by destroying the old one'.[14] Such all-or-nothing thinking has pervaded Western strategy towards China, as well as the belief that such a partial (economic) embrace would lead to the full embrace (of democracy). An alternative way of understanding China's dawning order is the *Ship of Theseus* thought experiment, wherein a ship used by Theseus in a famous battle is kept in a harbour as a museum piece. As the years went by some of the wooden parts began to rot and were replaced by new ones; then, after a century or so, every part had been replaced. The question then is whether the 'restored' ship is still the same object as the original.[15]

If understood from this perspective, we can see how China's rise does not deploy force to challenge the existing order, as other great powers have done, but instead uses existing mechanisms to enhance its status – in particular concerning liberal capitalism and international institutions. Thus, rather than acting as the Soviet Union did during the Cold War when two dichotomous worldviews and blocs were pitted against each other (and which Moscow lost, as is well studied by the CCP), China has acted as a 'quasi-revolutionary state' that selectively chooses norms and practices to comply with in a utilitarian manner. Moreover, by becoming a legitimate member of the existing order, China is pursuing a more peaceful path for asserting its international order, as well as its continued economic development. Thus, China has signed up to a host of institutions crucial to the Western international order – such as the World Trade Organization and the United Nations – in which it is now an indispensable partner and which China is attempting to hone towards its own values and interests. In turn, even when crafting its own multilateral groupings, such as the AIIB and the SCO, on a superficial level they look the same as parts of the existing international order – in that they are rule-based institutions often with similar sets of members – but which on deeper inspection consist of divergent values that reflect Chinese characteristics.

In this sense, the existing liberal international order is slowly being replaced plank by plank, which maintains its semblance but whose actual substance is being irrevocably transformed. Such a transformation has not been – and will not be – sudden but creeping and incremental, and *most decisively* has been a process simultaneously carried out by China *and* the West (and if it results in a grand authoritarian union may actually dissuade conflict between them). It also reveals a different kind of revolution than that espoused by Mao, who argued that 'a revolution is not a dinner party, ... [it] is an insurrection, an act of violence by which one class overthrows another';[16] instead, for Xi, it is a long multi-coursed banquet resting on patience, attraction and subterfuge.

The *Ship of Theseus* argument also recognizes the current coexistence of the (il)liberal international order and China's preferred authoritarian version, and encompasses arguments pertaining to a dual hierarchical order wherein China dominates the economic sphere and the US the security sphere,[17] or of a 'blending' of Western and Chinese values to create a truly inclusive, peaceful and harmonious world.[18] Such a deep blurring is most evident in Western companies and governments continuing to trade with China, even if this means that entire industries are complicit in Beijing's policies in Xinjiang (most notably textiles, wherein one in five cotton products are tainted by forced labour and human rights violations[19]). Moreover, by being heavily dependent on Beijing for their continued economic success, Western companies selling anything made in China – and indeed, anybody buying such products – are also complicit in the country's authoritarian reality, as they are by trading with other authoritarian regimes.

Despite the extent to which deepening authoritarian practices differ across China and other autocratic regimes – as well as among many of the international system's great powers and Western countries – the facts point to an accelerating and explicitly authoritarian future. From this basis, and if this convergence – and its driving centrifugal force – is not curtailed, then certain eventualities for the international system can be seen. In all of them – an *Asian century* (led by China or not), a *competent demagogue* in the US or a *global panopticon* enacted by Big Tech – an authoritarian international order and an authoritarian century seemingly beckon.

The Asian century

With the majority of economic power being created in Asia, along with the majority of military spending occurring in the region (although collectively still much lower than what the US spends alone), a much-heralded Asian century is upon us. China's role as the essential fulcrum of global trade and largest economy is at the heart of this emergence and is creating significant interdependencies that not only embolden Beijing's superlative regional – and global – positioning above all other countries but also bolster Asia as a whole. As we have seen, these relations implicitly recreate the hierarchies of the Middle Kingdom and those underpinning a *tian xia* outlook. The presence of the world's third, fourth and sixth largest economies in the guise of India, Japan and Russia, and through its Indo-Pacific borders the world's second largest economy courtesy of the US,[20] attest to this future positioning of the region. As the most convertible and translatable form of power, China's economic strength will also confirm the decline of the West and surmount Washington's ownership of the previously unchallenged economic pillar of the liberal international order. India's own rapid economic rise and its potential to replace or at the very least replicate China as a hub for global investment and trade also underscores the long-term significance of the region. With its own authoritarian proclivities expanding, New Delhi's authoritarian basis only reaffirms the broader authoritarian century.

Of note too is that the future of modern China under the CCP is by no means assured. As we saw in the earliest sections of this book, much of the CCP's authoritarian rule is in response to stamping out any perceived threats of instability and disharmony within the country, as per Mao's adage that 'a single spark can start a prairie fire'.[21] These insecurities are magnified by widespread environmental pollution that killed in excess of 1.1 million people in 2018 and led to major economic losses,[22] as well as widespread corruption that threatens the legitimacy of the CCP.[23] Xi also seemingly faces considerable opposition in the CCP amid fears that his unchecked political power will result in national collapse, whereby 'after a wrong decision is made ... those below are too afraid to tell him and wrong decisions [will] continue to be made until the situation is out of control. In this vicious cycle, there is no way to stop the country from sliding towards disaster.'[24]

Such a dynamic could precipitate the collapse of CCP rule (potentially towards the end of Xi's second term in power in 2022) and China's global pre-eminence, and in the short term will result in an even more authoritarian China that attempts to eradicate all anti-CCP dissent. This could include the splintering of the internet and Chinese authorities declaring an independent China-only cyberspace. Greater levels of protest, say in response to environmental destruction and consequent increased mass migrations and pressure on resources,[25] will also likely result in stricter measures to control the population, as would also clearly be the case in the West if it also undergoes similar (inter)national crises. Likewise, a severe economic recession within China (sparked, perhaps, by an imminent – and earth-shaking – stock market collapse in the US[26]) would quickly affect the whole world, and potentially precipitate further draconian responses by Beijing and other (including Western) governments.

Even if China were to lose its regional pre-eminence in these ways, the veracity of a China-inspired authoritarian century would remain because it was Beijing that first inculcated this shift in the international order. Likewise, given China's disposition for a multipolar international order, which is also shared by India and Russia, it will be the political and social basis of this order that matters most, not who leads it. As such, if India were to take over the helm of the Asian century, as the foremost economy in the region – if not the world – after Beijing's decline, New Delhi's authoritarianism politics would inherently serve to uphold the authoritarian century.

Competent US demagogue

To the casual observer, the greatest antidote to an authoritarian international order, especially if it were under the aegis of China, would be the US as the originator of the liberal international order. As we have seen in this book, however, the US has a well-established track record of not always protecting its liberal values either on the international or domestic level, and moreover is displaying an increasing proclivity for authoritarian politics. Thus, we have seen a significant decline in liberal rights within the US that has been facilitated by both sides of the political spectrum but most clearly by the Republican Party. The election of Donald Trump as president in 2016 only exacerbated this pro-authoritarian trend, which meant, as summed up by Adam Curtis, that 'the pantomime has become reality and starts rampaging around. And then we are fucked.'[27] In turn, the conduct of the 2020 election, and the consistent denial of the result by Trump, also drew harsh international criticism with the chair of Russia's Duma saying 'It's a show, you can't call it anything but that', Colombia's *Publimetro* newspaper observing 'Who's the banana republic now?', and Chinese state media pithily noting that the US looked a 'bit like a developing country'.[28] Such dynamics have undercut President Biden's attempts to frame competition between Washington and Beijing as being the world's democracies versus the world's authoritarian regimes, or as a public and media-friendly narrative concerning the emergence of a 'second Cold War'.

Nor did Trump's 2020 election loss to Joe Biden herald a return to politics as normal in the US, as the many deficiencies in its political system persisted and were exacerbated by bipartisan politics. Thus, the defeat did not 'remove the threats and social changes that trigger the "action side" of authoritarianism. The authoritarians will still be there ... [and] will still look for candidates who will give them the strong, punitive leadership they desire'.[29] When this observation is combined with a Republican Party that refuses to accept the result of the 2020 election and continues to advocate for voter repression, as well as attacking the media and academia, the spectre of another election victory by Trump or by a Trump-esque successor is highly possible. More tellingly, either eventuality could result in a more experienced, better organized and more ideologically driven Republican leader, who as president would rule as a competent demagogue who quickly and irrevocably disassembles the pillars of US democracy.

Such a leader would govern not via rule of law but by rule by law, would seek to eliminate the plurality of US politics, jail all political opponents and dismantle the universal human rights essential to a correctly functioning and accountability-inducing civil society. In particular, if Trump were to return as president in 2024, we can expect such a dismantling to be extremely rapid and to be driven by a deep-seated vengeance against any and all of his political and media opponents. From this basis, it is entirely conceivable that American democracy could collapse by 2028, heralding a populist autocratic regime and potentially resulting in a wider civil war. As a leading civil rights activist said of Trump, 'He's willing to kill democracy. ... He is willing to kill America's international and global relationships. He is a destroyer.'[30] If a similar leader were to emerge, and an authoritarian (even fascist) US to emerge, then a new authoritarian international order would also be swiftly confirmed along with a China-inspired authoritarian century. At the time of writing (in April 2022), the Democrats' wafer-thin majorities in the Senate and the House provide little succour that such unwelcome eventualities will be avoided.

Global panopticon

The major unifying factor between authoritarianism in China and that being increasingly manifest in other countries across the world is the use of increasingly powerful surveillance technology. Driven by Big Tech and advances in AI, they are fusing together the social and economic lives of the world's population with authoritarian outlooks centred on monitoring, manipulation and control. At the forefront of this fusing are social media companies whose interest in market share, data harvesting and acquiring content are increasingly surmounting political and moral considerations.

First among these is Facebook, which in 2019 exempted political advertisements from a ban on making false claims,[31] and which along with Twitter and Google allow the propagation of extremism and misinformation – including the glorification of violence during the 2020 election and the attack on the US Capitol in January 2021.[32] Such actions by Facebook have, for example, subverted freedoms of expression and speech in Vietnam and Thailand, and have enabled authoritarian regimes to attack civil rights activists and political opponents, as well as to incite violence in Myanmar, whereby Facebook 'follow[s] state-sponsored censorship so that it can conduct operations, businesses and sales in that country'.[33] Collectively, these authoritarian practices influence billions of daily social media users across the world, which in April 2021 included 2.797 billion on Facebook, 2.291 billion on YouTube, 2 billion on WhatsApp, 1.287 billion on Instagram, 1.225 billion on Weixin and WeChat, 0.732 billion on TikTok and 0.600 billion on Douyin, among others.[34] The neoliberal business practices of Big Tech are also anti-pluralistic – and hence authoritarian – as they protect their monopolies by buying up smaller companies, and from 2005 to 2020 Alphabet, Apple, Amazon and Facebook were all prolific in this regard as they reportedly acquired 385 other US companies[35] between them.

Such capabilities are backed up by increasing political sway in the West. Big Tech firms are now among the biggest corporate donors in the US, outstripping Big Pharma, Big Tobacco and the arms industry. In 2020, Amazon and Facebook also spent nearly twice as much as Exxon and Philip Morris on lobbying, had the highest number of lobbyists and spent $124 million in lobbying and campaign contributions during the 2020 presidential election.[36] All of these elements point to these companies' increasing supranational influence that is able to shape global politics and opinion, and which aims to permanently cement the presence of Big Tech into the political, social and economic fabric of the world.

Their actions are also reflective of the key themes relating to international order in this book, in that they are actively *facilitating, assimilating* and *normalizing* authoritarian tendencies. In these dynamics, their owners possess incredible power, whereby, for example, Mark Zuckerberg 'alone can decide how to configure Facebook's algorithms to determine what people see in their news feeds, what privacy settings they can use, ... he can choose to shut down a competitor by acquiring, blocking or copying it'.[37] Such control over vast swathes of the global population points to a future wherein the power of Big Tech exceeds that of most – if not all – countries, especially if it is intertwined with the maintenance of authoritarian-oriented regimes. In 2005, Zuckerberg pertinently noted a preference for 'companies over countries',[38] and in 2004 called users 'dumb fucks'[39] for trusting him with their data. With ever cheaper and more advanced technology, and more countries like China and Russia willing to use it to watch and control their populations, Edward Snowden noted in 2015 that 'if we do nothing, we ... sleepwalk into a total surveillance state where we have both a super-state that has unlimited capacity to apply force with an unlimited ability to know [about the people it is targeting], ... that's the dark future'.[40] Such a future would be unrelentingly authoritarian and would confirm the authoritarian international order, both economically as enabled by Big Tech and politically when such technology is widely used. With Beijing as its key harbinger, it would also consecrate a China-inspired authoritarian century and international order.

Descent, resistance and re-learning

As H.G. Wells noted in another era, 'there will be no day of days when a new world order comes into being. Step by step and here and there it will arrive ...'.[41] In this way, and as this book has consistently evidenced, we are now on the cusp of – if not already descending into – an authoritarian international order. When we recall that this shift is occurring not just in China and like-minded autocracies but also across the world's largest and most powerful democracies, this prognosis is astoundingly bleak. Such a scenario is reinforced by the prevalence of social media and technology that have become omnipresent surveillance tools across the world's population and which globally magnify – frequently hate-filled and divisive – authoritarian desires. Set against a neoliberal background, the logic and attraction of such inclinations has never been higher and, as shown by hyper-crises such as COVID-19, are proving irresistible – even necessary – to many of our leaders, be they in autocracies or democracies.

Within this shift, there is however some space for democracies to survive, if not thrive. China's preferred international order, while conclusively authoritarian in nature in that it reflects such domestic values and tacitly legitimizes them in global politics, does not seek to actively promote authoritarianism. When combined with Beijing's preference for a multipolar international order that respects and recognizes China's superiority within such a system, democratic regimes can exist so long as they accept such an inherent hierarchy. Notable too is that Beijing, as much as it dislikes and tries to dissuade criticism of its internal politics, does not proudly proclaim to be authoritarian in nature, and thus can be seen as a somewhat consistent geopolitical actor (especially versus an ambiguous US) – and especially given its clearly non-ideological attitude to conducting its trade relations. Chinese narratives concerning the creation of a more representative, equal and harmonious international order underscore how democracies can fruitfully coexist in a China-centric order, one which – for the time being – Beijing is not backing up with brute military force. Indeed, by not explicitly seeking (for the moment at least) global hegemony, working towards a multipolar international order would solve Kissinger's conundrum, which he noted after visiting China in 1971, that 'the mystery to be overcome is one all peoples share – how divergent historic experiences and values can be shaped into a common order'.[42]

In terms of resisting the world's wholesale descent into authoritarianism – a descent which would be exceptionally difficult, if not impossible, to extricate ourselves from – what is therefore needed is the maintenance and protection of democratic practices and values. Part of this process requires countries to confront China concerning its own authoritarian practices, but also involves nurturing democratic ones at home and making them attractive for other countries to work with and to imitate. As former US President Barack Obama has argued, in democracy, 'there has to be citizens who insist on it and participate to make sure it happens. Democracy is a garden that has to be tended.'[43] Such cultivation not only requires dissuading policies and political entities that are authoritarian or proto-authoritarian but also making sure that all individuals and groups embrace and respect key liberal norms. We must also remind ourselves that, in the words of John Buchan, democracy is 'primarily an attitude of mind, a spiritual testament, and not an economic structure or a political machine'.[44]

As such, liberal democratic societies 'require more than the formal institutions of democracy. They also depend on a broad and deep commitment to the underlying values of a liberal society, most notably tolerance'.[45] In order to prevent any slippage towards authoritarianism, national political, social and moral values require regular maintenance. Populations need to be actively (and regularly) informed through publicity campaigns and mandatory ongoing civic education classes (for both children and adults) of their rights, and how such rights were originally won historically. Influential individuals – such as television producers, directors, authors, artists, musicians, teachers, journalists and any kind of elected official – need to pre-emptively use their positions *now* to insist on the production and promotion of such educational campaigns. Without a knowledge basis concerning what democracy is, citizens will be ever-more vulnerable to alternative narratives, especially in periods of tumult – in the form of profound social or economic shocks and depressions – that frequently only serve to further accentuate and speed up a country's assimilation to authoritarianism and populism. We must also remember that with enough time, and as in modern China, *any dissenting voices will be targeted by a control-hungry authoritarian regime* and thus we all need to take action regardless of our political beliefs. Such action is necessary *against any democratic backsliding*, so as to maintain all democratic systems to the very highest standards.

Most fundamentally of all, what this bolstering requires are virtuous leaders who reject intolerance, division and self-interest and who can focus our national energies to create positive change that celebrates and augments liberal democratic politics. These leaders must also help us 'to re-learn the tools of reason, logic, clarity, dissent, civility, and debate … those things [which] are the non-partisan basis of democracy, … without them you can kiss this thing goodbye'.[46] Deprived of such leaders – and without such re-learning and individuals actively facilitating it – our global autocratic descent and the dawn of a new *Pax Autocratica* may well be irrevocably complete.

Notes

Preface

[1] Ogden, C. (2020) 'Must Britain be more like China to halt coronavirus outbreak?', *The Guardian*, [online] 27 February.

[2] Ogden, C. (2020) 'Starting a conversation: how far can the UK take authoritarian measures against coronavirus?', BBC Radio 4 (on PM), 2 March.

Introduction

[1] CACR (2021) 'Weekly report', *Center for Advanced China Research*, 26 June.

[2] Economist Intelligence Unit (2016) *Democracy Index 2016: Revenge of the 'Deplorables'*, London: Economist Intelligence Unit; Freedom House (2017) *Freedom in the World 2017 – Populists and Autocrats: The Dual Threat to Global Democracy*, Washington, DC: Freedom House; Polity IV (2014) *Polity IV Project: Political Regime Characteristics and Transitions 1800–2013*, Vienna: Center for Systemic Peace.

[3] *The Economist* (2021) 'Global democracy has a very bad year', *The Economist*, 2 February.

[4] Freeland, J. (2021) 'In plain sight, Boris Johnson is rigging the system to stay in power', *The Guardian*, [online] 1 October.

[5] AFP (2021) 'US added to "backsliding" democracies for first time', *The Guardian*, [online] 22 November.

[6] Katzenstein, P.J. (1996) *Cultural Norms and National Security: Police and Military in Post-War Japan*. Ithaca: Cornell University Press, p 6.

[7] Snyder, J. (1977) *The Soviet Strategic Culture: Implications for Limited Nuclear Operations*, Washington, DC: Defense Technical Information Center, p v.

[8] Adler, E. (2013) 'Constructivism in international relations: sources, contributions, and debates', in W. Carlsnaes, T. Risse Kappen, T. Risse, B.A. Simmons (eds), *Handbook of International Relations*, London: SAGE, p 113.

[9] Schamis, H.F. and Armony, A.C. (2015) 'Babel in democratization studies', *Journal of Democracy*, 16(4): 114.

[10] Alvarez, M., Cheibub, J.A., Limongi, F. and Przeworski, A. (1996) 'Classifying political regimes', *Studies in Comparative International Development*, 31(2): 3–36; Hadenius, A. and Teorell, J. (2006) *Authoritarian*

Regimes: Stability, Change, and Pathways to Democracy, 1972–2003, Helen Kellogg Institute for International Studies.

[11] Linz, J.J. (2000) *Totalitarian and Authoritarian Regimes*, Boulder: Lynne Rienner Publishers, p 60.

[12] Diamond, L.J. (2002) 'Thinking about hybrid regimes', *Journal of Democracy*, 13(2): 23.

[13] Brooker, P. (2014) *Non-Democratic Regimes*, London: Palgrave Macmillan.

[14] Schedler, A. (2002) 'The nested game of democratization by elections', *International Political Science Review*, 23(1): 103–22.

[15] Levitsky, S. and Way, L.A. (2010) *Competitive Authoritarianism: Hybrid Regimes after the Cold War*, Cambridge University Press, p 5.

[16] Zakaria, F. (1997) 'The rise of illiberal democracy', *Foreign Affairs*, 76(6): 22.

[17] Polity IV (2014).

[18] Economist Intelligence Unit (2016).

[19] Levitsky, S. and Ziblatt, D. (2016) 'Opinion: is Donald Trump a threat to democracy?', *New York Times*, 16 December.

[20] Schedler (2002) 103–22.

[21] Ikenberry, G.J. (2011) *Liberal Leviathan: The Origins, Crisis and Transformation of the American World Order*, Princeton: Princeton University Press, p 11.

[22] quoted in Acharya, A. (2014) *The End of American World Order*, Cambridge: Polity, p 12.

[23] Ikenberry, G.J. (2015) 'Introduction', in G.J. Ikenberry, Wang Jisi and Zhu Feng (eds) *America, China, and the Struggle for World Order: Ideas, Traditions, Historical Legacies, and Global Visions*, Basingstoke: Palgrave Macmillan, p 5.

[24] Patman, R.G. (2006) 'Globalization, the new US exceptionalism and the war on terror', *Third World Quarterly*, 27(6): 964.

[25] Acharya (2014) 34.

[26] Ikenberry (2011) xi.

[27] Charvet, J. and Kaczynska-Nay, E. (2008) *The Liberal Project and Human Rights: The Theory and Practice of a New World Order*, Cambridge: Cambridge University Press, p 2.

[28] Charvet and Kaczynska-Nay (2008) 2.

[29] Truman quoted in Smith, T. (1994) *America's Mission: The United States and the Worldwide Struggle for Democracy in the Twentieth Century*, Princeton: Princeton University Press, p 200.

[30] Johnson, L.B. (1967) 'Speech on Vietnam, September 29, 1967', Miller Center, University of Virginia, 29 September.

[31] Vine, D. (2015) *Base Nation: How US Military Bases Overseas Harm America and the World*, New York: Metropolitan Books.

[32] Roosevelt quoted in EB (2017) 'Big stick policy', *Encyclopædia Britannica*, 27 December.

[33] Ikenberry (2011) 174.

[34] Fukuyama, F. (1989) 'The end of history?', *The National Interest*, (16): 4.

[35] Krauthammer quoted in Acharya (2014) 12.

[36] see Kissinger, H. (2015) *World Order*, London: Penguin; Mearsheimer, J. (2001) *The Tragedy of Great Power Politics*, New York: W.W. Norton & Company.

[37] Economist Intelligence Unit (2016).

Chapter 1

[1] Janoski, T. (2014) 'Citizenship in China: a comparison of rights with the East and West', *Journal of Chinese Political Science*, 19(4): 365.

[2] Abrahamson, P. (2017) 'East Asian welfare regime: obsolete ideal-type or diversified reality', *Journal of Asian Public Policy*, 10(1): 90–103.

[3] Keenan, B.C. (2014) 'Economic markets and higher education: ethical issues in the United States and China', *Frontiers of Education in China*, 9(1): 63.

[4] Ogden, C. (2019) *A Dictionary of Politics and International Relations in China*, Oxford: Oxford University Press.

[5] All monetary values are in US dollars.

[6] Textor, C. (2020) 'China's public security expenditure 2009–2019', *Statista*, [online], 27 November.

[7] Strittmatter, K. (2019) *We Have Been Harmonised: Life in China's Surveillance State*, Exeter: Old Street, p 7.

[8] Xunzi and Knoblock, J. (1990) *Xunzi: A Translation and Study of the Complete Works*, Stanford: Stanford University Press, p 234.

[9] quoted in Song Xinning (2001) 'Building international relations theory with Chinese characteristics', *Journal of Contemporary China*, 10(26): 70.

[10] Suisheng Zhao (2010) 'The China model: can it replace the Western model of modernization?', *Journal of Contemporary China*, 19(65): 423.

[11] Lovell, J. (2016) '*The Cultural Revolution: A People's History 1962–1976* by Frank Dikotter – Review', *The Guardian*, [online] 11 August.

[12] MacFarquhar, R. (2016) Leadership styles at the party centre: from Mao Zedong to Xi Jinping', in S. Hellmann and M. Stepan (eds) *China's Core Executive*, Berlin: Mercator Institute for China Studies, pp 14–17.

[13] quoted in Phillips, T. (2017) 'Xi Jinping heralds "new era" of Chinese power at Communist Party congress', *The Guardian*, [online] 18 October.

[14] O'Brien, K.J. and Han, R. (2009) 'Path to democracy? Assessing village elections in China', *Journal of Contemporary China*, 18(60): 359–78.

[15] Owen, C. (2018) 'State transformation and authoritarian governance: the emergence of participatory authoritarianism?', Foreign Policy Centre, [online], 14 September.

[16] quoted in Phillips, T. (2016) '"Love the party, protect the party": how Xi Jinping is bringing China's media to heel', *The Guardian*, [online] 28 February.

[17] Hattenstone, S. (2020) 'Ai Weiwei on his new life in Britain: "People are at least polite. In Germany, they weren't"', *The Guardian*, [online] 21 January; Phillips, T. (2017) 'A human rights activist, a secret prison and a tale from Xi Jinping's new China', *The Guardian*, [online] 3 January.

[18] Vincent quoted in Waterson, J. (2021) 'Oppression of journalists in China may have been a factor in Covid pandemic', *The Guardian*, [online] 20 April.

[19] National Endowment for Democracy in Washington quoted in Tisdall, S. (2021) 'Xi's change of heart is too late to stop China's collision with the West', *The Guardian*, [online] 6 June.

[20] Lim, L. and Bergin, J. (2018) 'Inside China's audacious global propaganda campaign', *The Guardian*, [online] 7 December.

[21] CCP General Office and State Council (2015) 'CCP General Office and State Council General Office Opinions concerning strengthening the construction of new types of think tanks with Chinese characteristics', China Copyright and Media, [online] 21 January.

[22] Xue, L., Xufeng Zhu and Wanqu Han (2018) 'Embracing scientific decision making: the rise of think-tank policies in China', *Pacific Affairs*, 91(1): 52.

[23] Wayt, T. (2019) 'NYU Shanghai quietly added pro-government course at behest of Chinese government', *Vice*, [online] 20 November.

[24] Wintour, P. (2019) 'Alarming Chinese meddling at UK universities exposed in report', *The Guardian*, [online] 5 November.

[25] Hume, T. (2019) 'Pro-Beijing thugs are vandalizing Hong Kong protests in Australia now', *Vice*, [online] 7 August.

[26] AFP (2020) 'China insists Genghis Khan exhibit not use words "Genghis Khan"', *The Guardian*, [online] 14 October.

[27] see Kuo, L. (2018) 'China's anti-spy campaign: cash rewards and warnings about red heads' *The Guardian*, [online] 10 May; RSF (2021) 'China', *Reporters Without Borders*, [online]; Phillips (2017) 'A human rights activist'.

[28] ESPN (2020) 'NBA ends relationship with academy in China', [online] 22 July.

[29] Wintour, P. (2021) 'China sanctions UK businesses, MPS and lawyers in Xinjiang row', *The Guardian*, [online] 26 March.

[30] Graham-Harrison, E. (2021) 'Chinese actor quits as Burberry ambassador as Xinjiang cotton row escalates', *The Guardian*, [online] 26 March.

[31] Lawrence, D. and Patterson, J. (2018) 'FPC Briefing. Rule of law in China: a priority for businesses and Western governments', Foreign Policy Centre, [online] 24 September.

[32] Woo, M.Y.K. (2013) 'Justice', in C. Ogden (ed.) *Handbook of China's Governance and Domestic Politics*, London: Routledge, p 66.

[33] WJP (2020) *China – World Justice Project Rule of Law Index*, World Justice Project, [online].

[34] Chen, G.G. (2017), 'Le droit, c'est moi: Xi Jinping's new rule-by-law approach', Oxford Human Rights Hub, [online] 26 July.

[35] Glavin, T. (2017) 'China is no friend to Canada', *Macleans*, [online] 17 April.

[36] Lawrence and Patterson (2018).

[37] Lawrence and Patterson (2018).

[38] Charvet and Kaczynska-Nay (2008) 331.

[39] Charvet and Kaczynska-Nay (2008) 334.

[40] AI (2020) 'Death penalty in 2019: facts and figures', Amnesty International, [online] 21 April.

[41] WPB (2021) 'Welcome', World Prison Brief, [online].

[42] Fei-Ling Wang (2015) 47.

[43] Kalathil, S. and Boas, T.C. (2003) *Open Networks, Closed Regimes: The Impact of the Internet on Authoritarian Rule*, Carnegie Endowment, p 2.

[44] Mueller, M.L. (2012) 'China and global internet governance: a tiger by the tail', in R. Deibert, J. Palfrey, R. Rohozinski and J. Zittrain (eds) *Access Contested: Security, Identity, and Resistance in Asian Cyberspace*, Cambridge: MIT Press, p 182.

[45] Esarey, A. (2015) 'Winning hearts and minds? Cadres as microbloggers in China', *Journal of Current Chinese Affairs*, 44(2): 69–103.

[46] Thomala, L.L. (2021) 'Number of internet users in China 2008–2020', Statista, [online] 12 August.

[47] King, G., Pan, J. and Roberts, M.E. (2017) 'How the Chinese government fabricates social media posts for strategic distraction, not engaged argument', *American Political Science Review*, 111(3): 494.

[48] Griffiths, J. (2019) *The Great Firewall of China: How to Build and Control an Alternative Version of the Internet*, London: Zed Books, p 10.

[49] Kaiman, J. (2016) 'China cracks down on social media with threat of jail for "online rumours"', *The Guardian*, [online] 10 September.

[50] Luo, Y. (2014) 'The internet and agenda setting in China: the influence of online public opinion on media coverage and government policy', *International Journal of Communication*, 8(1): 1291.

[51] Haas, B. (2018) 'Peppa Pig, subversive symbol of the counterculture, in China video site ban', *The Guardian*, [online] 1 May; Haas, B. and Phillips, T. (2017) 'China cracks down on foreign children's books', *The Guardian*, [online] 13 March; Phillips, T. (2018) 'Ce*sored: China bans letter n (briefly) from internet as Xi Jinping extends grip on power', *The Guardian*, [online] 28 February; Kuo, L. (2018) 'No joke: have China's censors gone too far with ban on humour app?', *The Guardian*, [online] 21 April.

[52] Graham-Harrison, E. and Garside, J. (2019) '"Allow no escapes": leak exposes reality of China's vast prison camp network', *The Guardian*, [online] 24 November.

[53] Zenz quoted in Graham-Harrison and Garside (2019).

[54] quoted in Kuo, L. (2018) 'China claims Muslim detention camps are education centres', *The Guardian*, [online] 14 September.

[55] quoted in Simmons, K. (2019) 'Inside Chinese camps thought to be detaining a million Muslim Uighurs', NBC News, [online] 4 October.

[56] RFA (2017) 'China bans Uighur language in schools in key Xinjiang prefecture', Radio Free Asia, [online] 28 July.

[57] Kuo, L. (2019) 'Revealed: new evidence of China's mission to raze the mosques of Xinjiang', *The Guardian*, [online] 7 May.

[58] HRW (2019) 'China: Xinjiang children separated from families', Human Rights Watch, [online] 15 September.

59 Haas, B. (2017) 'China bans religious names from Muslim babies in Xinjiang', *The Guardian*, [online] 25 April.

60 quoted in Reuters (2017) 'China sets rules on beards, veils to combat extremism in Xinjiang', [online] 30 March.

61 HRW (2017) 'China: minority region collects DNA from millions', Human Rights Watch, [online] 13 December.

62 HRW (2018) 'China: big data fuels crackdown in minority region', Human Rights Watch, [online] 26 February.

63 Parton, C. (2018) 'The fourth weapon', *The Spectator*, [online] 17 November.

64 Zenz quoted in Strittmatter (2019) 193.

65 quoted in Byler, D. (2019) 'China's hi tech war on its Muslim minority', *The Guardian*, [online] 11 April.

66 13th Five Year Plan quoted in Hamilton, G.C. (2015) 'China's social credit score system is doomed to fail', *Financial Times*, [online] 16 November.

67 Byler (2019).

68 Parton (2018).

69 Strittmatter (2019) 173.

70 Strittmatter (2019) 183.

71 Strittmatter (2019) 7.

72 State Council quoted in Hatton, C. (2015) 'China "social credit": Beijing sets up huge system', BBC News, [online] 26 October.

73 Strittmatter (2019) 211.

74 BBC (2019) 'Huawei faces US charges: the short, medium and long story', BBC News, [online] 7 May.

75 National Public Credit Information Centre quoted in BBC (2019) 'Huawei'.

76 Strittmatter (2019) 49.

77 BBC (2019) 'Hong Kong protests: President Xi warns of "bodies smashed"', BBC News, [online] 14 October.

78 Rui Hou (2018) 'The booming industry of Chinese state internet control', openDemocracy, [online] 21 November.

79 With Armenia, Azerbaijan, Ecuador, Germany, Kazakhstan, Kenya, Kyrgyzstan, Malaysia, Pakistan, Rwanda, Singapore, Sri Lanka, Ukraine, the United Arab Emirates, Uzbekistan, Venezuela, Zambia and Zimbabwe.

80 With Angola, Bangladesh, Belarus, Brazil, Cambodia, Egypt, Ethiopia, The Gambia, Georgia, India, Indonesia, Iran, Jordan, Kenya, Lebanon, Libya, Malawi, Morocco, Myanmar, Nigeria, Pakistan, Philippines, Russia, Rwanda, Saudi Arabia, Singapore, South Africa, Sri Lanka, Sudan, Syria, Thailand, United Arab Emirates, Venezuela, Vietnam, Zambia and Zimbabwe.

81 With Angola, Australia, Bahrain, Bangladesh, Belarus, Cambodia, Canada, Cuba, Ecuador, Egypt, Ethiopia, France, Germany, Hungary, India, Iran, Italy, Japan, Kenya, Lebanon, Libya, Malawi, Mexico, Morocco, Myanmar, Nigeria, Pakistan, Rwanda, Saudi Arabia, South Africa, Sri Lanka, Sudan, Tunisia, Uganda, United Kingdom, Venezuela, Zambia and Zimbabwe.

82 Shahbaz, A. (2018) 'Freedom on the net 2018: the rise of digital authoritarianism', Freedom House, [online] October.

83 Owen (2018).

84 Fukuyama (1989).

85 Levin, D. (2019) 'Partisan electoral interventions by the great powers: introducing the PEIG Dataset', *Conflict Management and Peace Science*, 36(1): 88–106.

86 O'Rourke, L.A. (2020) 'The strategic logic of covert regime change: US-backed regime change campaigns during the Cold War', *Security Studies*, 29(1): 92–127.

87 Hedges, C. (2010) *Death of the Liberal Class*, New York: Nation Books.

88 Kaminski, M.E. and Witnov, S. (2014) 'The conforming effect: first amendment implications of surveillance, beyond chilling speech', *University of Richmond Law Review*, 49(2): 465–518.

89 quoted in Morris, R. (2022) '*Flooding the zone*: the Bannon playbook governing British politics', *Byline Times*, [online] 21 March.

90 Cohen, N. (2021) 'Gove and co were once thrilled to be close to Trump. Now see them run', *The Guardian*, [online] 9 January.

91 Yan Xuetong (2018) 'Chinese values versus liberalism: what ideology will shape the international normative order?', *The Chinese Journal of International Politics*, 11(1): 6.

92 Graham-Harrison, E. (2021) 'Beijing cuts Hong Kong's directly elected seats in radical overhaul', *The Guardian*, [online] 30 March.

Chapter 2

1   Wang Jisi and Zhu Feng (2015) 'Conclusion: the United States, China, and world order', in G.J. Ikenberry, Wang Jisi and Zhu Feng (eds) *America, China, and the Struggle for World Order: Ideas, Traditions, Historical Legacies, and Global Visions*, Basingstoke: Palgrave Macmillan, p 373.

2   Wang Yangzhong (1999) 'Chinese values, governance and international relations: historical development and present situation', in Han Sung-Joo (ed.) *Changing Values in Asia – Their Impact on Governance and Development*, Tokyo: Japan Centre for Political Exchange, p 24.

3   Eno, R. (2015) *The Analects of Confucius: An Online Teaching Translation*, Bloomington: Indiana University Press, p vi.

4   Grondona, M. (2000) 'A cultural typology of economic development', in L.E. Harrison and S.P. Huntingdon (eds) *Culture Matters: How Values Shape Human Progress*, New York: Basic Books, 2000), p 39.

5   quoted in Ivanhoe, P.J. and Van Norden, B.W. (eds) (2005) *Readings in Classical Chinese Philosophy*, Indianapolis: Hackett Publishing Company, p 37.

6   Fei-Ling Wang (2015) 'From *Tianxia* to Westphalia: the evolving Chinese conception of sovereignty and world order', in G.J. Ikenberry, Wang Jisi and Zhu Feng (eds) *America, China, and the Struggle for World Order: Ideas, Traditions, Historical Legacies, and Global Visions*, Basingstoke: Palgrave Macmillan, p 44.

[7] Tingyang Zhao (2006) 'Rethinking empire from a Chinese concept of "all-under-heaven (tian-xia)"', *Social Identities*, 12(1): 30.

[8] quoted in Acharya (2014) 2.

[9] Fei-Ling Wang (2015) 57.

[10] Zhao quoted in Acharya (2014) 128 (emphasis added).

[11] De Bary, W.T. (2000) *Asian Values and Human Rights: A Confucian Communitarian Perspective*, Cambridge, MA: Harvard University Press, p 343.

[12] Fei-Ling Wang (2015) 46.

[13] Kang, D.C. (2007) *China Rising: Power, Peace and Order in East Asia*, New York: Columbia University Press, p 41.

[14] Kang (2007) 43.

[15] Acharya (2014) 2.

[16] Kang (2007) 43.

[17] Kang (2007) 29.

[18] Madisson, A. (2003) *The World Economy: Historical Statistics*, Paris: OECD Publishing, p 261.

[19] Kaufman, A.A. (2010) 'The "century of humiliation," then and now: Chinese perceptions of the international order', *Pacific Focus*, 25(1): 5.

[20] Kaufman (2010) 1–33.

[21] Mao Zedong (1949) 'The Chinese people have stood up!', USC US–China Institute, [online] 21 September.

[22] Fei-Ling Wang (2015) 53.

[23] quoted in Callahan, W.A. (2004) 'Remembering the future: Utopia, empire, and harmony in 21st-century international theory', *European Journal of International Relations*, 10(4): 577.

[24] Tingyang Zhao (2006) 30.

[25] Acharya (2014) 46.

[26] Ikenberry (2015) 9.

[27] Johnston, A.I. (1995) 'Thinking about strategic culture', *International Security*, 19(4): 32–64.

[28] Wang Jisi and Zhu Feng (2015) 367.

[29] quoted in Acharya (2014) 47.

[30] Ogden, C. (2019) *A Dictionary of Politics and International Relations in China*, Oxford: Oxford University Press.

[31] Xi Jinping (2012) 'China's new party chief Xi Jinping's speech', BBC News, [online] 15 November.

[32] Xi Jinping (2015) 'Full text of Chinese president's speech on commemoration of 70th anniversary of war victory', Xinhua, [online] 3 September.

[33] Xi Jinping (2018) *The Governance of China*, Shanghai: Shanghai Book Traders.

[34] Callahan, W.A. (2016) 'China's "Asia dream": the Belt Road initiative and the new regional order', *Asian Journal of Comparative Politics*, 1(3): 238.

[35] Xi quoted in Bisley, N. (2017) 'Be in no doubt, Xi Jinping wants to make China great again', *The Guardian*, [online] 18 October.

36 Ogden (2019).

37 Carnegie-Tsinghua (2018) 'What does "great power diplomacy with Chinese characteristics" mean?', Carnegie-Tsinghua Centre for Global Policy, 20 April.

38 Cabestan quoted in ChinaFile (2017) 'Is the Trump era really the Xi era?', *ChinaFile*, [online] 18 February.

39 Carnegie-Tsinghua (2018).

40 see Ogden, C. (with Ioannou, M.) (2020) *Great Power Attributes: A Compendium of Historical Data*, Edinburgh: Fifth Hammer.

41 quoted in Kuo, L. (2020) 'China orders US consulate in Chengdu to close as tensions rise', *The Guardian*, [online] 24 July.

42 both quoted in Kuo (2020) 'China orders'.

Chapter 3

1 *CIA World Factbook* (2021) 'GDP PPP', [online].

2 Kupchan quoted in Acharya (2014) 50.

3 Berger quoted in Callahan, W.A. (2003) 'Beyond cosmopolitanism and nationalism: diasporic Chinese and neo-nationalism in China and Thailand', *International Organisation*, 57(3): 488.

4 see Baumann, C., Hamin, H., Tung, R. and Hoadley, S. (2016) 'Competitiveness and workforce performance: Asia vis-à-vis the "West"', *International Journal of Contemporary Hospitality Management*, 28(10): 2197.

5 see Kwock, B., James, M. and Anthony Shu Chuen, T. (2014) 'The psychology of auditing in China: the need to understand *guanxi* thinking and feelings as applied to contractual disputes', *Journal of Business Studies Quarterly*, 5(3): 10–18.

6 see Firoz, N. and Topchaya, O. (2016) 'East and West: understanding consumer behavior in China, implications and practical applications for international marketing of US-based companies', *Franklin Business & Law Journal*, 4: 67–82.

7 see Jijie Wang, Keil, M., Lih-bin Oh and Yide Shen (2017) 'Impacts of organizational commitment, interpersonal closeness, and Confucian ethics on willingness to report bad news in software projects', *Journal of Systems & Software*, 125: 220.

8 quoted in Wallace, M. (1986) 'Deng Xiaoping interview with Mike Wallace', CBS, [online] 2 September.

9 Xie Tao (2017) 'Chinese foreign policy with Xi Jinping characteristics', Carnegie-Tsinghua Centre for Global Policy, [online] 20 November.

10 quoted in Phillips, T. (2017) '"A huge deal" for China as the era of Xi Jinping Thought begins', *The Guardian*, [online] 19 October.

11 Barnett, A. (2017) *The Lure of Greatness: England's Brexit and America's Trump*, London: Unbound, p 249.

12 quoted in Mason, E.S. and Asher, R.E. (1974) *The World Bank Since Bretton Woods: The Origins, Policies, Operations and Impact of the International Bank for Reconstruction*, Washington, DC: Brookings Institution, p 29.

13 Goddard, C.R., Cronin, P. and Dash, K.C. (2006) *International Political Economy: State-Market Relations in a Changing Global Order*, Basingstoke: Palgrave Macmillan, p 353.

14 Carew, A. (1987) *Labour under the Marshall Plan: The Politics of Productivity and the Marketing of Management Science*, Manchester: Manchester University Press.

15 Ikenberry (2011) 208–9.

16 Hedges (2010) 19–58.

17 Friedman, M. (1951) 'Neo-liberalism and its prospects', *Farmand*, 89–93.

18 Harvey, D. (2005) *A Brief History of Neoliberalism*, Oxford: Oxford University Press, p 22.

19 Flew, T. (2014) 'Six theories of neoliberalism', *Thesis Eleven*, 122(1): 67.

20 Trilateral Commission quoted in De Sousa Santos, B. (2005) 'Beyond neoliberal governance: the World Social Forum as subaltern cosmopolitan politics and legality', in B. de Sousa Santos and C.A. Rodríguez-Garavito (eds) *Law and Globalization from Below – Towards a Cosmopolitan Legality*, Cambridge: Cambridge University Press, pp 29–63.

21 Worth, O. (2015) *Rethinking Hegemony*, London: Palgrave, p 91.

22 Barnett (2017) 197.

23 quoted in Plehwe, D., Walpen, B. and Neunhöffer, G. (eds) (2007) *Neoliberal Hegemony: A Global Critique*, London: Routledge, p 1.

24 Reagan, R. (2004) *Speaking My Mind: Selected Speeches*, New York: Simon & Schuster, p 419.

25 Brown, W. (2015) *Undoing the Demos: Neoliberalism's Stealth Revolution*, New York: Zone Books, p 28.

26 Hedges (2010) 173, 42–3.

27 Van de Graaf, T., Sovacool, B.K., Ghosh, A. and Klare, M.T. (2016) 'States, markets, and institutions: integrating international political economy and global energy politics', in T. Van de Graaf, B.K. Sovacool, A. Ghosh and M.T. Klare (eds) *The Palgrave Handbook of the International Political Economy of Energy*, London: Palgrave Macmillan, pp 3–45.

28 Stiglitz, J.E. (2017) *Globalization and Its Discontents Revisited – Anti-Globalization in the Era of Trump*, London: Penguin Random House, p 149.

29 Guimaraes, B. and Iazdi, O. (2015) 'IMF conditionalities, liquidity provision, and incentives for fiscal adjustment', *International Tax and Public Finance*, 22(5): 705–22.

30 Klein, N. (2007) *The Shock Doctrine: The Rise of Disaster Capitalism*, New York: Henry Holt and Company.

31 Barnett (2017) 316.

32 Barnett (2017) 349.

33 Chomsky, N. (1973) 'One man's view: Noam Chomsky interviewed by an anonymous interviewer', *Business Today*, [online] May.

34 Barnett (2017) 186.

35 Crouch, C. (2004) *Post-Democracy*, Cambridge: Cambridge University Press.

36 Tony Blair quoted in Barnett (2017) 26.

37 Clinton, W.J. (2000) *Public Papers of the Presidents of the United States: William J. Clinton, 2000–2001*, New York: Best Books, p 135.

38 Gordon Brown quoted in Barnett (2017) 26.

39 Wolin quoted in Hedges (2010) 25–6.

40 Hedges (2010) 24.

41 Schwartz, B. (2020) 'Total 2020 election spend to hit nearly $14 billion, more than double 2016's sum', CNBC, [online] 28 October.

42 Schwartz (2020).

43 Barnett (2017) 13.

44 Raiser, M. (2019) 'China's rise fits every developmental model', Brookings, [online] 17 October.

45 Yitao Tao (2017) 'Special economic zones and China's path', in Yiming Yuan (ed.) *Studies on China's Special Economic Zones*, London: Springer, pp 1–13.

46 Deng Xiaoping (1982) *Build Socialism with Chinese Characteristics*, Beijing: Foreign Languages Press.

47 World Bank (2021) 'Open data', [online].

48 World Bank (2021).

49 World Bank (2021).

50 Fang Cai (2015) *Demystifying China's Economy Development*, Heidelberg: Springer, p 61.

51 Wolff, R.C. (2016) *Capitalism's Crisis Deepens*, Chicago: Haymarket Books, p 8.

52 Harmon, G.E. (2021) 'We must reverse drop in US life expectancy that preceded pandemic', AMA, [online] 20 August.

53 Schiavenza, M. (2013) 'China's dominance in manufacturing in one chart', *The Atlantic*, [online] 5 August.

54 Richter, F. (2021) 'China is the world's manufacturing superpower', Statista, [online] 4 May.

55 Desjardins, J. (2018) 'China's staggering demand for commodities', *Visual Capitalist*, [online] 2 March.

56 UNCTAD (2021) 'Database', United Nations Conference on Trade and Development, [online].

57 Sutter, K.M., Schwarzenberg, A.B. and Sutherland, M.D. (2021) 'China's "One Belt, One Road" initiative: economic issues', US Congressional Research Service, [online] 22 January.

58 World Bank (2021).

59 Hedges (2010) 10.

60 quoted in Carpenter, T.G. (2020) 'George H.W. Bush's shameful kowtow to China: a cautionary tale', *The American Conservative*, [online] 27 May.

61 Kaplan, L.F. (2001) 'Trade barrier', *The New Republic*, [online] 9 July.

62 US Census (2021) 'Top trading partners – December 2020', United States Census Bureau, [online].

63 Bell, D.A. (2016) *The China Model: Political Meritocracy and the Limits of Democracy*, Princeton: Princeton University Press, pp 163–4.

64 Harvey (2005) 120.

[65] Tsai, K.S. (2007) *Capitalism Without Democracy: The Private Sector in Contemporary China*, Ithaca: Cornell University Press, p 17.

[66] Fukuyama (1989) 3.

[67] Ramo, J.C. (2004) '*The Beijing Consensus*', Foreign Policy Centre, [online] 18 March.

[68] Suisheng Zhao (2010) 422.

[69] Dirlik, A. (2011) 'The idea of a "Chinese model": a critical discussion', *International Critical Thought*, 1(2): 130.

[70] Pena, D. (2015) 'Comparing the Chinese dream with the American dream', *International Critical Thought*, 5(3): 292–3.

[71] Kennedy, S. (2010) 'The myth of the Beijing Consensus', *Journal of Contemporary China*, 19(65): 468.

[72] Guan Lijie and Ji Yushan (2015) 'From the Beijing consensus to the China model: a suggested strategy for future economic reform', *International Critical Thought*, 5(2): 138.

[73] Feng Zhang (2011) 'The rise of Chinese exceptionalism in international relations', *European Journal of International Relations*, 19(2): 312.

[74] Callahan, W.A. (2015) 'History, tradition and the China dream: socialist modernisation in the world of great harmony', *Journal of Contemporary China*, 24(96): 994.

[75] Suisheng Zhao (2010) 424.

[76] Davies, R. and Davidson, H. (2021) 'The strange case of Alibaba's Jack Ma and his three month vanishing act', *The Guardian*, [online] 23 January.

[77] Wolff (2016).

[78] He Huifeng (2018) 'In a remote corner of China, Beijing is trying to export is model by training foreign officials the Chinese way', *South China Morning Post*, [online] 14 July.

[79] Yun Sun (2016) 'Party political training: China's ideological push in Africa?', Brookings, [online] 5 July.

[80] Textor, C. (2020) 'Total number of foreign students studying in China 2014–18', Statista, [online] 29 April.

[81] Dai Bingguo (2010) 'Adhere to the path of peaceful development', USC US–China Institute, [online] 6 December.

[82] Wasara quoted in Kuo, L. (2017) 'Beijing is cultivating the next generation of African elites by training them in China', Quartz Africa, [online] 14 December.

[83] NDRC (2015) *Vision and Actions on Jointly Building Silk Road Economic Belt and 21st-Century Maritime Silk Road*, Beijing: National Development and Reform Commission.

[84] NDRC (2015).

[85] Callahan (2016).

[86] NDRC (2016) *The 13th Five Year Plan for Economic and Social Development of the PRC (2016–2020)*, Beijing: National Development and Reform Commission.

87 Hong Yu (2017) 'Motivation behind China's "One Belt, One Road" initiatives and establishment of the Asian Infrastructure Investment Bank', *Journal of Contemporary China*, 26(105): 354.

88 Macikenaite, V. (2020) 'China's economic statecraft: the use of economic power in an interdependent world', *Journal of Contemporary East Asia Studies*, 9(2): 117.

89 Fei Gao and Li Li (2019) 'The Belt and Road Initiative under the diplomacy perspective of the Great Power with Chinese characteristics', in Wei Liu and Hui Zhang (eds) *Regional Mutual Benefit and Win-Win under the Double Circulation of Global Value*, Shanghai: Peking University Press, p 110.

90 Nedopil, C. (2021) 'Countries of the Belt and Road Initiative', *IIGF Green BRI Center*, Beijing.

91 Nolan, P. (2017) 'State, market and infrastructure: the new Silk Road', *Croatian International Relations Review*, 23(78): 7–18.

92 Rolland, N. (2019) 'A concise guide to the Belt and Road Initiative', National Bureau of Asian Research, [online] 11 April.

93 Rajah, R., Dayant, D. and Pryke, J. (2019) 'Ocean of debt? Belt and Road and debt diplomacy in the Pacific', Lowy Institute, [online] 21 October.

94 Eisenman, J. and Stewart D.T. (2017) 'China's new Silk Road is getting muddy', *Foreign Policy*, [online] 9 January.

95 Bearak, M. (2019) 'In strategic Djibouti, a microcosm of China's growing foothold in Africa', *The Washington Post*, [online] 29 December.

96 Rajah et al (2019).

97 Marsh, J. (2018) 'How a Hong Kong millionaire's bribery case exposes China's corruption problem in Africa', CNN, [online] 9 February.

98 Laruelle, M. (2018) *China's Belt and Road Initiative and Its Impact in Central Asia*, Washington, DC: George Washington University, p xi.

99 Kärkkäinen, A. (2016) 'Does China have a geoeconomic strategy towards Zimbabwe? The case of the Zimbabwean natural resource sector', *Asia Europe Journal*, 14(2): 185–202.

100 Lawrence and Patterson (2018).

101 Sigmar Gabriel quoted in Chazan, G. (2018) 'Backlash grows over Chinese deals for Germany's corporate jewels', *Financial Times*, [online] 5 March.

102 Ho-Fong Hung (2016) *The China Boom: Why China Will Not Rule the World*, New York: Columbia University Press, p 43.

103 quoted in Rushe, D. and Kuo, L. (2019) 'US designates China as a currency manipulator', *The Guardian*, [online] 5 August.

104 Acharya (2014) 47.

105 quoted in GT (2020) 'China and US not in war for power, US on wrong side of history: Chinese FM during Europe visit', *Global Times*, [online] 31 August.

106 Rolland, N. (2017) *China's Eurasian Century? Political and Strategic Implications of the Belt and Road Initiative*, Seattle: National Bureau of Asian Research.

107 Xie Tao (2017).

Chapter 4

1 Lanteigne, M. (2005) *China and International Institutions*, London: Routledge, p 5.

2 Shin-wha Lee (2011) 'The theory and reality of soft power: practical approaches in East Asia', in J. Melissen (ed.) *Public Diplomacy and Soft Power in East Asia*, New York: Palgrave Macmillan, p 11.

3 Nye, J.S. (1990) 'Soft power', *Foreign Policy*, 80: 166.

4 Dig Mandarin (2021) 'Confucius Institutes around the world', [online] 22 February.

5 Confucius (2014) (translated by Legge, J.) *The Analects of Confucius*, Adelaide: University of Adelaide.

6 Lien, D., Oh, C.H. and Selmier, W.T. (2012) 'Confucius Institute effects on China's trade and FDI: isn't it delightful when folks afar study Hanyu?', *International Review of Economics & Finance*, 21(1): 147.

7 Ding, S. and Saunders, R. (2006) 'Talking up China: an analysis of China's rising cultural power and global promotion of the Chinese language', *East Asia*, 23(2): 3.

8 Global Times quoted in Dettmer, J. (2020) 'China's "wolf warrior" diplomacy prompts international backlash', *Voice of America*, [online] 6 May.

9 Gui quoted in Dettmer (2020).

10 Armijo, L. (2007) 'The BRIC countries as an analytical category: mirage or insight?', *Asian Perspective*, 31(4): 35.

11 Ikenberry (2011) 213.

12 Lake, D.A. (2009) *Hierarchy in International Relations*, Ithaca: Cornell University Press, p 182.

13 Hanlon, J. (2012) 'Governance as "kicking away the ladder"', *New Political Economy*, 17(5): 691–8.

14 Ikenberry (2011) 185.

15 UNC (2021) 'United Nations Charter', [online].

16 R2P (2021) 'Right to Protect and the UN', United Nations, [online].

17 NATO (1949) 'The North Atlantic Treaty', North Atlantic Treaty Organization, [online].

18 NATO (2021) 'Operations and missions: past and present', North Atlantic Treaty Organization, [online] 23 August.

19 quoted in MacAskill, E. and Borger, J. (2004) 'Iraq war was illegal and breached UN charter, says Annan', *The Guardian*, [online] 16 September.

20 Esfandiari, S. (2019) 'The United Nations warned that it may not be able to pay its staff on time because the US owes it $1 billion', Business Insider, [online] 10 October.

21 UNPK (2021) 'Troop and police contributors', United Nations Peacekeeping, [online].

22 Barnett, A. (2021) 'The end of closed democracy?', openDemocracy, [online] 20 March.

23 Ikenberry (2011) 331.

24 Ikenberry (2011) 11.

25 Kent, A. (2013) 'China's participation in international organisations', in Yongjin Zhang and G. Austin (eds) *Power and Responsibility in Chinese Foreign Policy*, Canberra: Australian National University Press, p 133.

26 Scott, J. and Wilkinson, R. (2011) 'China and the WTO', Indiana University Research Center for Chinese Politics and Business Working Paper, 5: 11.

27 Ogden, C. (2017) *China & India: Asia's Emergent Great Powers*, Cambridge: Polity, p 136.

28 Acharya (2014) 108.

29 Ikenberry (2011) 336.

30 Ikenberry (2011) 357.

31 Shambaugh, D.L. (2013) *China Goes Global: The Partial Power*, Oxford: Oxford University Press.

32 Buzan, B. (2018) 'China's rise in English school perspective', *International Relations of the Asia-Pacific*, 18(3): 456.

33 Mencius quoted in Acharya (2014) 75.

34 BRIC (2010) 'BRIC Summit Joint Statement (Brasilia, Brazil)', BRICS, [online] April.

35 Suzuki, S. (2015) 'Will the AIIB Trigger Off a New Round of Rivalry in Economic Diplomacy Between China and Japan?', CSGR Working Paper No. 279/15, Coventry: Centre for the Study of Globalisation and Regionalisation, p 5.

36 quoted in Callaghan, M. and Hubbard, P. (2016) 'The Asian Infrastructure Investment Bank: multilateralism on the Silk Road', *China Economic Journal*, 9(2): 125.

37 quoted in Ming Wan (2016) *The Asian Infrastructure Investment Bank: The Construction of Power and the Struggle for the East Asian International Order*, New York: Palgrave Macmillan, p 63.

38 Murphy, C. (2005) *Global Institutions, Marginalization, and Development*, New York: Routledge, p 135.

39 quoted in AIIB (2016) 'President's Opening Statement 2016 Annual Meeting of the Board of Governors Asian Infrastructure Investment Bank', Asian Infrastructure Investment Bank, [online] 25 June.

40 Xi quoted in Xinhua (2016) 'Full text of Chinese President Xi Jinping's address at AIIB inauguration ceremony', [online] 16 January.

41 Horta, K. (2019) *The Asian Infrastructure Investment Bank (AIIB): A Multilateral Bank where China Sets the Rules*, Heinrich Böll Stiftung Publication Series on Democracy, 52: 35.

42 ADB (2021) 'Who we are', Asian Development Bank, [online].

43 AIIB (2021) 'Frequently asked questions', Asian Infrastructure Investment Bank, [online].

44 quoted in AIIB (2016).

45 AIIB (2021) 'Members of bank', Asian Infrastructure Investment Bank, [online].

46 ADB (2021).

47 Xiao Ren (2016) 'China as an institution-builder: the case of the AIIB', *The Pacific Review*, 29(3): 435–6.

48 Peng Zhongzhou and Sow Keat Tok (2016) 'The AIIB and China's normative power in international financial governance structure', *Chinese Political Science Review*, 1(4): 740.

49 Shearman, P. (2014) *Power Transition and International Order in Asia*, London: Routledge, p 21.

50 Eswar Prasad, former head of the China division at the IMF, quoted in Perlez, J. (2015) 'China creates a World Bank of Its own, and the US balks', *The New York Times*, 4 December.

51 Mastanduno, M. (2012) 'The richness of the contributions of Robert G. Gilpin', in W.F. Danspeckgruber (ed.) *Robert Gilpin and International Relations: Reflections*, Princeton: Princeton University Press, p 16.

52 Hongying Wang (2015) 'The Asian Infrastructure Investment Bank: a new Bretton Woods moment? A total Chinese triumph?', *Centre for International Governance Innovation Policy Brief*, 59, p 1.

53 Raman, K.R. (2009) 'Asian Development Bank, policy conditionalities and social democratic governance: Kerala model under pressure?', *Review of International Political Economy*, 16(2): 286.

54 ADB (2021).

55 Breslin, S. (2018) 'Global reordering and China's rise: adoption, adaptation and reform', *The International Spectator*, 53(1): 67.

56 quoted in Prestowitz, C. (2015) 'Our incoherent China policy', *The American Prospect*, 21 September.

57 Beeson, M. and Jinghan Zeng (2018) 'The BRICS and global governance: China's contradictory role', *Third World Quarterly*, 39(10): 1–2

58 quoted in Ministry of Foreign Affairs (2015) 'Xi Jinping holds talks with representatives of Chinese and foreign entrepreneurs attending BFA Annual Conference', Ministry of Foreign Affairs of the People's Republic of China, [online] 29 March.

59 SCO (2021) 'About SCO', Shanghai Cooperation Organisation, [online].

60 State Council quoted in Gill, B. (2007) *Rising Star: China's New Security Diplomacy*, Washington, DC: Brookings Institution Press, p 5.

61 SCO (2021).

62 Pan Guang (2007) 'A Chinese perspective on the Shanghai Cooperation Organization', in A.J.K. Bailes, P. Dunay, Pan Guang and M. Troitskiy (eds) *The Shanghai Cooperation Organization*, Stockholm: Stockholm International Peace Research Institute, p 46.

63 Cohen quoted in Aris, S. (2011) *Eurasian Regionalism: The Shanghai Cooperation Organisation*, London: Palgrave Macmillan, p 6.

64 Jingdong Yuan (2010) 'China's role in establishing and building the Shanghai Cooperation Organization (SCO)', *Journal of Contemporary China*, 19(67): 862.

65 Bailes, A. and Pan Dunay (2007) 'The Shanghai Cooperation Organization as a regional security institution', in A.J.K. Bailes, P. Dunay, Pan Guang

and M. Troitskiy (eds) *The Shanghai Cooperation Organization*, Stockholm: Stockholm International Peace Research Institute, p 6.

66 Ambrosio, T. (2008) 'Catching the "Shanghai spirit": how the Shanghai Cooperation Organization promotes authoritarian norms in Central Asia', *Europe-Asia Studies*, 60(8): 1322.

67 SCO (2021).

68 Ogden (2017).

69 Wintour, P. (2018) 'China starts to assert its worldview at UN as influence grows', *The Guardian*, [online] 24 September.

70 Lee, P.K., Chan, G. and Chan, L. (2010) 'China in Darfur: humanitarian rule-maker or rule-taker?', *Review of International Studies*, 38(2): 21.

71 ICISS (2001) *Research and Consultations: Supplementary Volume to The Responsibility to Protect*, Ottawa: International Development Research Centre.

72 Zheng Chen (2016) 'China and the responsibility to protect', *Journal of Contemporary China*, 25(101): 692.

73 Fung, C. (2019) *China and Intervention at the UN Security Council: Reconciling Status*, Oxford: Oxford University Press.

74 Foot, R. (2020) *China, the UN, and Human Protection: Beliefs, Power, Image*, Oxford: Oxford University Press, pp 163–4.

75 Garwood-Gowers, A. (2016) 'China's "responsible protection" concept: reinterpreting the Responsibility to Protect (R2P) and military intervention for humanitarian purposes', *Asian Journal of International Law*, 6(1): 92.

76 Piccone quoted in Wintour (2018).

77 Wintour (2018).

78 Piccone, T. (2018) 'China's long game on human rights at the United Nations', Brookings Institution, [online] September 2018.

79 Charbonneau quoted in Borger, J. (2018) 'China and Russia accused of waging war on human rights at the UN', *The Guardian*, [online] 27 March.

80 Gowan quoted in Borger (2018).

81 Lina Liu (2021) 'Beyond the status quo and revisionism: an analysis of the role of China and the approaches of China's Belt and Road Initiative (BRI) to the global order', *Asian Journal of Political Science*, 29(1): 88, emphases in original.

82 Balabán, M. (2017) 'From the end of history to the post-American world: global politics, economy and security at the turn of the epoch', *Central European Journal of International & Security Studies*, 11(3): 9.

83 Berzina, K., Kovalcikova, N., Salvo, D. and Soula, E. (2019) *European Policy Blueprint for Countering Authoritarian Interference in Democracies*, Washington, DC: German Marshall Fund of the United States, p 5.

84 Kim, S.W., Fidler, D.P. and Ganguly, S. (2009) 'Eastphalia rising? Asian influence and the fate of human security', *World Policy Journal*, 26(2): 53.

Chapter 5

1 Kang, D.C. (2005) 'Hierarchy in Asian international relations: 1300–1900', *Asian Security*, 1(1): 61.

2   AIIB (2021).
3   Nedopil (2021).
4   Womack, B. (2013) 'Beyond win-win – rethinking China's international relationship in an era of economic uncertainty', *International Affairs*, 89(4): 918.
5   WTO (2021) 'Data', World Trade Organization, [online].
6   Ames, R.T. and Hershock, P.D. (2018) *Confucianisms for a Changing World Cultural Order*, Honolulu: University of Hawaii Press, p i.
7   Kreuzer, P. (2016) 'A comparison of Malaysian and Philippine responses to China in the South China Sea', *Chinese Journal of International Politics*, 9(3): 239.
8   Jacques, M. (2009) *When China Rules the World: The End of the Western World and the Birth of a New Global Order*, New York: Penguin, p 381.
9   Dalton, R.J. and Ong, N.T. (2005) 'Authority orientations and democratic attitudes: a test of the "Asian values" hypothesis', *Japanese Journal of Political Science*, 6(2): 5.
10 Rozman, G. (1991) 'The East Asian region in comparative perspective', in G. Rozman (ed.) *The East Asian Region: Confucian Heritage and Its Modern Adaptation*, Princeton: Princeton University Press, p 5.
11 Hobson, C. (2009) 'The limits of liberal-democracy promotion', *Alternatives: Global, Local, Political*, 34(4): 387.
12 Freedom House (2021) 'Global freedom status', [online].
13 Lee Kuan Yew (1992) 'Speech by Mr Lee Kuan Yew, senior minister of Singapore', *Asahi Forum*, 20 November.
14 Jacques (2009) 375.
15 Yixiong Huang (2013) 'The return of Confucianism in China: legitimacy and the rule of the Communist Party of China', *Fudan Journal of the Humanities & Social Sciences*, 6(1): 33.
16 Moore, G.J. (2014) 'The power of "sacred commitments": Chinese interests in Taiwan', *Foreign Policy Analysis*, 12(2): 22.
17 Brown, M.E. (2000) *The Rise of China*, Boston: MIT Press, p 42.
18 Beeson, M. and Higgott, R. (2005) 'Hegemony, institutionalism and US foreign policy: theory and practice in comparative historical perspective', *Third World Quarterly*, 26(7): 1175.
19 Including in Mexico (1845, 1914), Honduras (1903), Cuba (1906, 1961), Nicaragua (1912, 1927, 1981), Haiti (1915, 1994), Germany (1917), Russia (1918), Iran (1953, 2007, 2020), Indonesia (1957), Syria (1957, 2011), Lebanon (1958), Congo (1960, 1965), Laos (1963), Brazil (1964), Chile (1964, 1973), Dominican Republic (1965), Cambodia (1969), Bolivia (1971), Angola (1975), Afghanistan (1979, 2001), El Salvador (1980), Chad (1981), Poland (1982), Grenada (1983), Panama (1989), Bosnia and Herzegovina (1992), Iraq (1996, 1998, 2003), Yugoslavia (1999), the Palestinian Territories (2006), Libya (2011), Yemen (2015) and Venezuela (2017).
20 Herring, G. (2011) *From Colony to Superpower: US Foreign Relations since 1776*, New York: Oxford University Press, p 100.

21 POTUS (1823) 'Presidential Speeches: December 2, 1823: Seventh Annual Message (Monroe Doctrine)', Miller Center, University of Virginia, [online] 2 December.

22 POTUS (1947) 'Presidential Speeches: March 12, 1947: Truman Doctrine', Miller Center, University of Virginia, [online] 12 March.

23 USDOS (1950) 'National Security Council Report, NSC 68: United States Objectives and Programs for National Security', Washington DC: USDOS.

24 POTUS (1957) 'Presidential Speeches: January 5, 1957 – Eisenhower Doctrine', Miller Center, University of Virginia, [online] 5 January.

25 White House (2002) *The National Security Strategy of the United States of America*, Washington, DC: Office of the President of the United States, p i.

26 SIPRI (2021) 'Military expenditure', Stockholm International Peace Research Institute, [online].

27 SIPRI (2021) 'Military expenditure'.

28 SIPRI (2021) 'Military expenditure'.

29 SIPRI (2021) 'Military expenditure'.

30 SIPRI (2021) 'Military expenditure'.

31 DMDC (2021) 'Number of military and DoD Appropriated Fund (APF) civilian personnel permanently assigned by duty location and service/component', *Defense Manpower Data Center*, 31 March.

32 Lucas, J.A. (2007) 'Deaths in other nations since WWII due to US interventions', Countercurrents, [online] 24 April.

33 Dujmović, N. (2020) 'Review Essay: Covert action to promote democracy in China during the Cold War', *Studies in Intelligence*, 64(4): 31.

34 Mearsheimer (2001) 361–2.

35 Clinton, H.R. (2011) 'America's Pacific century', *US Department of State through Foreign Policy Magazine*, 11 October.

36 Campbell, K. and Ratner, E. (2018) 'The China reckoning: how Beijing defied American expectations', *Foreign Affairs*, 97(2): 61.

37 SIPRI (2021) 'Arms transfers', Stockholm International Peace Research Institute, [online].

38 SIPRI (2021) 'Arms transfers'.

39 SIPRI (2021) 'Arms transfers'.

40 SIPRI (2021) 'Arms transfers'.

41 Kang (2007) 36.

42 quoted in Beeson, M. and Fujian Li (2012) 'Charmed or alarmed? Reading China's regional relations', *Journal of Contemporary China*, 21(73): 37.

43 Yong Deng and Fei-Ling Wang (eds) (2005) *China Rising: Power and Motivation in Chinese Foreign Policy*, Lanham: Rowman and Littlefield, p viii.

44 Hoo Tiang Boon (2017) 'Hardening the hard, softening the soft: assertiveness and China's regional strategy', *Journal of Strategic Studies*, 40(5): 639.

45 quoted in Phillips, T. (2017) ' Xi Jinping tests eyelids – and bladders – with three-and-a-half-hour speech', *The Guardian*, [online] 18 October.

[46] Tseng, K.H-Y. (2017) *Rethinking South China Sea Disputes: The Untold Dimensions and Great Expectations*, London: Routledge.

[47] Lim, Y.-H. (2014) *China's Naval Power: An Offensive Realist Approach*, Farnham: Ashgate, p 4.

[48] Friedburg, A.L. (2005) 'The future of US–China relations: is conflict inevitable?', *International Security*, 30(2): 7–45.

[49] ICG (2012) 'Stirring up the South China Sea', Asia Report no. 223, International Crisis Group, 23 April.

[50] Gao Zhi Guo and Jia Bing Bing (2013) 'The nine-dash line in the South China Sea: history, status, and implications', *The American Journal of International Law*, 107(1): 100.

[51] UNCLOS (1982) *United Nations Convention on the Law of the Sea*, United Nations.

[52] DOC (2002) 'Declaration on the Conduct of Parties in the South China Sea', The Governments of the Member States of ASEAN and the Government of the People's Republic of China, 4 November.

[53] Shambaugh, D. (2005) 'China engages Asia: reshaping the regional order', *International Security*, 29(3): 75.

[54] The Hague (2016) *The South China Sea Arbitration*, Permanent Court of Arbitration, The Hague, 12 July.

[55] DWP (2019) 'Full text of 2019 Defense White Paper: "China's National Defense in the New Era"', State Council Information Office of the People's Republic of China, [online] 24 July.

[56] Pradt, T. (2016) *China's New Foreign Policy: Military Modernisation, Multilateralism and the China Threat*, Basingstoke: Palgrave Macmillan, pp 137–9.

[57] Pradt (2016) 137–9.

[58] Harris, H.B. (2015) 'US perspectives on coalition maritime operations in the Indo-Pacific', speech by Commander, US Pacific Fleet, Australian Strategic Policy Institute conference dinner, Canberra, [online] 31 March.

[59] Vuving, A.L. (2017) 'How America can take control in the South China Sea', *Foreign Policy*, 14 February.

[60] ChinaPower (2018) 'How much trade transits the South China Sea?', [online].

[61] ChinaPower (2017) 'Are maritime law enforcement forces destabilizing Asia?', [online].

[62] ChinaPower (2018).

[63] USEIA (2013) *South China Sea*, Washington, DC: US Energy Information Administration.

[64] Akos, K. and Peragovics, T. (2018) 'Overcoming the poverty of Western historical imagination: alternative analogies for making sense of the South China Sea conflict', *European Journal of International Relations*, 25(2): 372–6.

[65] quoted in Mollman, S. (2018) '"Ignore the missiles": Duterte says China's South China Sea militarization is no problem', *Quartz*, [online] 20 February.

[66] Jacques (2009) 347.

67 Mollman (2018).

68 quoted in Davidson, H. (2021) 'Xi Jinping warns China won't be bullied in speech marking 100-year anniversary of CCP', *The Guardian*, [online] 1 July.

69 IOCSS (2015) *China's Military Strategy 2015*, Beijing: The Information Office of China's State Council of the People's Republic of China.

70 DWP (1998) *China Defence White Paper 1998*, Beijing: The Information Office of the State Council of the PRC.

71 quoted in BBC (2019) 'Hong Kong protests'.

72 Hua quoted in O'Connor, T. (2019) 'Which countries still recognise Taiwan?', *Newsweek*, [online] 20 September.

73 quoted in Bush, R.C. (2017) 'What Xi Jinping said about Taiwan at the 19th Party Congress', Brookings, [online] 19 October.

74 Xi Jinping (2017) 'Secure a decisive victory in building a moderately prosperous society in all respects and strive for the great success of socialism with Chinese characteristics for a new era', *China Daily*, [online] 18 October.

75 O'Connor (2019).

76 MOFA (2015) 'Japanese territory: Senkaku Islands information', Ministry of Foreign Affairs of Japan, [online] 6 March.

77 Brady, A.-M. (2020) 'New Zealand needs to show it is serious about addressing Chinese interference', *The Guardian*, [online] 24 January.

78 Taylor, J. (2020) 'China's Belt and Road Initiative: what it is and why is Victoria under fire for its involvement?', *The Guardian*, [online] 25 May.

Chapter 6

1 Giuffrida, A., Safi, M. and Kalia, A. (2018) 'The populist social media playbook: the battle for Facebook, Twitter and Instagram', *The Guardian*, [online] 17 December.

2 ATV (2021) *Autocratization Turns Viral*, University of Gothenberg, V-Dem Institute.

3 Keyu quoted in Wintour, P. (2020) 'US versus China: is this the start of a new Cold War?', *The Guardian*, [online] 22 June.

4 Wintour (2020) 'US versus China'.

5 Olander quoted in Olewe, D. (2021) 'Why African countries back China on human rights', BBC News, [online] 2 May.

6 quoted in Adams, T. (2021) 'Ai Weiwei on colonialism and statues, Churchill, China and Covid', *The Guardian*, [online] 29 May.

7 US Census (2021).

8 Elagina, D. (2021) 'Major trade partners of Russia, 2020', Statista, [online] 17 August.

9 BBC (2021) 'China regains slot as India's top trade partner despite tensions', BBC News, [online] 23 February.

10 quoted in Barber, L. and Foy, H. (2019) 'Vladimir Putin says liberalism has "become obsolete"', *Financial Times*, [online] 28 June.

11 Schedler (2002).

12. Safi, M. (2020) 'George Floyd protests: reporters targeted by police and crowds', *The Guardian*, [online] 31 May.

13. Waterson, J. (2019) 'US classed as "problematic place" for journalists to work', *The Guardian*, [online] 18 April.

14. Kaye quoted in Safi (2020).

15. Wardle, executive director of First Draft, quoted in Beckett, L. (2021) 'Facts won't fix this: experts on how to fight America's disinformation crisis', *The Guardian*, [online] 1 January.

16. *Harpers* (2020) 'A letter on justice and open debate', *Harpers*, [online] 7 July.

17. Dhillon, A. (2019) 'Indian PM lampooned for "manufactured" interview', *The Guardian*, [online] 5 January.

18. ATV (2021).

19. Graham-Harrison, E. et al (2021) 'The world in 2021 – how global politics will change this year', *The Guardian*, [online] 3 January.

20. BBC (2017) 'Gauri Lankesh: India journalist shot dead in Bangalore', BBC News, [online] 6 September.

21. Varadarajan quoted in Ellis-Petersen, H. (2020) 'India's COVID-19 app fuels worries over authoritarian surveillance', *The Guardian*, [online] 4 May.

22. Graham-Harrison et al (2021).

23. Graham-Harrison et al (2021).

24. WikiR (2021) 'List of journalists killed in Russia', Wikipedia, [online].

25. quoted in Harding, L. (2008) '"To be a journalist in Russia is suicide"', *The Guardian*, [online] 24 November.

26. quoted in Phillips, T. (2018) '"Maybe we'll give that a shot": Donald Trump praises Xi Jinping's power grab', *The Guardian*, [online] 4 March.

27. Cillizza, C. and Williams, B. (2019) '15 times Donald Trump praised authoritarian leaders', CNN, [online] 2 July.

28. Snyder, T. (2018) 'Vladimir Putin's politics of eternity', *The Guardian*, [online] 16 March.

29. Mukhopadhyay quoted in Doshi, V. and Ratcliffe, R. (2019) 'India's strongman PM: Modi to appear on Bear Grylls' Man vs wild', *The Guardian*, [online] 29 July.

30. LCCHR (2021) 'Trump administration civil and human rights rollbacks', The Leadership Conference on Civil and Human Rights, [online].

31. Ocasio-Cortez quoted in Kelly, C. (2019) 'Ocasio-Cortez compares migrant detention facilities to concentration camps', CNN, [online] 18 June.

32. Stanton quoted in Werleman, C.J. (2020) '"Love jihad" another step towards India's Nazification', *Byline Times*, [online] 23 November.

33. AI (2006) 'Russian Federation: violent racism out of control', Amnesty International, [online] 3 May.

34. Schifeling quoted in Pilkington, E. (2020) 'America's flawed democracy: the five key areas where it is failing', *The Guardian*, [online] 16 November.

35. Repucci quoted in Levine, S. (2021) 'US sinks to new low in ranking of world's democracies', *The Guardian*, [online] 24 March.

36 Smith, D. (2021) '"Have you no shame?" Biden decries Republican attacks on voting rights', *The Guardian*, [online] 13 July.

37 USPLT (2022) 'US protest law tracker', International Center for Not-For-Profit Law, [online].

38 Biden quoted in Thomas, K. and Siddiqui, S. (2021) 'Biden says rioters who stormed Capitol were domestic terrorists', *Wall Street Journal*, [online] 7 January.

39 see II (2022) Insurrection Index, [online].

40 Haass quoted in Browne, A. (2021) 'Trump's last days raise comparisons with Mao', *Bloomberg*, [online] 9 January.

41 Rodrigues, J., Chaudhary, A. and Dormido, H. (2019) 'A murky flood of money pours into world's largest election', *Bloomberg*, [online] 16 March.

42 Weiden, D.L. (2011) 'Judicial politicization, ideology, and activism at the high courts of the United States, Canada, and Australia', *Political Research Quarterly*, 64(2): 335–47.

43 *Ballotpedia* (2021) 'Federal judges appointed by Donald Trump', [online].

44 Long, E. (2020) 'Where the politicisation of the US supreme court could lead', *The Conversation*, [online] 29 October.

45 Libération quoted in Henley, J. (2020) '"A pretence of justice": the global press on Trump's acquittal', *The Guardian*, [online] 6 February.

46 Die Zeit quoted in Henley (2020).

47 Toobin quoted in Borger, J. (2017) '"Terrifying, Nixonian": Comey's firing takes democracy to new dark territory', *The Guardian*, [online] 10 May.

48 McCarthy, T. (2020) 'Baby faced assassin: the 29 year old at the heart of Trump's "deep state" purge', *The Guardian*, [online] 26 February.

49 quoted in Gabbatt, A. (2017) 'Anti-protest bills would "attack right to speak out" under Trump', *The Guardian*, [online] 8 May.

50 Ogden (2017) 49–50.

51 Mehta, P.B. (2020) 'SC was never perfect but the signs are that it is slipping into judicial barbarism', *The Indian Express*, [online] 18 November.

52 ATV (2021).

53 ATV (2021).

54 Ellis-Petersen (2020).

55 ATV (2021).

56 Sakwa, R. (2011) *The Crisis of Russian Democracy: The Dual State, Factionalism and the Medvedev Succession*, Cambridge: Cambridge University Press, p 1.

57 Luttwak, E.N. (1990) 'From geopolitics to geo-economics: logic of conflict, grammar of commerce', *The National Interest*, 20: 19.

58 Barnett (2021).

59 AI (2019) 'Surveillance giants: How the business model of Google and Facebook threatens human rights', Amnesty International, [online] 21 November.

60 Wong, J.C. (2021) 'How Facebook let fake engagement distort global politics: a whistle-blower's account', *The Guardian*, [online] 12 April.

61 Wong, J.C. and Ellis-Petersen, H. (2021) 'Facebook planned to remove fake accounts in India – until it realized a BJP politician was involved', *The Guardian*, [online] 15 April.

62 Shahbaz (2018).

63 Rui Hou (2018).

64 Woolley, S.C. and Howard, P.N. (2019) 'Introduction: computational propaganda worldwide', in S.C. Woolley and P.N. Howard (eds) *Computational Propaganda: Political Parties, Politicians and Political Manipulation on Social Media*, Oxford: Oxford University Press, p 4.

65 Jukes, P. (2019) 'Brexit, Trump, Russia scandal', *Byline Times*, [online] 18 February.

66 Tucker, E. and Jalonick, M.C. (2020) 'Senate panel finds Russia interfered in 2016 election', PBS, [online] 18 August.

67 AI (2019).

68 O'Neil, C. (2016) *Weapons of Math Destruction: How Big Data Increases Inequality and Threatens Democracy*, London: Penguin.

69 Baltrusaitis, J. (2020) 'Top 10 countries and cities by numbers of CCTV cameras', Precise Security, [online] 4 December.

70 Access Now (2021) 'Internet shutdowns report: shattered dreams and lost opportunities – a year in the fight to #KeepItOn', [online] 3 March.

71 Logsdon, K.R. (2008) 'Who knows you are reading this – United States' domestic electronic surveillance in a post-9/11 world', *University of Illinois Journal of Law, Technology & Policy*, 2: 409–38.

72 NPR (2006) 'CONINTELPRO and the history of domestic spying', [online] 18 January.

73 Chang, N. (2011) *Silencing Political Dissent: How Post-September 11 Anti-Terrorism Measures Threaten Our Civil Liberties*, New York: Seven Stories Press, pp 47–8.

74 American Civil Liberties Union (2007) ACLU Fact Sheet on the 'Police America Act', [online].

75 Kadidal, S. (2014) 'NSA surveillance: the implications for civil liberties', *I/S: A Journal of Law and Policy for the Information Society*, 10(2): 435–6.

76 Saito, N.T. (2002) 'Whose liberty? Whose security? The USA PATRIOT Act in the context of COINTELPRO and the unlawful repression of political dissent', *Oregon Law Review*, 81(4): 1051–132.

77 Chang, N. (2001) 'The USA Patriot Act: what's so patriotic about trampling on the Bill of Rights', *Guild Practitioner*, 145.

78 see Kadidal (2014) 443–5.

79 Bradbury, S.G. (2013) 'Understanding the NSA programs: bulk acquisition of telephone metadata under Section 215 and foreign-targeted collection under Section 702', Research Paper, Washington, DC: Lawfare Research Paper Series, p 3.

80 Kadidal (2014) 446.

81 Greenwald, G. and MacAskill, E. (2013) 'NSA Prism Program taps in to user data of Apple, Google and others', *The Guardian*, [online] 6 June.

82 CNN (2005) 'Cheney: Bush has right to authorize secret surveillance', [online] 20 December.

83 Dorling, P. (2013) 'Snowden reveals Australia's links to US spy web', *Sydney Morning Herald*, [online] 8 July.

84 GCHQ lawyers quoted in MacAskill, E., Borger, J., Hopkins, N. and Davies, N. (2013) 'GCHQ taps fibre-optic cables for secret access to world's communications', *The Guardian*, [online] 21 June.

85 quoted in Borger, J. (2020) 'CIA controlled global encryption company for decades, says report', *The Guardian*, [online] 11 February.

86 Borger (2020).

87 quoted in Davies, N. (2009) *Flat Earth News*, London: Vintage, p 225.

88 BBC (2019) 'Huawei'.

89 Feldstein, S. (2019) 'The global expansion of AI surveillance', Carnegie Endowment for International Peace, [online] 17 September.

90 Ahmed, N. (2019) 'Smart cities and automated racism: how IBM designed China's surveillance regime', *Byline Times*, [online] 24 May.

91 Davidson, H. and Kuo, L. (2020) 'Zoom admits cutting off activists' accounts in obedience to China', *The Guardian*, [online] 12 June.

92 Tang, R. (2018) 'Google to seek return to China with a censored search engine; Reuters', ABC, [online] 3 August.

93 Feldstein (2019).

94 Palfrey, J. (2020) 'The ever-increasing surveillance state', *Georgetown Journal of International Affairs*, [online] 2 March.

95 Hern, A. (2020) 'What is facial recognition and how to police use it?', *The Guardian*, [online] 24 January.

96 Duffy, N. (2015) 'Internet freedom in Vladimir Putin's Russia: the noose tightens', American Enterprise Institute, 12 January; Sodatov, A. (2016) 'The taming of the internet', *Russian Politics & Law*, 53 (5–6): 63–83.

97 Duffy (2015).

98 Duffy (2015).

99 HRW (2020) 'Russia: growing internet isolation, control, censorship', Human Rights Watch, [online] 18 June.

100 Maréchal, N. (2017) 'Networked authoritarianism and the geopolitics of information: understanding Russian internet policy', *Media and Communication*, 5(1): 29.

101 Pallin, C.V. (2017) 'Internet control through ownership: the case of Russia', *Post-Soviet Affairs*, 33(1): 16–33.

102 Deibert, R. and Rohozinski, R. (2010) 'Control and subversion in Russian Cyberspace', in R. Deibert, J. Palfrey, R. Rohozinski and J. Zittrain (eds) *Access Controlled: The Shaping of Power, Rights, and Rule in Cyberspace*, Cambridge, MA: MIT Press, p 15.

103 HRW (2020).

104 Best, S. (2019) 'Russia will disconnect from the internet tomorrow to test cyber-war defences', *The Mirror*, [online] 31 October.

105 Subramanian, R. (2020) 'Historical consciousness of cyber security in India', *IEEE Annals of the History of Computing*, 42(4): 71–93.

[106] Chandran, M. (2010). 'The democratisation of censorship: books and the Indian public', *Economic and Political Weekly*, 45(40): 27–31.

[107] Chacko, P. (2018) 'The right turn in India: authoritarianism, populism and neoliberalisation', *Journal of Contemporary Asia*, 48(4): 541–65.

[108] HRW (2021) 'India: tech firms should uphold privacy, free speech', Human Rights Watch, [online] 11 March.

[109] Arun, C. (2014) 'Paper-thin safeguards and mass surveillance in India', *National Law School of India Review*, 26(2): 105–14.

[110] Bhardwaj, P. and Kumar, A. (2014) 'Comparing two inchoate conceptions: balancing privacy and security by e-surveillance laws in India', *National Law University Delhi Student Law Journal*, 3(1): 14.

[111] Litton, A. (2015) 'The state of surveillance in India: the Central Monitoring System's chilling effect on self-expression', *Washington University Global Studies Law Review*, 14(4): 821.

[112] Litton (2015) 820.

[113] Arun, P. (2017) 'Uncertainty and insecurity in privacyless India: a despotic push towards digitalisation', *Surveillance & Society*, 15(3/4): 462.

[114] G Ed (2020) 'The Guardian view on Trump tracking phones: it could happen here', *The Guardian*, [online] 9 March.

[115] Khosla, M. (2019) 'India's founding values are threatened by sinister new forms of oppression', *The Guardian*, [online] 28 December.

[116] Khosla (2019).

[117] quoted in Ellis-Petersen (2020).

[118] Wiki (2021) 'Social credit system', Wikipedia, [online].

[119] Ni, V. (2021) 'China denounces US Senate's $250 billion move to boost tech and manufacturing', *The Guardian*, [online] 9 June.

[120] Doshi, R., de la Bruyère, E., Picarsic, N. and Ferguson, J. (2021) *China as a 'Cyber Great Power': Beijing's Two Voices in Telecommunications*, Brookings, [online] April.

[121] Tiezzi, S. (2015) 'China vows no compromise on "cyber sovereignty"', *The Diplomat*, [online] 16 December.

[122] Murgia, M. and Gross, A. (2020) 'Inside China's controversial mission to reinvent the internet', *Financial Times*, [online] 27 March.

[123] Kenyon, F. (2021) 'China's "splinternet" will create a state-controlled alternative internet', *The Guardian*, [online] 3 June.

[124] quoted in Naughton, J. (2019) '"The goal is to automate us": welcome to the age of surveillance capitalism', *The Guardian*, [online] 20 January (emphases in original).

[125] Zuboff quoted in Murgia and Gross (2020).

[126] Wintour, P. (2021) 'US seen as bigger threat to democracy than Russia or China, global poll finds', *The Guardian*, [online] 5 May.

Conclusion

[1] quoted in Kelly, A. and Pattisson, P. (2021) '"A pandemic of abuses": human rights under attack during Covid, says UN head', *The Guardian*, [online] 22 February.

2   Kelly and Pattisson (2021).

3   Kuo, L. (2020) 'The new normal: China's excessive coronavirus public monitoring could be here to stay', *The Guardian*, [online] 9 March.

4   Kuo (2020) 'The new normal'.

5   Graham-Harrison, E. and Phillips, T. (2020) 'China hopes "vaccine diplomacy" will restore its image and boost its influence', *The Guardian*, [online] 29 November; Safi, M. (2021) 'Vaccine diplomacy: west falling behind in race for influence', *The Guardian*, [online] 19 February.

6   Ortiz, J. (2021) '"Blood on his hands": as US surpasses 400,000 COVID-19 deaths, experts blame Trump administration for "preventable" loss of life', USA Today News, [online] 17 January.

7   Walt quoted in Tisdall, S. (2021) 'US's global reputation hits rock bottom over Trump's coronavirus response', *The Guardian*, [online] 12 April.

8   Ogden, C. (2020) 'The role of competing narratives in China and the west's response to COVID-19', *British Journal of Chinese Studies*, 10, July: online.

9   Snyder, T. (2018) 'Vladimir Putin's politics of eternity', *The Guardian*, [online] 16 March.

10 Allison, G. and Ferguson, N. (2016) 'Why the US President needs a council of historians', *The Atlantic*, [online] September.

11 Xi Jinping (2014) 'Speech by Xi Jinping', *Körber Foundation, Berlin*, 28 March.

12 Wintour, P. (2020) '"Westlessness": is the west really in a state of peril?', *The Guardian*, [online] 16 February.

13 Jin Liqun (2015) 'Bretton Woods: the system and the institutions', in M. Uzan (ed.) *Bretton Woods: The Next 70 Years*, New York: Reinventing Bretton Woods Committee, pp 211–15.

14 PD (2021) 'Why did Ai Weiwei break this million dollar Han Dynasty vase?', *Public Delivery* [online] 10 February.

15 Wiki ST (2021) 'Ship of Theseus', Wikipedia, [online].

16 quoted in Tax, M. (2016) 'A revolution is not a dinner party', openDemocracy [online] 23 August.

17 Ikenberry (2015) 1–4.

18 Yan Xuetong (2018) 22.

19 see Kelly, A. (2020) '"Virtually entire" fashion industry complicit in Uighur forced labour, say rights group', *The Guardian*, [online] 23 July.

20 CIA World Factbook (2021).

21 Yu, V. (2019) '"They will definitely take revenge": how China could respond to the Hong Kong protests', *The Guardian*, [online] 30 June.

22 Kao, E. (2018) 'Air pollution is killing 1 million people and costing the Chinese economy 267 billion yuan a year, research from CUHK shows', *South China Morning Post*, [online] 2 October.

23 Ogden (2019).

24 Cai quoted in Kuo, L. (2020) 'Xi Jinping facing widespread opposition in his own party claims insider', *The Guardian*, [online] 18 August.

25 Ahmed, N. (2018) 'Scientists warn the UN of capitalism's imminent demise', *Vice*, [online] 27 August.

26 Grantham, J. (2022) 'Let the wild rumpus begin', GMO, [online] 20 January.

27 quoted in Adams, T. (2016) 'Adam Curtis continues search for hidden forces behind a century of chaos', *The Guardian*, [online] 9 October.

28 all quoted in Roth, A. and Phillips, T. (2020) '"What a spectacle! US adversaries revel in post-election chaos', *The Guardian*, [online] 5 November.

29 Taub, A. (2016) 'The rise of American authoritarianism', Vox, [online] 1 March.

30 Brown quoted in Smith, D. (2020) '"He is a destroyer": how the George Floyd protests left Donald Trump exposed', *The Guardian*, [online] 1 June.

31 Hern, A. (2019) 'Facebook exempts political ads from ban on making false claims', *The Guardian*, [online] 4 October.

32 Smith (2021).

33 Shaw, S. (2020) 'How Facebook is aiding authoritarian regimes', *Byline Times*, [online] 16 December.

34 Statista (2021) 'Global social networks ranked by number of users', [online] 2 August.

35 Gwyther, M. (2020) 'The rise and rise of the big tech empire', *Byline Times*, [online] 30 December.

36 Chung, J. (2021) 'Big tech, big cash: Washington's new power players', Public Citizen, [online] 24 March.

37 Hughes quoted in Shaw (2020).

38 quoted in Losse, K. (2018) 'I was Zuckerberg's speechwriter. "Companies over countries" was his early motto', Vox, [online] 16 April.

39 quoted in Keach, S. and Shah, S. (2018) 'Mark Zuckerberg once called Facebook users "dumb f★★★s" for handing over personal data to him – as fears over major hack grows', *The Sun*, [online] 1 October.

40 quoted in Roy, A. (2015) 'Edward Snowden meets Arundhati Roy and John Cusack: "He was small and lithe, like a house cat"', *The Guardian*, [online] 28 November.

41 Wells, H.G. (2014) *The New World Order*, Hong Kong: Hesperides Press, p 105.

42 Kissinger (2015) 10.

43 quoted in Visser, N. (2019) 'Obama takes subtle jab at Trump: "democracy is a garden that has to be tended"', *Huffington Post*, [online] 7 March.

44 Buchan, J. (1940) *Pilgrim's Way*, London: Houghton Mifflin, p 222.

45 Walt, S.M. (2016) 'The collapse of the liberal world order', *Foreign Policy*, [online] 26 June.

46 Dreyfuss, R. (2006) Real time with Bill Maher, YouTube, [online] 17 November.

References

Abrahamson, P. (2017) 'East Asian welfare regime: obsolete ideal-type or diversified reality', *Journal of Asian Public Policy*, 10(1): 90–103.

Access Now (2021) 'Internet shutdowns report: shattered dreams and lost opportunities – a year in the fight to #KeepItOn', 3 March, www.accessnow.org/keepiton-report-a-year-in-the-fight.

Acharya, A. (2014) *The End of American World Order*, Cambridge: Polity.

Adams, T. (2016) 'Adam Curtis continues search for hidden forces behind a century of chaos', *The Guardian*, 9 October, www.theguardian.com/tv-and-radio/2016/oct/09/adam-curtis-donald-trump-documentary-hypernormalisation.

Adams, T. (2021) 'Ai Weiwei on colonialism and statues, Churchill, China and Covid', *The Guardian*, 29 May, www.theguardian.com/artanddesign/2021/may/29/ai-weiwei-on-colonialism-and-statues-churchill-china-and-covid.

ADB (2021) 'Who we are', Asian Development Bank, www.adb.org/who-we-are/about.

Adler, E. (2013) 'Constructivism in international relations: sources, contributions, and debates', in W. Carlsnaes, T. Risse Kappen, T. Risse and B.A. Simmons (eds) *Handbook of International Relations*, London: SAGE, pp 112–44.

AFP (2020) 'China insists Genghis Khan exhibit not use words "Genghis Khan"', *The Guardian*, 14 October, www.theguardian.com/world/2020/oct/14/china-insists-genghis-khan-exhibit-not-use-words-genghis-khan.

AFP (2021) 'US added to "backsliding" democracies for first time', *The Guardian*, 22 November, www.theguardian.com/us-news/2021/nov/22/us-list-backsliding-democracies-civil-liberties-international.

Ahmed, N. (2018) 'Scientists warn the UN of capitalism's imminent demise', *Vice*, 27 August, www.vice.com/en/article/43pek3/scientists-warn-the-un-of-capitalisms-imminent-demise.

Ahmed, N. (2019) 'Smart cities and automated racism: how IBM designed China's surveillance regime', *Byline Times*, 24 May, https://bylinetimes.com/2019/05/24/smart-cities-and-automated-racism-how-ibm-designed-chinas-surveillance-regime.

AI (2006) 'Russian Federation – violent racism out of control', Amnesty International, 3 May, www.amnesty.org/en/documents/EUR46/022/2006/en.

AI (2019) 'Surveillance giants: how the business model of Google and Facebook threatens human rights', Amnesty International, 21 November, www.amnesty.org/en/documents/pol30/1404/2019/en.

AI (2020) 'Death penalty in 2019: facts and figures', Amnesty International, 21 April, www.amnesty.org/en/latest/news/2020/04/death-penalty-in-2019-facts-and-figures.

AIIB (2016) 'President's opening statement, 2016 Annual Meeting of the Board of Governors Asian Infrastructure Investment Bank', Asian Infrastructure Investment Bank, 25 June, www.aiib.org/en/news-events/news/2016/20160625_001.html.

AIIB (2021) 'Frequently asked questions', *Asian Infrastructure Investment Bank*, www.aiib.org/en/general/faq/index.html.

AIIB (2021) 'Members of bank', Asian Infrastructure Investment Bank, www.aiib.org/en/about-aiib/governance/members-of-bank/index.html.

Akos, K. and Peragovics, T. (2018) 'Overcoming the poverty of Western historical imagination: alternative analogies for making sense of the South China Sea conflict', *European Journal of International Relations*, 25(2): 360–82.

Allison, G. and Ferguson, N. (2016) 'Why the US president needs a council of historians', *The Atlantic*, September, www.theatlantic.com/magazine/archive/2016/09/dont-know-much-about-history/492746.

Alvarez, M., Cheibub, J.A., Limongi, F. and Przeworski, A. (1996) 'Classifying political regimes', *Studies in Comparative International Development*, 31(2): 3–36.

Ambrosio, T. (2008) 'Catching the "Shanghai spirit": how the Shanghai Cooperation Organization promotes authoritarian norms in Central Asia', *Europe-Asia Studies*, 60(8): 1321–44.

American Civil Liberties Union (2007) ACLU Fact Sheet on the 'Police America Act', www.aclu.org/other/aclu-fact-sheet-police-america-act?redirect=cpredirect/31203.

Ames, R.T. and Hershock, P.D. (2018) *Confucianisms for a Changing World Cultural Order*, Honolulu: University of Hawaii Press.

Aris, S. (2011) *Eurasian Regionalism: The Shanghai Cooperation Organisation*, London: Palgrave Macmillan.

Armijo, L. (2007) 'The BRIC countries as an analytical category: mirage or insight?', *Asian Perspective*, 31(4): 7–42.

Arun, C. (2014) 'Paper-thin safeguards and mass surveillance in India', *National Law School of India Review*, 26(2): 105–14.

Arun, P. (2017) 'Uncertainty and insecurity in privacyless India: a despotic push towards digitalisation', *Surveillance & Society*, 15(3/4): 456–64.

ATV (2021) *Autocratization Turns Viral*, University of Gothenberg, V-Dem Institute. www.v-dem.net/files/25/DR 2021.pdf.

Bailes, A. and Pan Dunay (2007) 'The Shanghai Cooperation Organization as a regional security institution', in A.J.K. Bailes, P. Dunay, P. Guang and M. Troitskiy (eds) *The Shanghai Cooperation Organization*, Stockholm: Stockholm International Peace Research Institute, pp 1–27.

Balabán, M. (2017) 'From the end of history to the post-American world: global politics, economy and security at the turn of the epoch', *Central European Journal of International & Security Studies*, 11(3): 9–36.

Ballotpedia (2021) 'Federal judges appointed by Donald Trump', *Ballotpedia*, https://ballotpedia.org/Federal_judges_nominated_by_Donald_Trump.

Baltrusaitis, J. (2020) 'Top 10 countries and cities by numbers of CCTV cameras', Precise Security, 4 December, www.precisesecurity.com/articles/Top-10-Countries-by-Number-of-CCTV-Cameras.

Barber, L. and Foy, H. (2019) 'Vladimir Putin says liberalism has "become obsolete"', *Financial Times*, 28 June, www.ft.com/content/670039ec-98f3-11e9-9573-ee5cbb98ed36.

Barnett, A. (2017) *The Lure of Greatness: England's Brexit and America's Trump*, London: Unbound.

Barnett, A. (2021) 'The end of closed democracy?', openDemocracy, 20 March, www.opendemocracy.net/en/end-closed-democracy.

Baumann, C., Hamin, H., Tung, R. and Hoadley, S. (2016) 'Competitiveness and workforce performance: Asia vis-à-vis the "West"', *International Journal of Contemporary Hospitality Management*, 28(10): 2197.

BBC (2017) 'Gauri Lankesh: India journalist shot dead in Bangalore', BBC News, 6 September, www.bbc.co.uk/news/world-asia-india-41169817

BBC (2019) 'Hong Kong protests: President Xi warns of "bodies smashed"', BBC News, 14 October, www.bbc.com/news/world-asia-china-50035229.

BBC (2019) 'Huawei faces US charges: the short, medium and long story', BBC News, 7 May, www.bbc.com/news/world-us-canada-47046264.

BBC (2021) 'China regains slot as India's top trade partner despite tensions', BBC News, 23 February, www.bbc.co.uk/news/business-56164154.

Bearak, M. (2019) 'In strategic Djibouti, a microcosm of China's growing foothold in Africa', *The Washington Post*, 29 December.

Beckett, L. (2021) 'Facts won't fix this: experts on how to fight America's disinformation crisis', *The Guardian*, 1 January, www.theguardian.com/us-news/2021/jan/01/disinformation-us-election-covid-pandemic-trump-biden.

Beeson, M. and Fujian Li (2012) 'Charmed or alarmed? Reading China's regional relations,' *Journal of Contemporary China*, 21(73): 35–51.

Beeson, M. and Higgott, R. (2005) 'Hegemony, institutionalism and US foreign policy: theory and practice in comparative historical perspective', *Third World Quarterly*, 26(7): 1173–88.

Beeson, M. and Jinghan Zeng (2018) 'The BRICS and global governance: China's contradictory role', *Third World Quarterly*, 39(10): 1962–78.

Bell, D.A. (2016) *The China Model: Political Meritocracy and the Limits of Democracy*, Princeton: Princeton University Press.

Berzina, K., Kovalcikova, N., Salvo, D. and Soula, E. (2019) *European Policy Blueprint for Countering Authoritarian Interference in Democracies*, Washington, German Marshall Fund of the United States.

Best, S. (2019) 'Russia will disconnect from the internet tomorrow to test cyber-war defences', *The Mirror*, 31 October, www.mirror.co.uk/tech/russia-disconnect-internet-tomorrow-test-20763305.

Bhardwaj, P. and Kumar, A. (2014) 'Comparing two inchoate conceptions: balancing privacy and security by e-surveillance laws in India', *National Law University Delhi Student Law Journal*, 3(1): 1–19.

Bisley, N. (2017) 'Be in no doubt, Xi Jinping wants to make China great again', *The Guardian*, 18 October, www.theguardian.com/world/2017/oct/18/be-in-no-doubt-xi-jinping-wants-to-make-china-great.

Borger, J. (2017) '"Terrifying, Nixonian": Comey's firing takes democracy to new dark territory', *The Guardian*, 10 May, www.theguardian.com/us-news/2017/may/10/terrifying-astonishing-nixonian-james-comeys-termination-by-trump.

Borger, J. (2018) 'China and Russia accused of waging war on human rights at the UN', *The Guardian*, 27 March, www.theguardian.com/world/2018/mar/27/china-and-russia-accused-of-waging-war-on-human-rights-at-un.

Borger, J. (2020) 'CIA controlled global encryption company for decades, says report', *The Guardian*, 11 February, www.theguardian.com/us-news/2020/feb/11/crypto-ag-cia-bnd-germany-intelligence-report.

Bradbury, S.G. (2013) 'Understanding the NSA programs: bulk acquisition of telephone metadata under Section 215 and foreign-targeted collection under Section 702', Research Paper, Washington, DC: Lawfare Research Paper Series.

Brady, A-M. (2020) 'New Zealand needs to show it is serious about addressing Chinese interference', *The Guardian*, 24 January, www.theguardian.com/world/commentisfree/2020/jan/24/new-zealand-needs-to-show-its-serious-about-addressing-chinese-interference.

Breslin, S. (2018) 'Global reordering and China's rise: adoption, adaptation and reform', *The International Spectator*, 53(1): 57–75.

BRIC (2010) 'BRIC Summit Joint Statement (Brasilia, Brazil)', BRICS, April, https://infobrics.org/document/21.

Brooker, P. (2014) *Non-Democratic Regimes*, London: Palgrave Macmillan.

Brown, M.E. (2000) *The Rise of China*, Boston: MIT Press.

Brown, W. (2015) *Undoing the Demos: Neoliberalism's Stealth Revolution*, New York: Zone Books.

Browne, A. (2021) 'Bloomberg New Economy: Trump's last days raise comparisons with Mao', *Bloomberg*, 9 January, www.bloomberg.com/news/newsletters/2021-01-09/bloomberg-new-economy-trump-s-last-days-raise-comparisons-to-mao.

Buchan, J. (1940) *Pilgrim's Way*, London: Houghton Mifflin

Bush, R.C. (2017) 'What Xi Jinping said about Taiwan at the 19th Party Congress', Brookings, 19 October, www.brookings.edu/blog/order-from- chaos/2017/10/19/what-xi-jinping-said-about-taiwan-at-the-19th-party-congress.

Buzan, B. (2018) 'China's rise in English school perspective', *International Relations of the Asia-Pacific*, 18(3): 449–76.

Byler, D. (2019) 'China's hi tech war on its Muslim minority', *The Guardian*, 11 April, www.theguardian.com/news/2019/apr/11/china-hi-tech-war-on-muslim-minority-xinjiang-uighurs-surveillance-face-recognition.

CACR (2021) 'Weekly report', Centre for Advanced China Research, 26 June, www.ccpwatch.org/single-post/weekly-report-4-33-6-26-2021-7-16-2021.

Callaghan, M. and Hubbard, P. (2016) 'The Asian Infrastructure Investment Bank: multilateralism on the Silk Road', *China Economic Journal*, 9(2): 116–39.

Callahan, W.A. (2003) 'Beyond cosmopolitanism and nationalism: diasporic Chinese and neo-nationalism in China and Thailand', *International Organisation*, 57(3): 481–517.

Callahan, W.A. (2004) 'Remembering the future: utopia, empire, and harmony in 21st-century international theory', *European Journal of International Relations*, 10(4): 569–601.

Callahan, W.A. (2015) 'History, tradition and the China dream: socialist modernisation in the world of great harmony', *Journal of Contemporary China*, 24(96): 983–1001.

Callahan, W.A. (2016) 'China's "Asia dream": The Belt Road initiative and the new regional order', *Asian Journal of Comparative Politics*, 1(3): 226–43.

Campbell. K. and Ratner, E. (2018) 'The China reckoning: how Beijing defied American expectations', *Foreign Affairs*, 97(2): 60–70.

Carew, A. (1987) *Labour Under the Marshall Plan: The Politics of Productivity and the Marketing of Management Science*, Manchester: Manchester University Press.

Carnegie-Tsinghua (2018) 'What does "great power diplomacy with Chinese characteristics" mean?', *Carnegie-Tsinghua Centre for Global Policy*, 20 April, https://carnegietsinghua.org/2018/04/20/what-does-great-power-diplomacy-with-chinese-characteristics-mean-event-6866.

Carpenter, T.G. (2020) 'George H.W. Bush's shameful kowtow to China: a cautionary tale', *The American Conservative*, 27 May, www.theamericanconservative.com/articles/george-h-w-bushs-shameful-kowtow-to-china-a-cautionary-tale.

CCP General Office and State Council (2015) 'CCP General Office and State Council General Office Opinions concerning strengthening the construction of new types of think tanks with Chinese characteristics', [blog], China Copyright and Media, 21 January, https://chinacopyrightandmedia.wordpress.com/2015/01/20/ccp-general-office-and-state-council-general-office-opinions-concerning-strengthening-the-construction-of-new-types-of-think-tanks-with-chinese-characteristics.

Chacko, P. (2018) 'The right turn in India: authoritarianism, populism and neoliberalisation', *Journal of Contemporary Asia*, 48(4): 541–65.

Chandran, M. (2010). 'The democratisation of censorship: books and the Indian public', *Economic and Political Weekly*, 45(40): 27–31.

Chang, N. (2001) 'The USA Patriot Act: what's so patriotic about trampling on the Bill of Rights', *Guild Practitioner*, 142–58.

Chang, N. (2011) *Silencing Political Dissent: How Post-September 11 Anti-Terrorism Measures Threaten Our Civil Liberties*, New York: Seven Stories Press.

Charvet, J. and Kaczynska-Nay, E. (2008) *The Liberal Project and Human Rights: The Theory and Practice of a New World Order*, Cambridge: Cambridge University Press.

Chazan, G. (2018) 'Backlash grows over Chinese deals for Germany's corporate jewels', *Financial Times*, 5 March, www. ft.com/content/391637d2-215a-11e8-a895-1ba1f72c2c11.

Chen, G.G. (2017) 'Le droit, c'est moi: Xi Jinping's new rule-by-law approach', Oxford Human Rights Hub, 26 July, http:// ohrh.law.ox.ac.uk/le-droit-cest-moi-xi-jinpings-new-rule-by-law-approach.

ChinaFile (2017) 'Is the Trump era really the Xi era?', *ChinaFile*, 18 February, www.chinafile.com/conversation/trump-era-really-xi-era.

ChinaPower (2017) 'Are maritime law enforcement forces destabilizing Asia?', https://chinapower.csis.org/maritime-forces-destabilizing-asia.

ChinaPower (2018) 'How much trade transits the South China Sea?', https://chinapower.csis.org/much-trade-transits-south-china-sea.

Chomsky, N. (1973) 'One man's view: Noam Chomsky interviewed by an anonymous interviewer', *Business Today*, May, www.chomsky.info/interviews/197305--.htm.

Chung, J. (2021) 'Big Tech, big cash: Washington's new power players', Public Citizen, 24 March, www.citizen.org/article/big-tech-lobbying-update.

CIA World Factbook (2021) 'GDP PPP', www.cia.gov/the-world-factbook/field/real-gdp-purchasing-power-parity/country-comparison.

Cillizza, C. and Williams, B. (2019) '15 times Donald Trump praised authoritarian leaders', CNN, 2 July, https://edition.cnn. com/2019/07/02/politics/donald-trump-dictators-kim-jong-un-vladimir-putin/index.html.

Clinton, H.R. (2011) 'America's Pacific century', *US Department of State through Foreign Policy Magazine*, 11 October.

Clinton, W.J. (2000) *Public Papers of the Presidents of the United States: William J. Clinton, 2000–2001*, New York: Best Books.

CNN (2005) 'Cheney: Bush has right to authorize secret surveillance', 20 December, www.cnn.com/2005/POLITICS/12/20/cheney. wiretaps.

Cohen, N. (2021) 'Gove and co were once thrilled to be close to Trump. Now see them run', *The Guardian*, 9 January, www. theguardian.com/commentisfree/2021/jan/09/gove-and-co-were-once-thrilled-to-be-close-to-trump-now-see-them-run.

Confucius (2014) (translated by Legge, J.) *The Analects of Confucius*, Adelaide: University of Adelaide.

Crouch, C. (2004) *Post-Democracy*, Cambridge: Cambridge University Press.

Dai Bingguo (2010) 'Adhere to the path of peaceful development', USC US-China Institute, 6 December, http://china.usc. edu/dai-bingguo-%E2%80%9Cadhere-path-peaceful-development%E2%80%9D-dec-6-2010.

Dalton, R.J. and Ong, N.T. (2005) 'Authority orientations and democratic attitudes: a test of the "Asian values" hypothesis', *Japanese Journal of Political Science*, 6(2): 1–21.

Davidson, H. (2021) 'Xi Jinping warns China won't be bullied in speech marking 100-year anniversary of CCP', *The Guardian*, 1 July, www.theguardian.com/world/2021/jul/01/xi-jinping-warns-china-wont-be-bullied-100-year-anniversary-chinese-communist-party-.

Davidson, H. and Kuo, L. (2020) 'Zoom admits cutting off activists' accounts in obedience to China', *The Guardian*, 12 June, www. theguardian.com/world/2020/jun/12/zoom-admits-cutting-off-activists-accounts-in-obedience-to-china.

Davies, N. (2009) *Flat Earth News*, London: Vintage.

Davies, R. and Davidson, H. (2021) 'The strange case of Alibaba's Jack Ma and his three month vanishing act', *The Guardian*, 23 January, www.theguardian.com/business/2021/jan/23/the-strange-case-of-alibabas-jack-ma-and-his-three-month-vanishing-act.

De Bary, W.T. (2000) *Asian Values and Human Rights: A Confucian Communitarian Perspective*, Cambridge, MA: Harvard University Press.

De Sousa Santos, B. (2005) 'Beyond neoliberal governance: the World Social Forum as subaltern cosmopolitan politics and legality', in B. de Sousa Santos and C.A. Rodríguez-Garavito (eds) *Law and Globalization from Below – Towards a Cosmopolitan Legality*, Cambridge: Cambridge University Press, pp 29–63.

Deibert, R. and Rohozinski, R. (2010) 'Control and subversion in Russian cyberspace', in R. Deibert, J. Palfrey, R. Rohozinski and J. Zittrain (eds) *Access Controlled: The Shaping of Power, Rights, and Rule in Cyberspace*, Cambridge, MA: MIT Press, pp 15–34.

Deng Xiaoping (1982) *Build Socialism with Chinese Characteristics*, Beijing: Foreign Languages Press.

Desjardins, J. (2018) 'China's staggering demand for commodities', *Visual Capitalist*, 2 March, www.visualcapitalist.com/chinas-staggering-demand-commodities.

Dettmer, J. (2020) 'China's "wolf warrior" diplomacy prompts international backlash', *Voice of America*, 6 May, www.voanews.com/covid-19-pandemic/chinas-wolf-warrior-diplomacy-prompts-international-backlash.

Dhillon, A. (2019) 'Indian PM lampooned for "manufactured" interview', *The Guardian*, 5 January, www.theguardian.com/world/2019/jan/05/indian-pm-narendra-modi-lampooned-for-manufactured-interview.

Diamond, L.J. (2002) 'Thinking about hybrid regimes', *Journal of Democracy*, 13(2): 21–35.

Dig Mandarin (2021) 'Confucius Institutes around the world', 22 February, www.digmandarin.com/confucius-institutes-around-the-world.html.

Ding, S. and Saunders, R. (2006) 'Talking up China: an analysis of China's rising cultural power and global promotion of the Chinese language', *East Asia*, 23(2): 3–33.

Dirlik, A. (2011) 'The idea of a "Chinese model": a critical discussion', *International Critical Thought*, 1(2): 129–37.

DMDC (2021) 'Number of military and DoD Appropriated Fund (APF) civilian personnel permanently assigned by duty location and service/component', Defense Manpower Data Center, 31 March.

DOC (2002) 'Declaration on the Code of Parties in the South China Sea', *The Governments of the Member States of ASEAN and the Government of the People's Republic of China*, 2 November, www.files.ethz.ch/isn/125380/5066_South_China_Sea.pdf.

Dorling, P. (2013) 'Snowden reveals Australia's links to US spy web', *Sydney Morning Herald*, 8 July, www.smh.com.au/world/snowden-reveals-australias-links-to-us-spy-web-20130708-2plyg.html.

Doshi, R., de la Bruyère, E., Picarsic, N. and Ferguson, J. (2021) *China as a 'Cyber Great Power': Beijing's Two Voices in Telecommunications*, Brookings, April, www.brookings.edu/research/china-as-a-cyber-great-power-beijings-two-voices-in-telecommunications/?utm_campaign=Foreign%20Policy&utm_medium=email&utm_content=120516204&utm_source=hs_email.

Doshi, V. and Ratcliffe, R. (2019) 'India's strongman PM: Modi to appear on Bear Grylls' Man vs wild', *The Guardian*, 29 July, www.theguardian.com/global-development/2019/jul/29/indias-strongman-pm-modi-to-appear-on-bear-grylls-man-vs-wild.

Dreyfuss, R. (2006) Real time with Bill Maher, *YouTube*, 17 November, www.youtube.com/watch?v=t8C3MUDVn_I.

Duffy, N. (2015) 'Internet freedom in Vladimir Putin's Russia: the noose tightens', American Enterprise Institute, 12 January.

Dujmović, N. (2020) 'Review Essay: Covert action to promote democracy in China during the Cold War', *Studies in Intelligence*, 64(4): 31–5.

DWP (1998) *China Defence White Paper 1998*, Beijing: The Information Office of China's State Council of the People's Republic of China.

DWP (2019) 'Full text of 2019 Defense White Paper: "China's national defense in the new era"', State Council Information Office of the People's Republic of China, 24 July, www.andrewerickson.com/2019/07/full-text-of-defense-white-paper-chinas-national-defense-in-the-new-era-english-chinese-versions.

EB (2017) 'Big stick policy', *Encyclopædia Britannica*, 27 December, www.britannica.com/event/Big-Stick-policy.

Economist Intelligence Unit (2016) *Democracy Index 2016: Revenge of the 'Deplorables'*, London: Economist Intelligence Unit.

The Economist (2021) 'Global democracy has a very bad year', *The Economist*, 2 February, www.economist.com/graphic-detail/2021/02/02/global-democracy-has-a-very-bad-year.

Eisenman, J. and Stewart D.T. (2017) 'China's new Silk Road is getting muddy', *Foreign Policy*, 9 January, http://foreignpolicy.com/2017/01/09/chinas-newsilk-road-is-getting-muddy.

Elagina, D. (2021) 'Major trade partners of Russia, 2020', Statista, 17 August, www.statista.com/statistics/1100708/russia-leading-foreign-trade-partners-by-volume.

Ellis-Petersen, H. (2020) 'India's COVID-19 app fuels worries over authoritarian surveillance', *The Guardian*, 4 May, www.theguardian.com/world/2020/may/04/how-safe-is-it-really-privacy-fears-over-india-coronavirus-app.

Eno, R. (2015) *The Analects of Confucius: An Online Teaching Translation*, Bloomington: Indiana University Press.

Esarey, A. (2015) 'Winning hearts and minds? Cadres as microbloggers in China', *Journal of Current Chinese Affairs*, 44(2): 69–103.

Esfandiari, S. (2019) 'The United Nations warned that it may not be able to pay its staff on time because the US owes it $1 billion', Business Insider, 10 October, www.businessinsider.de/international/un-may-not-be-able-pay-staff-us-budget-cuts-2019-10/?r=US&IR=T.

ESPN (2020) 'NBA ends relationship with academy in China', 22 July, www.espn.com/nba/story/_/id/29517957/nba-ends-relationship-academy-china.

Fang Cai (2015) *Demystifying China's Economy Development*, Heidelberg: Springer.

Fei Gao and Li Li (2019) 'The Belt and Road Initiative under the diplomacy perspective of the Great Power with Chinese Characteristics', in Wei Liu and Hui Zhang (eds) *Regional Mutual Benefit and Win-Win under the Double Circulation of Global Value*, Shanghai: Peking University Press, pp 105–25.

Fei-Ling Wang (2015) 'From *Tianxia* to Westphalia: the evolving Chinese conception of sovereignty and world order' in G.J. Ikenberry, Wang Jisi and Zhu Feng (eds) *America, China, and the Struggle for World Order: Ideas, Traditions, Historical Legacies, and Global Visions*, Basingstoke: Palgrave Macmillan, pp 43–70.

Feldstein, S. (2019) 'The global expansion of AI surveillance', Carnegie Endowment for International Peace, 17 September, https://carnegieendowment.org/publications/interactive/ai-surveillance.

Feng Zhang (2011) 'The rise of Chinese exceptionalism in international relations', *European Journal of International Relations*, 19(2): 305–28.

Firoz, N. and Topchaya, O. (2016) 'East and West: understanding consumer behavior in China implications and practical applications for international marketing of US- based companies', *Franklin Business & Law Journal*, 4: 67–82.

Flew, T. (2014) 'Six theories of neoliberalism', *Thesis Eleven*, 122(1): 49–71.

Foot, R. (2020) *China, the UN, and Human Protection: Beliefs, Power, Image*, Oxford: Oxford University Press.

Freedom House (2017) *Freedom in the World 2017 – Populists and Autocrats: The Dual Threat to Global Democracy*, Washington, DC: Freedom House.

Freedom House (2021) 'Global freedom status', https://freedomhouse.org/explore-the-map?type=fiw&year=2021.

Freeland, J. (2021) 'In plain sight, Boris Johnson is rigging the system to stay in power', *The Guardian*, 1 October, www.theguardian.com/commentisfree/2021/oct/01/boris-johnson-rigging-the-system-power-courts-protest-elections.

Friedburg, A.L. (2005) 'The future of US–China relations: is conflict inevitable?', *International Security*, 30(2): 7–45.

Friedman, M. (1951) 'Neo-liberalism and its prospects', *Farmand*, 89–93.

Fukuyama, F. (1989) 'The end of history?', *The National Interest*, (16): 3–18.

Fung, C. (2019) *China and Intervention at the UN Security Council: Reconciling Status*, Oxford: Oxford University Press.

G Ed (2020) 'The Guardian view on Trump tracking phones: it could happen here', *The Guardian*, 9 March, www.theguardian.com/commentisfree/2020/mar/09/the-guardian-view-on-trump-tracking-phones-it-could-happen-here.

Gabbatt, A. (2017) 'Anti-protest bills would "attack right to speak out" under Trump', *The Guardian*, 8 May, www.theguardian.com/world/2017/may/08/donald-trump-anti-protest-bills.

Gao Zhi Guo and Jia Bing Bing (2013) 'The nine-dash line in the South China Sea: history, status, and implications', *The American Journal of International Law*, 107(1): 98–124.

Garwood-Gowers, A. (2016) 'China's "responsible protection" concept: reinterpreting the Responsibility to Protect (R2P) and military intervention for humanitarian purposes', *Asian Journal of International Law*, 6(1): 89–118.

Gill, B. (2007) *Rising Star: China's New Security Diplomacy*, Washington, DC: Brookings Institution Press.

Giuffrida, A., Safi, M. and Kalia, A. (2018) 'The populist social media playbook: the battle for Facebook, Twitter and Instagram', *The Guardian*, 17 December, www.theguardian.com/world/2018/dec/17/populist-social-media-playbook-who-is-best-facebook-twitter-instagram-matteo-salvini-narendra-modi.

Glavin, T. (2017) 'China is no friend to Canada', *Macleans*, 17 April, www.macleans.ca/politics/china-is-no-friend-to-canada.

Goddard, C.R., Cronin, P. and Dash, K.C. (2006) *International Political Economy: State-Market Relations in a Changing Global Order*, Basingstoke: Palgrave Macmillan.

Graham-Harrison, E. (2021) 'Beijing cuts Hong Kong's directly elected seats in radical overhaul', *The Guardian*, 30 March, www.theguardian.com/world/2021/mar/30/hong-kong-china-brings-in-voting-system-changes.

Graham-Harrison, E. (2021) 'Chinese actor quits as Burberry ambassador as Xinjiang cotton row escalates', *The Guardian*, 26 March, www.theguardian.com/world/2021/mar/26/chinese-actor-quits-as-burberry-ambassador-as-xinjiang-cotton-row-escalates.

Graham-Harrison, E. and Garside, J. (2019) '"Allow no escapes": leak exposes reality of China's vast prison camp network', *The Guardian*, 24 November, www.theguardian.com/world/2019/nov/24/china-cables-leak-no-escapes-reality-china-uighur-prison-camp.

Graham-Harrison, E. and Phillips, T. (2020) 'China hopes "vaccine diplomacy" will restore its image and boost its influence', *The Guardian*, 29 November, www.theguardian.com/world/2020/nov/29/china-hopes-vaccine-diplomacy-will-restore-its-image-and-boost-its-influence.

Graham-Harrison, E. et al (2021) 'The world in 2021 – how global politics will change this year', *The Guardian*, 3 January, www.theguardian.com/world/2021/jan/03/the-world-in-2021-how-global-politics-will-change-this-year.

Grantham, J. (2022) 'Let the wild rumpus begin', GMO, 20 January, www.gmo.com/globalassets/articles/viewpoints/2022/gmo_let-the-wild-rumpus-begin_1-22.pdf.

Greenwald, G. and MacAskill, E. (2013) 'NSA Prism program taps in to user data of Apple, Google and others', *The Guardian*, 6 June, www.theguardian.com/world/2013/jun/06/us-tech-giants-nsa-data.

Griffiths, James (2019) *The Great Firewall of China: How to Build and Control an Alternative Version of the Internet*, London: Zed Books.

Grondona, M. (2000) 'A cultural typology of economic development', in L.E. Harrison and S.P. Huntingdon (eds) *Culture Matters: How Values Shape Human Progress*, New York: Basic Books, pp 44–56.

GT (2020) 'China and US not in war for power, US on wrong side of history: Chinese FM during Europe visit', *Global Times*, 31 August, www.globaltimes.cn/content/1199390.shtml.

Guan Lijie and Ji Yushan (2015) 'From the Beijing consensus to the China model: a suggested strategy for future economic reform', *International Critical Thought*, 5(2): 135–47.

Guimaraes, B. and Iazdi, O. (2015) 'IMF conditionalities, liquidity provision, and incentives for fiscal adjustment', *International Tax and Public Finance*, 22(5): 705–22.

Gwyther, M. (2020) 'The rise and rise of the big tech empire', *Byline Times*, 30 December, https://bylinetimes.com/2020/12/30/the-rise-and-rise-of-the-big-tech-empire.

Haas, B. (2017) 'China bans religious names from Muslim babies in Xinjiang' *The Guardian*, 25 April, www.theguardian.com/world/2017/apr/25/china-bans-religious-names-for-muslims-babies-in-xinjiang.

Haas, B. (2018) 'Peppa Pig, subversive symbol of the counterculture, in China video site ban', *The Guardian*, 1 May, www.theguardian.com/world/2018/may/01/peppa-pig-banned-from-chinese-video-site.

Haas, B. and Phillips, T. (2017) 'China cracks down on foreign children's books', *The Guardian*, 13 March, www.theguardian.com/world/2017/mar/13/peppa-pig-pulled-china-cracks-down-on-foreign-childrens-books.

Hadenius, A. and Teorell, J. (2006) *Authoritarian Regimes: Stability, Change, and Pathways to Democracy, 1972–2003*, Helen Kellogg Institute for International Studies.

Hamilton, G.C. (2015) 'China's social credit score system is doomed to fail', *Financial Times*, 16 November, www.ft.com.

Hanlon, J. (2012) 'Governance as "kicking away the ladder"', *New Political Economy*, 17(5): 691–8.

Harding, L. (2008) '"To be a journalist in Russia is suicide"', *The Guardian*, 24 November, www.theguardian.com/media/2008/nov/24/anna-politkovskaya-russia-press-freedom.

Harmon, G.E. (2021) 'We must reverse drop in US life expectancy that preceded pandemic', AMA, 20 August, www.ama-assn.org/about/leadership/we-must-reverse-drop-us-life-expectancy-preceded-pandemic.

Harpers (2020) 'A letter on justice and open debate', *Harpers*, 7 July, https://harpers.org/a-letter-on-justice-and-open-debate.

Harris, H.B. (2015) 'US perspectives on coalition maritime operations in the Indo-Pacific' [video], speech by Commander, US Pacific Fleet, Australian Strategic Policy Institute conference dinner, Canberra, 31 March, www.aspi.org.au/index.php/video/us-perspectives-coalition-maritime-operations-indo-pacific.

Harvey, D. (2005) *A Brief History of Neoliberalism*, Oxford: Oxford University Press.

Hattenstone, S. (2020) 'Ai Weiwei on his new life in Britain: "People are at least polite. In Germany, they weren't"', *The Guardian*, 21 January, www.theguardian.com/artanddesign/2020/jan/21/ai-weiwei-on-his-new-life-in-britain-germany-virtual-reality-film.

Hatton, C. (2015) 'China "social credit": Beijing sets up huge system', BBC News, 26 October, www.bbc.co.uk/news/world-asia-china-34592186.

He Huifeng (2018) 'In a remote corner of China, Beijing is trying to export is model by training foreign officials the Chinese way', *South China Morning Post*, 14 July, www.scmp.com/news/china/economy/article/2155203/remote-corner-china-beijing-trying-export-its-model-training.

Hedges, C. (2010) *Death of the Liberal Class*, New York: Nation Books.

Henley, J. (2020) '"A pretence of justice": the global press on Trump's acquittal', *The Guardian*, 6 February, www.theguardian.com/us-news/2020/feb/06/hollow-pretence-justice-global-press-trump-impeachment-acquittal.

Hern, A. (2019) 'Facebook exempts political ads from ban on making false claims', *The Guardian*, 4 October, www.theguardian. com/technology/2019/oct/04/facebook-exempts-political-ads-ban-making-false-claims.

Hern, A. (2020) 'What is facial recognition and how do police use it?', *The Guardian*, 24 January, www.theguardian.com/technology/2020/jan/24/what-is-facial-recognition-and-how-do-police-use-it.

Herring, G. (2011) *From Colony to Superpower: U.S. Foreign Relations since 1776*, New York: Oxford University Press.

Ho-Fong Hung (2016) *The China Boom: Why China will not Rule the World*, New York: Columbia University Press.

Hobson, C. (2009) 'The limits of liberal-democracy promotion', *Alternatives: Global, Local, Political*, 34(4): 383–405.

Hong Yu (2017) 'Motivation behind China's "One Belt, One Road" initiatives and establishment of the Asian Infrastructure Investment Bank', *Journal of Contemporary China*, 26(105): 353–68.

Hongying Wang (2015) 'The Asian Infrastructure Investment Bank: a new Bretton Woods moment? A total Chinese triumph?', *Centre for International Governance Innovation Policy Brief*, 59.

Hoo Tiang Boon (2017) 'Hardening the hard, softening the soft: assertiveness and China's regional strategy', *Journal of Strategic Studies*, 40(5): 639–62.

Horta, K. (2019) 'The Asian Infrastructure Investment Bank (AIIB): a multilateral bank where China sets the rules', *Heinrich Böll Stiftung Publication Series on Democracy*, 52.

HRW (2017) 'China: minority region collects DNA from millions', Human Rights Watch, 13 December, www.hrw.org/news/2017/12/13/china-minority-region-collects-dna-millions.

HRW (2018) 'China: big data fuels crackdown in minority region', Human Rights Watch, 26 February, www.hrw.org/news/2018/02/26/china-big-data-fuels-crackdown-minority-region.

HRW (2019) 'China: Xinjiang children separated from families', Human Rights Watch, 15 September, www.hrw.org/news/2019/09/15/china-xinjiang-children-separated-families.

HRW (2020) 'Russia: growing internet isolation, control, censorship', Human Rights Watch, 18 June, www.hrw.org/news/2020/06/18/russia-growing-internet-isolation-control-censorship.

HRW (2021) 'India: tech firms should uphold privacy, free speech', Human Rights Watch, 11 March, www.hrw.org/news/2021/03/11/india-tech-firms-should-uphold-privacy-free-speech.

Hume, T. (2019) 'Pro-Beijing thugs are vandalizing Hong Kong protests in Australia now', *Vice*, 7 August, www.vice.com/en/article/evjgjn/pro-beijing-thugs-are-vandalizing-hong-kong-democracy-protests-in-australia-now.

ICG (2012) 'Stirring up the South China Sea', Asia Report no. 223, International Crisis Group, 23 April, https://d2071andvip0wj.cloudfront.net/223-stirring-up-the-south-china-sea-i.pdf.

ICISS (2001) *Research and Consultations: Supplementary Volume to the Responsibility to Protect*, Ottawa: International Development Research Centre.

II (2022) Insurrection Index, https://insurrectionindex.org/

Ikenberry, G.J. (2011) *Liberal Leviathan: The Origins, Crisis and Transformation of the American World Order*, Princeton: Princeton University Press.

Ikenberry, G.J. (2015) 'Introduction', in G.J. Ikenberry, Wang Jisi and Zhu Feng (eds) *America, China, and the Struggle for World Order: Ideas, Traditions, Historical Legacies, and Global Visions*, Basingstoke: Palgrave Macmillan, pp 1–18.

IOCSS (2015) *China's Military Strategy 2015*, Beijing: The Information Office of China's State Council of the People's Republic of China.

Ivanhoe, P.J. and Van Norden, B.W. (eds) (2005) *Readings in Classical Chinese Philosophy*, Indianapolis: Hackett Publishing Company.

Jacques, M. (2009) *When China Rules the World: The End of the Western World and the Birth of a New Global Order*, New York: Penguin.

Janoski, T. (2014) 'Citizenship in China: a comparison of rights with the East and West', *Journal of Chinese Political Science*, 19(4): 365–85.

Jijie Wang, Keil, M., Lih-bin Oh and Yide Shen (2017) 'Impacts of organizational commitment, interpersonal closeness, and Confucian ethics on willingness to report bad news in software projects', *Journal of Systems & Software*, 125: 220–33.

Jin Liqun (2015) 'Bretton Woods: the system and the institutions', in M. Uzan (ed.) *Bretton Woods: The Next 70 Years*, New York: Reinventing Bretton Woods Committee, pp 211–15.

Jingdong Yuan (2010) 'China's role in establishing and building the Shanghai Cooperation Organization (SCO)', *Journal of Contemporary China*, 19(67): 855–69.

Johnston, A.I. (1995) 'Thinking about strategic culture', *International Security*, 19(4): 32–64.

Johnson, L.B. (1967) 'Speech on Vietnam, September 29, 1967', Miller Center, University of Virginia, 29 September.

Jukes, P. (2019) 'Brexit, Trump, Russia scandal', *Byline Times*, 18 February, https://bylinetimes.com/2019/02/18/explosive-uk-parliamentary-report-exposes-the-molten-core-of-the-trump-brexit-russia-scandal.

Kadidal, S. (2014) 'NSA surveillance: the implications for civil liberties', *I/S: A Journal of Law and Policy for the Information Society*, 10(2): 433–80.

Kaiman, J. (2016) 'China cracks down on social media with threat of jail for "online rumours"', *The Guardian*, 10 September, www.theguardian.com/world/2013/sep/10/china-social-media-jail-rumours.

Kalathil, S. and Boas, T.C. (2003) *Open Networks, Closed Regimes: The Impact of the Internet on Authoritarian Rule*, Washington, DC: Carnegie Endowment.

Kaminski, M.E. and Witnov, S. (2014) 'The conforming effect: first amendment implications of surveillance, beyond chilling speech', *University of Richmond Law Review*, 49(2): 465–518.

Kang, D.C. (2005) 'Hierarchy in Asian international relations: 1300–1900', *Asian Security*, 1(1): 53–79.

Kang, D.C. (2007) *China Rising: Power, Peace and Order in East Asia*, New York: Columbia University Press.

Kao, E. (2018) 'Air pollution is killing 1 million people and costing the Chinese economy 267 billion yuan a year, research from CUHK shows', *South China Morning Post*, 2 October, www.scmp.com/news/china/science/article/2166542/air-pollution-killing-1-million-people-and-costing-chinese.

Kaplan, L.F. (2001) 'Trade barrier', *The New Republic*, 9 July, https://newrepublic.com/article/90711/trade-barrier.

Kärkkäinen, A. (2016) 'Does China have a geoeconomic strategy towards Zimbabwe? The case of the Zimbabwean natural resource sector', *Asia Europe Journal*, 14(2): 185–202.

Katzenstein, P.J. (1996) *Cultural Norms and National Security: Police and Military in Post-War Japan*, Ithaca: Cornell University Press.

Kaufman, A.A. (2010) 'The "century of humiliation", then and now: Chinese perceptions of the international order', *Pacific Focus*, 25(1): 1–33.

Keach, S. and Shah, S. (2018) 'Mark Zuckerberg once called Facebook users "dumb f***s" for handing over personal data to him – as fears over major hack grows', *The Sun*, 1 October, www.thesun.co.uk/tech/5845432/mark-zuckerberg-facebook-hack-dumb-users-privacy.

Keenan, B.C. (2014) 'Economic markets and higher education: ethical issues in the United States and China', *Frontiers of Education in China*, 9(1): 63–88.

Kelly, A. (2020) '"Virtually entire" fashion industry complicit in Uighur forced labour, say rights group', *The Guardian*, 23 July, www.theguardian.com/global-development/2020/jul/23/virtually-entire-fashion-industry-complicit-in-uighur-forced-labour-say-rights-groups-china.

Kelly, A. and Pattisson, P. (2021) '"A pandemic of abuses": human rights under attack during Covid, says UN head', *The Guardian*, 22 February, www.theguardian.com/global-development/2021/feb/22/human-rights-in-the-time-of-covid-a-pandemic-of-abuses-says-un-head.

Kelly, C. (2019) 'Ocasio-Cortez compares migrant detention facilities to concentration camps', *CNN*, 18 June, https://edition.cnn.com/2019/06/18/politics/alexandria-ocasio-cortez-concentration-camps-migrants-detention/index.html.

Kennedy, S. (2010) 'The myth of the Beijing consensus', *Journal of Contemporary China*, 19(65): 461–77.

Kent, A. (2013) 'China's participation in international organisations', in Yongjin Zhang. and G. Austin (eds) *Power and Responsibility in Chinese Foreign Policy*, Canberra: Australian National University Press, pp 132–66.

Kenyon, F. (2021) 'China's "splinternet" will create a state-controlled alternative internet', *The Guardian*, 3 June, www.theguardian.com/global-development/2021/jun/03/chinas-splinternet-blockchain-state-control-of-cyberspace.

Khosla, M. (2019) 'India's founding values are threatened by sinister new forms of oppression', *The Guardian*, 28 December, www.theguardian.com/commentisfree/2019/dec/28/indias-founding-values-are-threatened-by-sinister-new-forms-of-oppression.

Kim, S.W., Fidler, D.P. and Ganguly, S. (2009) 'Eastphalia rising? Asian influence and the fate of human security', *World Policy Journal*, 26(2): 53–64.

King, G., Pan, J. and Roberts, M.E. (2017) 'How the Chinese government fabricates social media posts for strategic distraction, not engaged argument', *American Political Science Review*, 111(3): 484–501.

Kissinger, H. (2015) *World Order*, London: Penguin.

Klein, N. (2007) *The Shock Doctrine: The Rise of Disaster Capitalism*, New York: Henry Holt and Company.

Kreuzer, P. (2016) 'A comparison of Malaysian and Philippine responses to China in the South China Sea', *Chinese Journal of International Politics*, 9(3): 239–76.

Kuo, L. (2017) 'Beijing is cultivating the next generation of African elites by training them in China', Quartz Africa, 14 December, https://qz.com/africa/1119447/china-is-training-africas-next-generation-of-leaders.

Kuo, L. (2018) 'China claims Muslim detention camps are education centres', *The Guardian*, 14 September, www.theguardian.com/world/2018/sep/14/china-claims-muslim-internment-camps-provide-professional-training.

Kuo, L. (2018) 'China's anti-spy campaign: cash rewards and warnings about red heads', *The Guardian*, 10 May, www.theguardian.com/world/2018/may/10/chinas-anti-spy-campaign-cash-rewards-and-warnings-about-red-heads.

Kuo, L. (2018) 'No joke: have China's censors gone too far with ban on humour app?', *The Guardian*, 21 April, www.theguardian. com/world/2018/apr/21/no-joke-have-chinas-censors-gone-too-far-with-ban-on-humour-app.

Kuo, L. (2019) ' Revealed: new evidence of China's mission to raze the mosques of Xinjiang', *The Guardian*, 7 May, www.theguardian. com/world/2019/may/07/revealed-new-evidence-of-chinas-mission-to-raze-the-mosques-of-xinjiang.

Kuo, L. (2020) 'China orders US consulate in Chengdu to close as tensions rise', *The Guardian*, 24 July, www.theguardian.com/world/2020/jul/24/china-orders-us-consulate-in-chengdu-to-close-as-tensions-rise.

Kuo, L. (2020) 'The new normal: China's excessive coronavirus public monitoring could be here to stay', *The Guardian*, 9 March, www.theguardian.com/world/2020/mar/09/the-new-normal-chinas-excessive-coronavirus-public-monitoring-could-be-here-to-stay.

Kuo, L. (2020) 'Xi Jinping facing widespread opposition in his own party claims insider', *The Guardian*, 18 August, www.theguardian. com/world/2020/aug/18/china-xi-jinping-facing-widespread-opposition-in-his-own-party-claims-insider.

Kwock, B., James, M. and Anthony Shu Chuen, T. (2014) 'The psychology of auditing in China: the need to understand *guanxi* thinking and feelings as applied to contractual disputes', *Journal of Business Studies Quarterly*, 5(3): 10–18.

Lake, D.A. (2009) *Hierarchy in International Relations*, Ithaca: Cornell University Press.

Lanteigne, M. (2005) *China and International Institutions*, London: Routledge.

Laruelle, M. (2018) *China's Belt and Road Initiative and Its Impact in Central Asia*, Washington, DC: George Washington University.

Lawrence, D. and Patterson, J. (2018) 'FPC Briefing. Rule of law in China: a priority for businesses and Western governments', Foreign Policy Centre, 24 September, https://fpc.org.uk/fpc-briefing-rule-of-law-in-china-a-priority-for-businesses-and-western-governments/?mc_cid=75587e5327&mc_eid=1711b07e96.

LCCHR (2021) 'Trump administration civil and human rights rollback', Leadership Conference on Civil and Human Rights, https://civilrights.org/trump-rollbacks.

Lee Kuan Yew (1992) 'Speech by Mr Lee Kuan Yew, senior minister of Singapore', *Asahi Forum*, 20 November.

Lee, P.K., Chan, G. and Chan, L. (2010) 'China in Darfur: humanitarian rule-maker or rule-taker?', *Review of International Studies*, 38(2): 1–22.

Levin, D. (2019) 'Partisan electoral interventions by the great powers: Introducing the PEIG Dataset', *Conflict Management and Peace Science*, 36(1): 88–106.

Levine, S. (2021) 'US sinks to new low in ranking of world's democracies', *The Guardian*, 24 March, www.theguardian.com/us-news/2021/mar/24/us-world-democracy-rankings-freedom-house-new-low.

Levitsky, S. and Ziblatt, D. (2016) 'Opinion: is Donald Trump at threat to democracy?', *New York Times*, 16 December, www.nytimes.com/2016/12/16/opinion/sunday/is-donald-trump-a-threat-to-democracy.html?_r=0.

Levitsky, S. and Way, L.A. (2010) *Competitive Authoritarianism: Hybrid Regimes after the Cold War*, Cambridge: Cambridge University Press.

Lien, D., Oh, C.H. and Selmier, W.T. (2012) 'Confucius institute effects on China's trade and FDI: isn't it delightful when folks afar study Hanyu?', *International Review of Economics & Finance*, 21(1): 147–55.

Lim, L. and Bergin, J. (2018) 'Inside China's audacious global propaganda campaign', *The Guardian*, 7 December, www.theguardian.com/news/2018/dec/07/china-plan-for-global-media-dominance-propaganda-xi-jinping.

Lim, Y.-H. (2014) *China's Naval Power: An Offensive Realist Approach*, Farnham: Ashgate.

Lina Liu (2021) 'Beyond the status quo and revisionism: an analysis of the role of China and the approaches of China's Belt and Road Initiative (BRI) to the global order', *Asian Journal of Political Science*, 29(1): 88–109.

Linz, J.J. (2000) *Totalitarian and Authoritarian Regimes*, Boulder: Lynne Rienner Publishers.

Litton, A. (2015) 'The state of surveillance in India: the Central Monitoring System's chilling effect on self-expression', *Washington University Global Studies Law Review*, 14(4): 799–822.

Logsdon, K.R. (2008) 'Who knows you are reading this – United States' domestic electronic surveillance in a post-9/11 world', *University of Illinois Journal of Law, Technology & Policy*, 2: 409–38.

Long, E. (2020) 'Where the politicisation of the US supreme court could lead', *The Conversation*, 29 October, https://theconversation.com/where-the-politicisation-of-the-us-supreme-court-could-lead-149025.

Losse, K. (2018) 'I was Zuckerberg's speechwriter. "Companies over countries" was his early motto', Vox, 16 April, www.vox.com/first-person/2018/4/11/17221344/mark-zuckerberg-facebook-cambridge-analytica.

Lovell, J. (2016) '*The Cultural Revolution: A People's History 1962–1976* by Frank Dikotter – Review', *The Guardian*, 11 August.

Lucas, J.A. (2007) 'Deaths in other nations since WW II due to US interventions', 24 April, www.countercurrents.org/lucas240407.htm.

Luo, Y. (2014) 'The internet and agenda setting in China: the influence of online public opinion on media coverage and government policy', *International Journal of Communication*, 8(1): 1289–312.

Luttwak, E.N. (1990) 'From geopolitics to geo-economics: logic of conflict, grammar of commerce', *The National Interest*, 20: 17–23.

MacAskill, E. and Borger, J. (2004) 'Iraq war was illegal and breached UN charter, says Annan', *The Guardian*, 16 September, www.theguardian.com/world/2004/sep/16/iraq.iraq.

MacAskill, E., Borger, J., Hopkins, N. and Davies, N. (2013) 'GCHQ taps fibre-optic cables for secret access to world's communications', *The Guardian*, 21 June, www.theguardian.com/uk/2013/jun/21/gchq-cables-secret-world-communications-nsa.

MacFarquhar R. (2016) Leadership styles at the party centre: from Mao Zedong to Xi Jinping', in S. Hellmann and M. Stepan (eds) *China's Core Executive*, Berlin: Mercator Institute for China Studies, pp 14–17.

Macikenaite, V. (2020) 'China's economic statecraft: the use of economic power in an interdependent world', *Journal of Contemporary East Asia Studies*, 9(2): 108–26.

Madisson, A. (2003) *The World Economy: Historical Statistics*, Paris: OECD Publishing.

Mao Zedong (1949) 'The Chinese people have stood up!', USC US-China Institute, 21 September, https://china.usc.edu/Mao-declares-founding-of-peoples-republic-of-china-chinese-people-have-stood-up.

Maréchal, N. (2017) 'Networked authoritarianism and the geopolitics of information: understanding Russian internet policy', *Media and Communication*, 5(1): 29–41.

Marsh, J. (2018) 'How a Hong Kong millionaire's bribery case exposes China's corruption problem in Africa', CNN, 9 February, https://edition.cnn.com/2018/02/09/world/patrick-ho-corruption-china-africa.

Mason, E.S. and Asher, R.E. (1974) *The World Bank Since Bretton Woods: The Origins, Policies, Operations and Impact of the International Bank for Reconstruction*, Washington, DC: Brookings Institution.

Mastanduno, M. (2012) 'The richness of the contributions of Robert G Gilpin', in W.F. Danspeckgruber (ed.) *Robert Gilpin and International Relations: Reflections*, Princeton: Princeton University Press: 7–20.

McCarthy, T. (2020) 'Baby-faced assassin: the 29 year old at the heart of Trump's "deep state" purge', *The Guardian*, 26 February, www.theguardian.com/us-news/2020/feb/26/johnny-mcentee-trump-purge-civil-service-deep-state.

Mearsheimer, J. (2001) *The Tragedy of Great Power Politics*, New York: W.W. Norton & Company.

Mehta, P.B. (2020) 'SC was never perfect but the signs are that it is slipping into judicial barbarism', *The Indian Express*, 18 November, https://indianexpress.com/article/opinion/columns/supreme-court-arnab-goswami-bail-article-32-pratap-bhanu-mehta-7055067.

Ming Wan (2016) *The Asian Infrastructure Investment Bank: The Construction of Power and the Struggle for the East Asian International Order*, New York: Palgrave Macmillan.

Ministry of Foreign Affairs (2015) 'Xi Jinping holds talks with representatives of Chinese and foreign entrepreneurs attending BFA Annual Conference', Ministry of Foreign Affairs of the People's Republic of China, 29 March, www.fmprc.gov.cn/mfa_eng/zxxx_662805/t1250585.shtml.

MOFA (2015) 'Japanese territory: Senkaku Islands information', Ministry of Foreign Affairs of Japan, 6 March, www.mofa. go.jp/a_o/c_m1/senkaku/page1we_000009.html.

Mollman, S. (2018) '"Ignore the missiles": Duterte says China's South China Sea militarization is no problem", *Quartz*, 20 February, https://qz.com/1211014/south-china-sea-militarization-nothing-to-fret-over-says-philippines-president-rodrigo-duterte.

Moore, G.J. (2014) 'The power of "sacred commitments": Chinese interests in Taiwan', *Foreign Policy Analysis*, 12(2): 1–22.

Morris, R. (2022) '*Flooding the zone*: the Bannon playbook governing British politics', *Byline Times*, 21 March, https://bylinetimes.com/2022/03/21/flooding-the-zone-the-bannon-playbook-governing-british-politics.

Mueller, M.L. (2012) 'China and global internet governance: a tiger by the tail', in R. Deibert, J. Palfrey, R. Rohozinski and J. Zittrain (eds) *Access Contested: Security, Identity, and Resistance in Asian Cyberspace*, Cambridge, MA: MIT Press, pp 177–94.

Murgia, M. and Gross, A. (2020) 'Inside China's controversial mission to reinvent the internet', *Financial Times*, 27 March, www.ft.com/content/ba94c2bc-6e27-11ea-9bca-bf503995cd6f.

Murphy, C. (2005) *Global Institutions, Marginalization, and Development*, New York: Routledge.

NATO (1949) 'The North Atlantic Treaty', North Atlantic Treaty Organization, www.nato.int/cps/en/natolive/official_texts_17120.htm.

NATO (2021) 'Operations and missions: past and present', North Atlantic Treaty Organization, 23 August, www.nato.int/cps/en/natohq/topics_52060.htm.

Naughton, J. (2019) '"The goal is to automate us": welcome to the age of surveillance capitalism', *The Guardian*, 20 January, www.theguardian.com/technology/2019/jan/20/shoshana-zuboff-age-of-surveillance-capitalism-google-facebook.

NDRC (2015) *Vision and Actions on Jointly Building Silk Road Economic Belt and 21st-Century Maritime Silk Road*, Beijing: National Development and Reform Commission.

NDRC (2016) *The 13th Five Year Plan for Economic and Social Development of the PRC (2016–2020)*, Beijing: National Development and Reform Commission.

Nedopil, Christoph (2021) 'Countries of the Belt and Road Initiative', IIGF Green BRI Center, Beijing, www.green-bri.org.

Ni, V. (2021) 'China denounces US Senates' $250 billion move to boost tech and manufacturing', *The Guardian*, 9 June, www.theguardian.com/us-news/2021/jun/09/us-senate-approves-50bn-boost-for-computer-chip-and-ai-technology-to-counter-china

Nolan, P. (2017) 'State, market and infrastructure: the new Silk Road', *Croatian International Relations Review*, 23(78): 7–18.

NPR (2006) 'CONINTELPRO and the history of domestic spying', 18 January, www.npr.org/templates/story/story.php?storyId=5161811.

Nye, J.S. (1990) 'Soft power', *Foreign Policy*, 80: 153–71.

O'Brien, K.J. and Han, R. (2009) 'Path to democracy? Assessing village elections in China', *Journal of Contemporary China*, 18(60): 359–78.

O'Connor, T. (2019) 'Which countries still recognize Taiwan?', *Newsweek*, 20 September, www.newsweek.com/who-recognizes-taiwan-two-change-china-1460559.

O'Neil, C. (2016) *Weapons of Math Destruction: How Big Data Increases Inequality and Threatens Democracy*, London: Penguin.

O'Rourke, L.A. (2020) 'The strategic logic of covert regime change: US-backed regime change campaigns during the Cold War', *Security Studies*, 29(1): 92–127.

Ogden, C. (2017) *China and India: Asia's Emergent Great Powers*, Cambridge: Polity.

Ogden, C. (2019) *A Dictionary of Politics and International Relations in China*, Oxford: Oxford University Press.

Ogden, C. (2020) 'Must Britain be more like China to halt coronavirus outbreak?', *The Guardian*, 27 February, www.theguardian.com/world/2020/feb/27/coronavirus-must-britain-be-more-like-china-to-halt-outbreak.

Ogden, C. (2020) 'Starting a conversation: how far can the UK take authoritarian measures against coronavirus?', Radio 4 (on PM), 2 March, https://chrisogdendotorg.files.wordpress.com/2020/03/bbc-radio-4-chris-ogden-coronavirus-02032020.mp3.

Ogden, C. (2020) 'The role of competing narratives in China and the West's response to COVID-19', *British Journal of Chinese Studies*, 10, July, https://doi.org/10.51661/bjocs.v10i0.121.

Ogden, C. (with Ioannou, M.) (2020) *Great Power Attributes: A Compendium of Historical Data*, Edinburgh: Fifth Hammer.

Olewe, D. (2021) 'Why African countries back China on human rights', BBC News, 2 May, www.bbc.co.uk/news/world-africa-56717986.

Ortiz, J. (2021) '"Blood on his hands": as US surpasses 400,000 COVID-19 deaths, experts blame Trump administration for "preventable" loss of life', USA Today News, 17 January, https://eu.usatoday.com/story/news/nation/2021/01/17/covid-19-us-400-000-deaths-experts-blame-trump-administration/6642685002.

Owen, C. (2018) 'State transformation and authoritarian governance: the emergence of participatory authoritarianism?', Foreign Policy Centre, 14 September, https://fpc.org.uk/state-transformation-and-authoritarian-governance-the-emergence-of-participatory-authoritarianism.

Palfrey, J. (2020) 'The ever-increasing surveillance state', *Georgetown Journal of International Affairs*, 2 March, https://gjia.georgetown.edu/2020/03/02/the-ever-increasing-surveillance-state.

Pallin, C.V. (2017) 'Internet control through ownership: the case of Russia', *Post-Soviet Affairs*, 33(1): 16–33.

Pan Guang (2007) 'A Chinese perspective on the Shanghai Cooperation Organization', in A.J.K. Bailes, P. Dunay, Pan Guang and M. Troitskiy (eds) *The Shanghai Cooperation Organization*, Stockholm: Stockholm International Peace Research Institute, pp 45–58.

Parton, C. (2018) 'The fourth weapon', *The Spectator*, 17 November, www.spectator.co.uk/article/the-fourth-weapon.

Patman, R.G. (2006) 'Globalization, the new US exceptionalism and the war on terror', *Third World Quarterly*, 27(6): 963–986.

PD (2021) 'Why did Ai Weiwei break this million-dollar Han Dynasty vase?', *Public Delivery*, 10 February, https://publicdelivery.org/ai-weiwei-dropping-a-han-dynasty-urn.

Pena, D. (2015) 'Comparing the Chinese Dream with the American Dream', *International Critical Thought*, 5(3): 277–95.

Peng Zhongzhou and Sow Keat Tok (2016) 'The AIIB and China's normative power in international financial governance structure', *Chinese Political Science Review*, 1(4): 736–53.

Perlez, J. (2015) 'China creates a World Bank of its own, and the US balks', *The New York Times*, 4 December.

Phillips, T. (2016) '"Love the party, protect the party": how Xi Jinping is bringing China's media to heel', *The Guardian*, 28 February, www.theguardian.com/world/2016/feb/28/absolute-loyalty-how-xi-jinping-is-bringing-chinas-media-to-heel.

Phillips, T. (2017) ' Xi Jinping tests eyelids – and bladders – with three-and-a-half-hour speech', *The Guardian*, 18 October, www.theguardian.com/world/2017/oct/18/xi-jinping-tests-eyelids-and-bladders-with-three-and-a-half-hour-speech-congress.

Phillips, T. (2017) '"A huge deal" for China as the era of Xi Jinping Thought begins', *The Guardian*, 19 October, www.theguardian.com/world/2017/oct/19/huge-deal-china-era-of-xi-jinping-thought-politics.

Phillips, T. (2017) 'A human rights activist, a secret prison and a tale from Xi Jinping's new China', *The Guardian*, 3 January, www.theguardian.com/world/2017/jan/03/human-rights-activist-peter-dahlin-secret-black-prison-xi-jinpings-new-china.

Phillips, T. (2017) 'Xi Jinping heralds "new era" of Chinese power at Communist Party congress', *The Guardian*, 18 October, www.theguardian.com/world/2017/oct/18/xi-jinping-speech-new-era-chinese-power-party-congress.

Phillips, T. (2018) '"Maybe we'll give that a shot": Donald Trump praises Xi Jinping's power grab', *The Guardian*, 4 March, www.theguardian.com/us-news/2018/mar/04/donald-trump-praises-xi-jinping-power-grab-give-that-a-shot-china.

Phillips, T. (2018) 'Ce*sored: China bans letter n (briefly) from internet as Xi Jinping extends grip on power', *The Guardian*, 28 February, www.theguardian.com/world/2018/feb/28/china-bans-the-letter-n-internet-xi-jinping-extends-power.

Piccone, T. (2018) 'China's long game on human rights at the United Nations,' Brookings Institution, September 2018, www.brookings.edu/research/chinas-long-game-on-human-rights-at-the-united-nations.

Pilkington, E. (2020) 'America's flawed democracy: the five key areas where it is failing', *The Guardian*, 16 November, www.theguardian.com/us-news/2020/nov/16/america-flawed-democracy-five-key-areas.

Plehwe, D., Walpen, B. and Neunhöffer, G. (eds) (2007) *Neoliberal Hegemony: A Global Critique*, London: Routledge.

Polity IV (2014) *Polity IV Project: Political Regime Characteristics and Transitions 1800–2013*, Vienna: Center for Systemic Peace.

POTUS (1823) 'Presidential Speeches: December 2, 1823: Seventh Annual Message (Monroe Doctrine)', Miller Center, University of Virginia, 2 December, https://millercenter.org/the-presidency/presidential-speeches/december-2-1823-seventh-annual-message-monroe-doctrine.

POTUS (1947) 'Presidential Speeches: March 12, 1947: Truman Doctrine', Miller Center, University of Virginia, 12 March, https://millercenter.org/the-presidency/presidential-speeches/march-12-1947-truman-doctrine.

POTUS (1957) 'Presidential Speeches: January 5, 1957 – Eisenhower Doctrine', Miller Center, University of Virginia, 5 January, https://millercenter.org/the-presidency/presidential-speeches/january-5-1957-eisenhower-doctrine.

Pradt, T. (2016) *China's New Foreign Policy: Military Modernisation, Multilateralism and the China Threat*, Basingstoke: Palgrave Macmillan.

Prestowitz, C. (2015) 'Our incoherent China policy', *The American Prospect*, 21 September.

R2P (2021) 'Right to protect and the UN', United Nations, www.un.org/en/chronicle/article/r2p-and-un.

Raiser, M. (2019) 'China's rise fits every developmental model', Brookings, 17 October, www.brookings.edu/blog/future-development/2019/10/17/chinas-rise-fits-every-development-model.

Rajah, R., Dayant, D. and Pryke, J. (2019) 'Ocean of debt? Belt and Road and debt diplomacy in the Pacific', Lowy Institute, 21 October, www.lowyinstitute.org/publications/ocean-debt-belt-and-road-and-debt-diplomacy-pacific#_edn4.

Raman, K.R. (2009) 'Asian Development Bank, policy conditionalities and social democratic governance: Kerala model under pressure?" *Review of International Political Economy*, 16(2): 284–308.

Ramo, J.C. (2004) 'The Beijing Consensus', Foreign Policy Centre, 18 March, https://fpc.org.uk/publications/the-beijing-consensus.

Reagan, R. (2004) *Speaking My Mind: Selected Speeches*, New York: Simon & Schuster.

Reuters (2017) 'China sets rules on beards, veils to combat extremism in Xinjiang', 30 March, www.reuters.com/article/china-xinjiang-int/china-sets-rules-on-beards-veils-to-combat-extremism-in-xinjiang-idUSKBN1710DD.

RFA (2017) 'China bans Uighur language in schools in key Xinjiang prefecture', Radio Free Asia, 28 July, www.rfa.org/english/news/uyghur/language-07282017143037.html.

Richter, F. (2021) 'China is the world's manufacturing superpower', Statista, 4 May, www.statista.com/chart/20858/top-10-countries-by-share-of-global-manufacturing-output.

Rodrigues, J., Chaudhary, A. and Dormido, H. (2019) 'A murky flood of money pours into world's largest election', *Bloomberg*, 16 March, www.bloomberg.com/graphics/2019-india-election-funds.

Rolland, N. (2017) *China's Eurasian Century? Political and Strategic Implications of the Belt and Road Initiative*, Seattle: National Bureau of Asian Research.

Rolland, N. (2019) 'A concise guide to the Belt and Road Initiative', National Bureau of Asian Research, 11 April, www.nbr.org/publication/a-guide-to-the-belt-and-road-initiative.

Roth, A. and Phillips, T. (2020) '"What a spectacle!" US adversaries revel in post-election chaos', *The Guardian*, 5 November, www.theguardian.com/us-news/2020/nov/05/what-a-spectacle-the-uss-enemies-revel-in-the-post-election-chaos.

Roy, A. (2015) 'Edward Snowden meets Arundhati Roy and John Cusack: "He was small and lithe, like a house cat"', *The Guardian*, 28 November, www.theguardian.com/lifeandstyle/2015/nov/28/conversation-edward-snowden-arundhati-roy-john-cusack-interview.

Rozman, G. (1991) 'The East Asian region in comparative perspective', in G. Rozman (ed.) *The East Asian Region: Confucian Heritage and Its Modern Adaptation*, Princeton: Princeton University Press, pp 3–44.

RSF (2021) 'China', Reporters Without Borders, https://rsf.org/en/china.

Rui Hou (2018) 'The booming industry of Chinese state internet control', openDemocracy, 21 November, www.opendemocracy. net/en/booming-industry-of-chinese-state-internet-control.

Rushe, D. and Kuo, L. (2019) 'US designates China as a currency manipulator', *The Guardian*, 5 August, www.theguardian. com/us-news/2019/aug/05/us-designates-china-as-currency-manipulator.

Safi, M. (2020) 'George Floyd protests: reporters targeted by police and crowds', *The Guardian*, 31 May, www.theguardian.com/us-news/2020/may/31/george-floyd-protests-reporters-targeted-by-police-and-crowds.

Safi, M. (2021) 'Vaccine diplomacy: West falling behind in race for influence', *The Guardian*, 19 February, www.theguardian.com/world/2021/feb/19/coronavirus-vaccine-diplomacy-west-falling-behind-russia-china-race-influence.

Saito, N.T. (2002) 'Whose liberty? Whose security? The USA PATRIOT Act in the context of COINTELPRO and the unlawful repression of political dissent', *Oregon Law Review*, 81(4): 1051–132.

Sakwa, R. (2011) *The Crisis of Russian Democracy: The Dual State, Factionalism and the Medvedev Succession*, Cambridge: Cambridge University Press.

Schamis, H.F. and Armony, A.C. (2015) 'Babel in democratization studies', *Journal of Democracy*, 16(4): 113–26.

Schedler, A. (2002) 'The nested game of democratization by elections', *International Political Science Review*, 23(1): 103–22.

Schiavenza, M. (2013) 'China's dominance in manufacturing in one chart', *The Atlantic*, 5 August, www.theatlantic.com/china/archive/2013/08/chinas-dominance-in-manufacturing-in-one-chart/278366.

Schwartz, B. (2020) 'Total 2020 election spend to hit nearly $14 billion, more than double 2016's sum', CNBC, 28 October, www.cnbc.com/2020/10/28/2020-election-spending-to-hit-nearly-14-billion-a-record.html.

SCO (2021) 'About SCO', *Shanghai Cooperation Organisation*, http://eng.sectsco.org/about_sco.

Scott, J. and Wilkinson, R. (2011) 'China and the WTO', *Indiana University Research Center for Chinese Politics and Business*, Working Paper, 5: 1–26.

Shahbaz, A. (2018) 'Freedom on the net 2018: the rise of digital authoritarianism', Freedom House, October, https://freedomhouse.org/report/freedom-net/2018/rise-digital-authoritarianism.

Shambaugh, D. (2005) 'China engages Asia: reshaping the regional order', *International Security*, 29(3): 64–99.

Shambaugh, D.L. (2013) *China Goes Global: The Partial Power*, Oxford: Oxford University Press.

Shaw, S. (2020) 'How Facebook is aiding authoritarian regimes', *Byline Times*, 16 December, https://bylinetimes.com/2020/12/16/how-facebook-is-aiding-authoritarian-regimes.

Shearman, P. (2014) *Power Transition and International Order in Asia*, London: Routledge.

Shin-wha Lee (2011) 'The theory and reality of soft power: practical approaches in East Asia', in J. Melissen (ed.) *Public Diplomacy and Soft Power in East Asia*, New York: Palgrave Macmillan, pp 11–32.

Simmons, K. (2019) 'Inside Chinese camps thought to be detaining a million Muslim Uighurs', NBC News, 4 October, www.nbcnews.com/news/world/inside-chinese-camps-thought-detain-million-muslim-uighurs-n1062321.

SIPRI (2021) 'Arms Transfers', *Stockholm International Peace Research Institute*, https://sipri.org/databases/armstransfers.

SIPRI (2021) 'Military Expenditure', *Stockholm International Peace Research Institute*, https://sipri.org/databases/milex.

Smith, D. (2020) '"He is a destroyer": how the George Floyd protests left Donald Trump exposed', *The Guardian*, 1 June, www.theguardian.com/us-news/2020/jun/01/george-floyd-donald-trump-black-lives-matter.

Smith, D. (2021) '"Have you no shame?" Biden decries Republican attacks on voting rights', *The Guardian*, 13 July, www.theguardian.com/us-news/2021/jul/13/joe-biden-republicans-voting-rights-philadelphia.

Smith, T. (1994) *America's Mission: The United States and the Worldwide Struggle for Democracy in the Twentieth Century*, Princeton: Princeton University Press.

Snyder, J. (1977) *The Soviet Strategic Culture: Implications for Limited Nuclear Operations*, Washington, DC: Defense Technical Information Centre.

Snyder, T. (2018) 'Vladimir Putin's politics of eternity', *The Guardian*, 16 March, www.theguardian.com/news/2018/mar/16/vladimir-putin-russia-politics-of-eternity-timothy-snyder.

Sodatov, A. (2016) "The taming of the internet', *Russian Politics & Law*, 53(5–6): 63–83.

Song Xinning (2001) 'Building international relations theory with Chinese characteristics', *Journal of Contemporary China*, 10(26): 61–74.

Statista (2021) 'Global social networks ranked by number of users', 2 August, www.statista.com/statistics/272014/global-social-networks-ranked-by-number-of-users.

Stiglitz, J.E. (2017) *Globalization and Its Discontents Revisited – Anti-Globalization in the Era of Trump*, London: Penguin Random House.

Strittmatter, K. (2019) *We Have Been Harmonised: Life in China's Surveillance State*, Exeter: Old Street.

Subramanian, R. (2020) 'Historical consciousness of cyber security in India', *IEEE Annals of the History of Computing*, 42(4): 71–93.

Suisheng Zhao (2010) 'The China model: can it replace the Western model of modernization?', *Journal of Contemporary China*, 19(65): 419–36.

Sutter, K.M., Schwarzenberg, A.B. and Sutherland, M.D. (2021) 'China's "One Belt, One Road" Initiative: Economic Issues', US Congressional Research Service, 22 January, www.everycrsreport.com/reports/IF11735.html.

Suzuki, S. (2015) 'Will the AIIB Trigger off a New Round of Rivalry in Economic Diplomacy between China and Japan?', *CSGR Working Paper No. 279/15*, Coventry: Centre for the Study of Globalisation and Regionalisation.

Tang, R. (2018) 'Google to seek return to China with a censored search engine; Reuters', ABC, 3 August, https://abcnews.go.com/International/google-seek-return-china-censored-search-engine-reports/story?id=56991547.

Taub, A. (2016) 'The rise of American authoritarianism', Vox, 1 March, www.vox.com/2016/3/1/11127424/trump-authoritarianism#whatis.

Tax, M. (2016) 'A revolution is not a dinner party', openDemocracy, 23 August, www.opendemocracy.net/en/5050/revolution-is-not-dinner-party.

Taylor, J. (2020) 'China's Belt and Road Initiative: what it is and why is Victoria under fire for its involvement?', *The Guardian*, 25 May, www.theguardian.com/world/2020/may/25/chinas-belt-and-road-initiative-what-is-it-and-why-is-victoria-under-fire-for-its-involvement.

Textor, C. (2020) 'China's public security expenditure 2009–2019', Statista, 27 November, www.statista.com/statistics/1049749/china-public-security-spending-by-government-level.

Textor, C. (2020) 'Total number of foreign students studying in China 2014–18', Statista, 29 April, www.statista.com/statistics/1092488/china-total-number-of-foreign-students.

The Hague (2016) *The South China Sea Arbitration*, Permanent Court of Arbitration, The Hague, 12 July.

Thomala, L.L. (2021) 'Number of internet users in China 2008–2020', Statista, 12 August, www.statista.com/statistics/265140/number-of-internet-users-in-china.

Thomas, K. and Siddiqui, S. (2021) 'Biden says rioters who stormed Capitol were domestic terrorists', *Wall Street Journal*, 7 January, www.wsj.com/articles/biden-says-mob-that-stormed-capitol-were-domestic-terrorists-11610046962.

Tiezzi, S. (2015) 'China vows no compromise on "cyber sovereignty"', *The Diplomat*, 16 December, https://thediplomat.com/2015/12/china-vows-no-compromise-on-cyber-sovereignty.

Tingyang Zhao (2006) 'Rethinking empire from a Chinese concept of "all-under-heaven (tian-xia)"', *Social Identities*, 12(1): 29–41.

Tisdall, S. (2021) 'US's global reputation hits rock bottom over Trump's coronavirus response', *The Guardian*, 12 April, www.theguardian.com/us-news/2020/apr/12/us-global-reputation-rock-bottom-donald-trump-coronavirus.

Tisdall, S. (2021) 'Xi's change of heart is too late to stop China's collision with the West', *The Guardian*, 6 June, www.theguardian.com/commentisfree/2021/jun/06/xis-change-of-heart-is-too-late-to-stop-chinas-collision-with-the-west.

Tsai, K.S. (2007) *Capitalism Without Democracy: The Private Sector in Contemporary China*, Ithaca: Cornell University Press.

Tseng, K.H-Y. (2017) *Rethinking South China Sea Disputes: The Untold Dimensions and Great Expectations*, London: Routledge.

Tucker, E. and Jalonick, M.C. (2020) 'Senate panel finds Russia interfered in 2016 election', PBS, 18 August, www.pbs.org/newshour/politics/senate-panel-finds-russia-interfered-in-the-2016-us-election.

UNC (2021) *United Nations Charter*, United Nations, www.un.org/en/about-us/un-charter.

UNCLOS (1982) *United Nations Convention on the Law of the Sea*, United Nations, www.un.org/Depts/los/convention_agreements/texts/unclos/unclos_e.pdf.

UNCTAD (2021) 'Database', United Nations Conference on Trade and Development, http://unctadstat.unctad.org/wds/ReportFolders/reportFolders.aspx?sCS_referer=&sCS_ChosenLang=en

UNPK (2021) 'Troop and police contributors', United Nations Peacekeeping, https://peacekeeping.un.org/en/troop-and-police-contributors.

USPLT (2022) 'US protest law tracker', International Center for Not-For-Profit Law, www.icnl.org/usprotestlawtracker/

US Census (2021) 'Top trading partners – December 2020', United States Census Bureau, www.census.gov/foreign-trade/statistics/highlights/top/top2012yr.html.

USDOS (1950) 'National Security Council Report, NSC 68: United States objectives and programs for national security', Washington, DC: USDOS, https://digitalarchive.wilsoncenter.org/document/116191.pdf?v=2699956db534c1821edefa61b8c13ffe.

USEIA (2013) *South China Sea*, Washington, DC: US Energy Information Administration.

Van de Graaf, T., Sovacool, B.K., Ghosh, A. and Klare, M.T. (2016) 'States, markets, and institutions: integrating international political economy and global energy politics', in T. Van de Graaf, B.K. Sovacool, A. Ghosh and M.T Klare (eds) *The Palgrave Handbook of the International Political Economy of Energy*, London: Palgrave Macmillan, pp 3–45.

Vine, D. (2015) *Base Nation: How US Military Bases Overseas Harm America and the World*, New York: Metropolitan Books.

Visser, N. (2019) 'Obama takes subtle jab at Trump: "democracy is a garden that has to be tended"', *Huffington Post*, 7 March, www. huffingtonpost.co.uk/entry/barack-obama-rule-of-law-trump_ n_5c80aa7ee4b020b54d821484?ri18n=true&ncid=+edlinkusa olp00000029.

Vuving, A.L. (2017) 'How America can take control in the South China Sea', *Foreign Policy*, 14 February.

Wallace, M. (1986) 'Deng Xiaoping interview with Mike Wallace', CBS, 2 September, http://english.people.com.cn/dengxp/vol3/ text/c1560.html.

Walt, S.M. (2016) 'The collapse of the liberal world order', *Foreign Policy*, 26 June, https://foreignpolicy.com/2016/06/26/ the-collapse-of-the-liberal-world-order-european-union-brexit-donald-trump.

Wang Jisi and Zhu Feng (2015) 'Conclusion: the United States, China, and world order', in G.J. Ikenberry, Wang Jisi and Zhu Feng (eds) *America, China, and the Struggle for World Order: Ideas, Traditions, Historical Legacies, and Global Visions*, Basingstoke: Palgrave Macmillan, pp 359–76.

Wang Yangzhong (1999) 'Chinese values, governance and international relations: historical development and present situation', in Han Sung-Joo (ed.) *Changing Values in Asia – Their Impact on Governance and Development*, Tokyo: Japan Centre for Political Exchange, pp 24–36.

Waterson, J. (2019) 'US classed as "problematic place" for journalists to work', *The Guardian*, 18 April, www.theguardian.com/ media/2019/apr/18/united-states-classed-as-problematic-place-for-journalists-to-work.

Waterson, J. (2021) 'Oppression of journalists in China may have been a factor in Covid pandemic', *The Guardian*, 20 April, www. theguardian.com/media/2021/apr/20/oppression-of-journalists-in-china-may-have-been-factor-in-covid-pandemic.

Wayt, T. (2019) 'NYU Shanghai quietly added pro-government course at behest of Chinese government', *Vice*, 20 November, www.vice.com/en/article/43k9jn/nyu-shanghai-quietly-added-pro-government-course-at-behest-of-chinese-government.

Weiden, D.L. (2011) 'Judicial politicization, ideology, and activism at the high courts of the United States, Canada, and Australia', *Political Research Quarterly*, 64(2): 335–47.

Wells, H.G. (2014) *The New World Order*, Hong Kong: Hesperides Press.

Werleman, C.J. (2020) '"Love jihad": another step towards India's Nazification', *Byline Times*, 23 November, https://bylinetimes.com/2020/11/23/love-jihad-another-step-towards-indias-nazification.

White House (2002) *The National Security Strategy of the United States of America*, Washington, DC: Office of the President of the United States.

Wiki (2021) 'Social credit system', *Wikipedia*, https://en.wikipedia.org/wiki/Social_Credit_System#Comparison_to_other_countries.

Wiki ST (2021) 'Ship of Theseus', *Wikipedia*, https://en.wikipedia.org/wiki/Ship_of_Theseus.

WikiR (2021) 'List of journalists killed in Russia', *Wikipedia*, https://en.wikipedia.org/wiki/List_of_journalists_killed_in_Russia.

Wintour, P. (2018) 'China starts to assert its worldview at UN as influence grows', *The Guardian*, 24 September, www.theguardian.com/world/2018/sep/24/china-starts-to-assert-its-world-view-at-un-as-influence-grows.

Wintour, P. (2019) 'Alarming Chinese meddling at UK universities exposed in report', *The Guardian*, 5 November, www.theguardian.com/education/2019/nov/05/alarming-chinese-meddling-at-uk-universities-exposed-in-report.

Wintour, P. (2020) '"Westlessness": is the West really in a state of peril?', *The Guardian*, 16 February, www.theguardian.com/world/2020/feb/16/westlessness-is-the-west-really-in-a-state-of-peril.

Wintour, P. (2020) 'US versus China: is this the start of a new Cold War?', *The Guardian*, 22 June, www.theguardian.com/world/2020/jun/22/us-v-china-is-this-the-start-of-a-new-cold-war.

Wintour, P. (2021) 'China sanctions UK businesses, MPS and lawyers in Xinjiang row', *The Guardian*, 26 March, www.theguardian.com/world/2021/mar/26/china-sanctions-uk-businesses-mps-and-lawyers-in-xinjiang-row.

Wintour, P. (2021) 'US seen as bigger threat to democracy than Russia or China, global poll finds', *The Guardian*, 5 May, www.theguardian.com/world/2021/may/05/us-threat-democracy-russia-china-global-poll.

WJP (2020) *China – World Justice Project Rule of Law Index*, World Justice Project, https://worldjusticeproject.org/rule-of-law-index/country/China.

Wolff, R.C. (2016) *Capitalism's Crisis Deepens*, Chicago: Haymarket Books.

Womack, B. (2013) 'Beyond win-win – rethinking China's international relationship in an era of economic uncertainty', *International Affairs*, 89(4): 911–28.

Wong, J.C. (2021) 'How Facebook let fake engagement distort global politics: a whistle-blower's account', *The Guardian*, 12 April, www.theguardian.com/technology/2021/apr/12/facebook-fake-engagement-whistleblower-sophie-zhang.

Wong, J.C. and Ellis-Petersen, H. (2021) 'Facebook planned to remove fake accounts in India – until it realized a BJP politician was involved', *The Guardian*, 15 April, www.theguardian.com/technology/2021/apr/15/facebook-india-bjp-fake-accounts.

Woo, M.Y.K. (2013) 'Justice', in C. Ogden (ed.) *Handbook of China's Governance and Domestic Politics*, London: Routledge, pp 53–66.

Woolley, S.C. and Howard, P.N. (2019) 'Introduction: computational propaganda worldwide', in S.C. Woolley and P.N. Howard (eds) *Computational Propaganda: Political Parties, Politicians and Political Manipulation on Social Media*, Oxford: Oxford UP, pp 3–20.

World Bank (2021) 'Open data', https://data.worldbank.org.

Worth, O. (2015) *Rethinking Hegemony*, London: Palgrave.

WPB (2021) 'Welcome', World Prison Brief, www.prisonstudies.org.

WTO (2021) 'Data', World Trade Organization, https://data.wto.org.

Xi Jinping (2012) 'China's new party chief Xi Jinping's speech', BBC News, 15 November, www.bbc.co.uk/news/world-asia-china-20338586.

Xi Jinping (2014) 'Speech by Xi Jinping', Körber Foundation, Berlin, 28 March.

Xi Jinping (2015) 'Full text of Chinese president's speech on commemoration of 70th anniversary of war victory', Xinhua, 3 September, www.china.org.cn/china/2015-09/03/content_36489889.htm.

Xi Jinping (2017) 'Secure a decisive victory in building a moderately prosperous society in all respects and strive for the great success of socialism with Chinese characteristics for a new era', China Daily, 18 October, www.chinadaily.com.cn/china/19thcpc nationalcongress/2017-11/04/content_34115212.htm.

Xi Jinping (2018) The Governance of China, Shanghai: Shanghai Book Traders.

Xiao Ren (2016) 'China as an institution-builder: the case of the AIIB', The Pacific Review, 29(3): 435–42.

Xie Tao (2017) 'Chinese foreign policy with Xi Jinping characteristics', Carnegie-Tsinghua Centre for Global Policy, 20 November, https://carnegietsinghua.org/2017/11/20/chinese-foreign-policy-with-xi-jinping-characteristics-pub-74765.

Xinhua (2016) 'Full text of Chinese President Xi Jinping's address at AIIB inauguration ceremony', 16 January, www.xinhuanet.com/english/china/2016-01/16/c_135015661.htm.

Xue, L., Xufeng Zhu and Wanqu Han (2018) 'Embracing scientific decision making: the rise of think-tank policies in China', Pacific Affairs, 91(1): 49–71.

Xunzi and Knoblock, J. (1990) Xunzi: A Translation and Study of the Complete Works, Stanford: Stanford University Press.

Yan Xuetong (2018) 'Chinese values versus liberalism: what ideology will shape the international normative order?', The Chinese Journal of International Politics, 11(1): 1–22.

Yitao Tao (2017) 'Special Economic Zones and China's path', in Yiming Yuan (ed.) Studies on China's Special Economic Zones, London: Springer, pp 1–13.

Yixiong Huang (2013) 'The return of Confucianism in China: legitimacy and the rule of the Communist Party of China', Fudan Journal of the Humanities & Social Sciences, 6(1): 33–61.

Yong Deng and Fei-Ling Wang (eds) (2005) China Rising: Power and Motivation in Chinese Foreign Policy, Lanham: Rowman & Littlefield.

Yu, V. (2019) '"They will definitely take revenge": how China could respond to the Hong Kong protests', *The Guardian*, 30 June, www.theguardian.com/world/2019/jun/30/they-will-definitely-take-revenge-how-china-could-respond-to-the-hong-kong-protests.

Yun Sun (2016) 'Party political training: China's ideological push in Africa?', Brookings, 5 July, www.brookings.edu/blog/africa-in-focus/2016/07/05/political-party-training-chinas-ideological-push-in-africa.

Zakaria, F. (1997) 'The rise of illiberal democracy', *Foreign Affairs*, 76(6): 22–43.

Zheng Chen (2016) 'China and the responsibility to protect', *Journal of Contemporary China*, 25(101): 686–700.

Index